ON MEN

BY THE SAME AUTHOR

Psychiatry In Dissent
Let's Talk About Me (with Sally Thompson)
In The Psychiatrist's Chair, vols I, II & III
Lovelaw
Depression and How to Survive It (with Spike Milligan)

ON MEN

Masculinity in Crisis

ANTHONY CLARE

Chatto & Windus
LONDON

Published by Chatto & Windus 2000

2 4 6 8 10 9 7 5 3 1

First published in Great Britain in 2000 by
Chatto & Windus
Random House, 20 Vauxhall Bridge Road,
London SW1V 2SA

Random House Australia (Pty) Limited
20 Alfred Street, Milsons Point, Sydney,
New South Wales 2061, Australia

Random House New Zealand Limited
18 Poland Road, Glenfield,
Auckland 10, New Zealand

Random House (Pty) Limited
Endulini, 5A Jubilee Road, Parktown, 2193, South Africa

The Random House Group Limited Reg. No. 954009
www.randomhouse.co.uk

A CIP catalogue record for this book
is available from the British Library

ISBN 1 85619 633 X

Papers used by Random House are natural, recyclable products made from wood grown in sustainable forests. The manufacturing processes conform to the environmental regulations of the country of origin

Typeset by SX Composing DTP, Rayleigh, Essex
Printed and bound in Great Britain by
Mackays of Chatham plc, Chatham, Kent

Contents

In memory of my father

CHAPTER 1

THE DYING PHALLUS

As I get older and perhaps wiser, I realise more and more what I do not know. I still don't know what makes people happy although I am a good deal more knowledgeable about what makes them sad. I don't know now whether there is a God, when once I did believe and with a passionate conviction. I don't know whether good mothers are born or made, what turns some people into leaders and others into the led, nor whether in my lifetime we will see the cure for cancer, schizophrenia or Alzheimer's disease.

What I do know is what it is like to be a man. However, as I reflect on how I learned about masculinity and manhood, I realise that almost all the teaching was implicit and all the learning by way of a kind of osmotic process. I don't recall anyone, my father, my mother, my teachers, my peers, saying 'This is what it means to be a man, a son, a brother, a lover, a dad'. Yet I learned very early on that what a man does; his work is as important as, even more important than, who he is; that a man is defined in modern capitalistic society in terms not of being but doing.

My career, particularly my medical career, was always portrayed and interpreted, by others as much as by myself, as more important than spouse, family, friends. During my undergraduate and postgraduate training, first in medicine, then in psychiatry, I never ever witnessed a male colleague admitting to putting his family first. Male colleagues would blithely arrange late evening meetings of this or that committee and be surprised and irritated when female colleagues pointed out that domestic duties made their attendance impossible. For a male to make such a statement would have marked him as someone not committed to his job. Most male colleagues were busy demonstrating how they worked all the hours God gave them. It was like chimps beating their chests and baring their teeth. Often, it was just about as productive.

In an interview published in the *New York Times* back in 1912, Carl Jung observed that the libido of American men:

> is focused almost entirely on his business, so that as a husband he is glad to have no responsibilities. He gives the complete direction of his family life over to his wife. This is what you call giving independence to the American woman. It is what I call the laziness of the American man. That is why he is so kind and polite in his home and why he can fight so hard in his business. His real life is where his fight is. The lazy part of his life is where his family is.[1]

Jung was writing of American men at the turn of the last century. He could as easily have been writing of manhood, career and family life some 80 years later. He certainly could have been writing about mine. Yet, given the nature and extent of the feminist analysis and the sexual revolution of the second half of the twentieth century, much would appear to have changed for – women. But what has happened to men?

As a young psychiatrist in the late 1960s and 1970s I regularly encountered the phenomenon then known as the 'empty-nest syndrome'. It afflicted married women who, having given their lives to the rearing of their families, found when they reached their fifties that their children had grown up and gone and their spouses were off living a life of work and golf. Now, in the 1990s, I don't see so many women from empty nests. Rather I see middle-aged men, who gave their lives loyally to this company or that corporation, who sacrificed everything for it, now ruthlessly put out to grass, compulsorily retired, downsized, rendered redundant. Bewildered, they look around but their children have flown and their spouses are otherwise occupied. It is the women who now play the golf, who have jobs and friends at work. It is the men who cower in the empty nest, nervously facing what an eloquent Irish businessman friend has termed 'the forgotten future'.

From the outset of public life as a male – at school, university, medical school, debating union, postgraduate research centre, hospital – I learned to compete and pretend to a confidence I didn't often (didn't ever) feel. That is what men are required to do. As a result, one of the commonest fears of mature men is that they will be 'found out' in some mysterious fashion. As a young father, I shouted at my children in order to feel powerful, and covertly and sometimes overtly declared that manly boys didn't complain but had to be strong and responsible and suppress vulnerability, particularly if they were to avoid being bullied by other boys. As a young husband, I loved my wife and was, or so I believed, a sympathetic and liberated 'new' male. Now I am not so sure.

She sacrificed much to be a committed and full-time mother. I sacrificed little to be a peripheral and very part-time dad. But I was the family provider and that counted for a great deal – to me at any rate – and I was a father to my children, even if I would have been hard put to define precisely what being a father was.

Now, the whole issue of men – the point of them, their purpose, their value, their justification – is a matter for public debate. Serious commentators declare that men are redundant, that women do not need them and children would be better off without them. At the beginning of the twenty-first century it is difficult to avoid the conclusion that men are in serious trouble. Throughout the world, developed and developing, antisocial behaviour is essentially male. Violence, sexual abuse of children, illicit drug use, alcohol misuse, gambling all are overwhelmingly male activities. The courts and prisons bulge with men. When it comes to aggression, delinquent behaviour, risk taking and social mayhem, men win gold.

And yet, for all their behaving badly, they do not seem any the happier. Throughout North America, Europe and Australia, male suicides outnumber female by a factor of between 3 and 4 to 1.[2] The rise in the number of young men killing themselves in much of the developed world has been rightly termed an epidemic. For the old, the situation is no better. For every 6 elderly women in every 100,000 who kill themselves each year, 40 elderly men take their own lives. And these suicide figures are viewed as the tip of an iceberg of male depression, an iceberg hidden only because men are seen to be either too proud or too emotionally constipated to admit when their feelings are out of control. Men renowned for their ability and inclination to be stoned, drunk or sexually daring, appear terrified by the prospect of revealing that they can be – and often are – depressed, dependent, in need of help.

It will be said that it has always been thus and that all that is changing is that men are coming out of the emotional closet. Men, so this argument goes, having ridiculed, demeaned and patronised women's supposed emotionality, now accept the importance, the maturity, of not merely acknowledging feelings but expressing them in a civilised and open way.

Others argue that there is a genuine rise in male dissatisfaction for which there is no shortage of suggested causes. Top of the list is the growing assertiveness of women. As a consequence of the feminist revolution, so this argument goes, women are no longer prepared to be the property of patriarchal men. In this feminist revolution, male power is being overthrown. Men, like colonists seeing their empire crumble, don't like what is happening. Few women have much time for such an argument. After all, the gains that have accrued to women remain pretty miserly. Men still outnumber women in positions of power across the globe, still glower downwards through the glass ceiling, still strut the cabinet and boardrooms in every developed country in the world, the seeming masters of their fate and everybody else's. In the developing world the situation is even more unequal. The gender disparity in sharing the burden of unpaid work is stark, and for all the talk of equality women throughout the world continue to work longer hours than men and are paid very much less for it. The colonists are still in command.

In the circumstances, female impatience with male sensitivities is understandable. But it may be missing the point. It is true that patriarchy has not been overthrown. But its justification is in disarray. The colonists have not been displaced but the colonised are planning, discussing, organising, and, in a number of small, well-planned uprisings, have demonstrated their capability. There is a sense, certainly in the outlying areas of the patriarchal empire, that the time for male authority, dominance and control is up. Beneath the surface, male power is being subverted. Throughout Europe – in primary schools, through secondary education and right into the universities – girls are outperforming boys. In the European Union, 20 per cent more women are graduating than men. On leaving school and university, women's prospects of employment exceed men's. In Germany, for example, between 1991 and 1995 twice as many men as women lost their jobs. Women actually gained 210,000 jobs while men lost 400,000. Some teenage boys reassure themselves that later on, in their twenties and thirties, the right order reasserts itself, and men regain their rightful place – on top. But that reassurance, for a variety of reasons, is sounding increasingly hollow. Women are on the march and, even if they still have a long way to go, many men, already threatened, are reacting with aggression directed at women and at themselves.

And if changes in education, training and work are not sufficient to demoralise the average man, there is the sorry, dismal, public soap opera of man's relationship with his penis. Men, who in most other areas of their lives make such a fetish of being in control, seem unable to remain masters of their sexual appetites. More darkly, there is little respite from exposure to the more savage side of male sexuality – rape, molestation, sexual violence – manifested overwhelmingly in aggression by men against women and children. Not surprisingly, many innocent men, like the relatives of torturers and killers, find themselves apologising for crimes they have not themselves committed.

But are men fearful of their feelings and, if they are, have they good reason to be? Do men feel contempt for women and, if they do, what is fuelling such contempt? It has been argued that misogyny, the hatred of women, is an inescapable element in the development of men and that, quite simply, there are no good men.[3] Might the fear and contempt be related to a deeper fear, a more profound anxiety about male sexuality itself? Here one is treading on dangerous ground. Put a foot wrong and one risks being accused of blaming *women* for men's inability to control their sexual feelings and to harness their aggression. That is what many men believe and some act upon it. Women are feared, despised and sometimes even destroyed because of what men perceive women to be doing to them. To such men, their own sexuality is exciting precisely because it is unpredictable, capricious, dangerous – and women end up being blamed for provoking it. To such men, women, by their very presence, represent a most disturbing challenge to self-control. Given the extent to which control is for many men the defining mark of their masculinity, any suggestion or threat of being out of control challenges the very essence of what being a male is all about. Bill Clinton's sexual behaviour revealed that the Garden of Eden myth is alive and well and flourishing in the heart of the American empire. Men fall because women tempt them. This remains *the* explanation of male sexual behaviour most favoured by men. Rather than expose to a genuinely rigorous analysis the nature of male sexuality and its relationship to power, social status, aggression and control, most male commentators retreat into a self-pitying and ultimately depressing moan about the difficulty of being a full-bloodedly sexual man in a dynamic relationship with a woman in the new post-feminist world of gender equality.

In an interview with Germaine Greer in 1989 I wondered whether she accepted that behind the bluster and the posturing many men were not really as confident as they might appear. 'I don't care much about phallic insecurity', she tartly replied, adding that, after all,

> men created the dream of the phallus. It's men who are worried about whether the phallic department is adequate. The women are perfectly happy with all the other stuff – with social status, power, intelligence.[4]

She is absolutely right. Men do remain preoccupied with 'whether the phallic department is adequate'. They worry about the size, shape and erectile potential of their genitalia. Men, young and old, are disconcerted by mocking references to what Sylvia Plath dismissively referred to as 'old turkey neck and gizzards'. The highly successful British film, *The Full Monty*, explicitly drew an analogy between male inadequacy consequent on the loss of a job and male anxiety concerning genital potency. Men must bond, share, emotionally relate, must reveal themselves in full nakedness to each other and to women if they are to be fully human; so went the movie's message. Then came the ultimate cop-out in which everything was indeed revealed to the cinema audience – save 'old turkey neck and gizzards'!

Male preoccupation with their penises would appear to be based on fear, right enough: not on the Freudian fear of castration, but on the Adlerian fear of ridicule. Are we up to it? ask today's men anxiously, peering at their shrivelled cocks and analysing their social skills; are we up to competing, succeeding, achieving, conquering, controlling, asserting, pontificating, as well as getting it up? And there is of course the unavoidable gender inequality, the fact that, unlike the female orgasm, the male erection cannot be faked. The obvious visibility of the male genital organs, their state and size, roused and flaccid, are readily measurable and comparable. Hardly surprising, therefore, that the arrival of Viagra has been accompanied not merely by dodgy humour and gruesome *double entendres* but also by po-faced and panicky political discussions about the possible bankrupting of health finances due to a stampede by men to get their hands on the latest 'old turkey gizzard' stimulant.

The one biological difference between the sexes on which everybody is agreed is that whereas women possess two X-shaped sex chromosomes, men possess one X and a little Y-shaped chromosome. The Y chromosome accounts for superior male strength, stature, mass of muscle, sleight of hand, speed of foot. These attributes have been of considerable value in a world dominated by a need for physical power and energy and a raw, brutal, martial strength. We have become accustomed to thinking of 'real' men as those who labour in the iron, steel and coal industries, in shipbuilding, lumberjacking, pre-mechanised farming. Our martial heroes have been almost entirely male, in the fantasies and the realities of hand-to-hand combat, of sheer physical guts, the will to survive, athletic derring-do. What price all that brute strength, might and energy now, when more people are employed making Indian curries than mining coal, when computerised robots and not sweating men assemble cars and when the male predilection for violence, far from saving national pride, threatens world survival?

There is hardly anything to be done in today's society that cannot be done by women. 'So what!' say women, not unreasonably, given the age it has taken to establish such a state of affairs. So what, indeed. The problem is one for men and particularly for those men – and they have been the majority – who have defined their lives, their identities, the very essence of their masculinity in terms of professional and occupational achievement and have prided themselves on the work that only they as men could do. My father's generation prided themselves on being providers – for their spouses, families and themselves. Today, providing seems no longer required. Married women increasingly reap the benefit of education, harness their intelligence and generate their own incomes. In one-parent families women press hard for workplace crèches and better childcare facilities, as well as social security payments to compensate for male-generated finances. Not merely is the role of provider under siege, the role of father is threatened. The second millennium has ended with man's claim to a significant role in procreation and child-rearing seriously diminished. The rise in the number of single mothers suggests not merely that men are inadequate as partners and fathers but that they are simply redundant. Women are asserting that they can conceive and rear children on their own. They don't need men to father their children. The development of assisted reproduction, including techniques such as in vitro fertilisation, artificial insemination by anonymous donor and surrogate motherhood, together with the highly political and controversial assertion that single parenting is as good as that provided by two parents, raise the question – whither fatherhood? If conception, pregnancy, delivery and child-rearing can be perfectly well accomplished without the active participation of the male, then why bother with him at all, given the heartache, the trouble, the sheer cussedness of today's man? Once so proud of his penis (Freud, after all, argued that women envied it), contemporary man now finds he is being reduced to the role of support seed carrier, as women occupy centre stage not merely in the creation of new life (they have always been there) but in its nurturing. It is hardly surprising that there are some men who seriously suggest that the only way they can again play a reproductive and parental role of any significance is if they can be assisted by science to have babies themselves!

A century ago, a peevish Sigmund Freud, perplexed by a seeming epidemic of hysterical, depressed, lethargic and dissatisfied women, asked, 'What do women want?' He asked it at a time when to be a woman was to be pathological, to be male was to be health personified. A century later it is not women who are seen to be pathological, but men; it is not women's wants, but men's, that mystify us. But before we can begin to answer what men want, deserve or need, it is necessary to reassess what we know about men. What is it that the Y chromosome, the cause of all the trouble, is up to? Are men innately and incorrigibly violent? Must the issue between the sexes be for men a case of dominate or be dominated, for women a choice between being resistant or submissive? In a world of equal opportunity for the sexes, can men renegotiate the relationship with themselves and with women? Is there anything left of the male role as provider and protector? Do we need men? Do we need fathers? And if we do, what kind of men, what kind of fathers do we need?

The contemporary world is still, for the most part, divided into two spheres – the private sphere, inhabited for the most part by women, and a public sphere where men find and cultivate their identity and assert their dominance. The power of patriarchy, that set of relations of power that enable men to control women, is grounded in the belief that the public takes precedence over the private. Women struggling to escape the constraints of patriarchy are drawn into a tacit acceptance of the superior value of the public, the business, the profession and the office, and a devaluation of the private. Men, as a consequence, feel little need to reassess the priority they give to the public; indeed, the very desire of women to establish their own public legitimacy is interpreted as further proof that the public is indeed superior and the private is legitimately regarded as inferior.

In exploring the challenged state of masculinity in this book, I have chosen the term 'phallus' very deliberately. The *penis* is an anatomical term referring to the male generative organ. The *phallus* is an anthropological and theological term referring to its image. The penis is an organ with biological functions, the phallus is an idea venerated in various religions as a *symbol* of male power. Phallic refers not merely to the penis but incorporates notions of potency, virility, manliness, strength and power. It has been seen as the 'signifier of signifiers', the mark which positions the individual as male and locates him in terms of authority, control, dominance'.[5] The phallus 'signifies what men think they have and what women are believed to lack'.[6] Man's penis is not at issue, except for its possible redundancy as a tool of procreation. But phallic man, authoritative, dominant, assertive – man in control not merely of himself but of woman – is starting to die, and now the question is whether a new man will emerge phoenix-like in his place or whether man himself will become largely redundant.

CHAPTER 2

WHY THE Y?

What is it that increases your chances of ending up in remedial classes at school, in trouble with the police in adolescence and in jail in your twenties? What is it that makes you much more likely to inject heroin, abuse alcohol, betray your spouse and desert your children? What is it that increases threefold your risk of killing yourself and tenfold your chances of killing someone else? The answer – being a male. And what makes a male? A minute Y-shaped chromosome, invisible to the naked eye, the smallest of the chromosomes that carry all our human genes. The genes on the Y chromosome trigger the development of male characteristics including the formation of the penis and testes, the production of sperm and the development of secondary sexual characteristics including facial hair, a deep voice and pelvic shape and size.

In every human cell there are 46 chromosomes. Forty-four are identical pairs, but two are different – one X-shaped and one Y-shaped, (Figure 1). These two chromosomes regulate sexual development. Hundreds of millions of years ago, sex may well have been determined not by chromosomes but by some environmental factor, such as the temperature at which the egg was incubated. This is the way it still happens in animals such as crocodiles and sea turtles. But the sexuality of the human embryo is determined by the sex chromosomes. Females normally have two X-shaped sex chromosomes, males have one X and one Y. Under a microscope the Y chromosome appears about one-third the size of the X. It is the Y that holds the key to maleness. Without it the embryo develops as a female. Whereas there are thousands of genes to be found on the X chromosome, there are probably no more than a couple of dozen on the Y. To date, researchers have thus far identified only 21 of these genes. These genes can be divided into three groups based on the roles they play in the body.[1] One group contains a single gene that shapes the embryo's destiny to be a male by directing the formation of the testes. The second group, made up of about 10 genes, only becomes active at male puberty and influences the production of

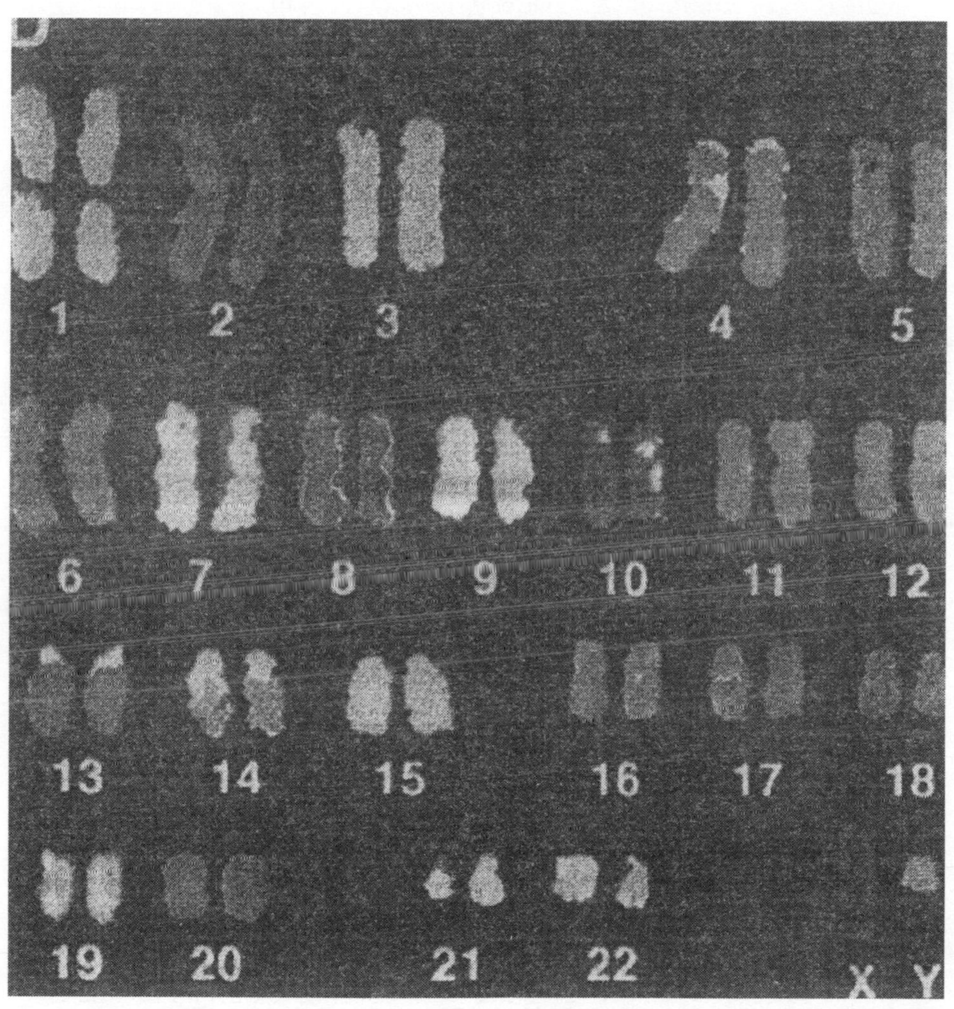

Figure 1 The 46 human chromosomes

sperm. The third group of the remaining 10 genes serves to ensure that cells in the body function efficiently and effectively.

In human reproduction, the male and female each contribute a sex chromosome to make up the embryo's sex chromosome pair. The female can only contribute one of her two X chromosomes, whereas the male can contribute an X (whereby the embryo will be female) or a Y (whereby the embryo will be male). Mixing and matching of parental genes is believed to enhance the survival of the species. Offspring genetically different from either parent are produced. The odds that their progeny can exploit new opportunities thrown up by a changing environment and survive the assaults of adverse biological and environmental factors are thereby increased.

Very early in the development of the human embryo can be seen a primitive structure called the Mullerian duct. This is a forerunner of the uterus and the inner portion of the vagina and *both* male and female embryos possess it. Until the foetal testis influenced by the Y chromosome begins to secrete hormones, there is no apparent sexual differentiation within the embryo. Even if the testis is present but does not secrete for some reason, a female embryo will develop. The basic state of human development is female. Unless and until the foetal testis gets to work, we are all embryonic women. A masterly review of the biology of sexual differences puts it bluntly:

> masculine differentiation occurs because the fetal testes, which are actively producing androgen (testosterone) and a substance that inhibits the development of the female anlagen (Mullerian inhibiting substance), impose masculinity upon the *basic feminine trend of the body*, whereas female differentiation proceeds in the relative absence of these influences. [my italics][2]

So from the very outset one of the oldest explanations of the creation of the sexes, indeed one of the foundation stones of patriarchy in Judaeo-Christianity, namely the story of Genesis in the Bible, gets it spectacularly wrong. Eve is not fashioned out of Adam's rib. Adam is made out of Eve. To be a male not only demands a Y chromosome but that a switch be turned on by one of the genes on the Y. If the switch fails then, Y or no Y, the embryo turns out female.

Most people are not particularly interested in the Y chromosome when it comes to explaining how men tick. Instead they focus on **testosterone** – the hormone produced by the male testis that results from the actions of the genes on the Y. There are respected scientists and political commentators, virtually all men, who endow this hormone with the most awesome of powers. Testosterone, they insist, underpins patriarchal societies, explains the predominance of men in governments and boardrooms, impels murderous youths to machine-gun American schoolchildren, fuels the sexual use and abuse of women and children. Testosterone is the reason men fly to the moon, climb Mount Everest, paint the Sistine Chapel and peddle pornography. Testosterone, quite simply, is the reason why, as one unabashed defender of patriarchy puts it,

> human biology precludes the possibility of a human social system whose authority structure is not dominated by males, and in which male aggression is not manifested in dominance and attainment of position, of status and power.[3]

And the social biologists are not alone. Though she is by no means as certain that testosterone is the whole explanation, Germaine Greer is in no doubt that the end result of all those embryonic interactions is pathetic when it is not repulsive. 'To be male', she declares in her most recent book:

> is to be a kind of idiot savant, full of queer obsessions about fetishistic activities and fantasy goals, single-minded in pursuit of arbitrary objectives, doomed to competition and injustice, not merely towards females but towards children, animals and other men.[4]

But what is the evidence that it is testosterone that holds the key to male aggression and violence? The hormone and its metabolites do explain why men are physically larger, stronger, faster and leaner on average than women, why they grow facial hair, have deeper voices, and narrower hips. In addition to its *masculinising* effects, testosterone and related male sex hormones (together termed *androgens*) have *anabolic* (protein tissue building) properties. The anabolic steroids used by athletes to build muscle mass, reduce fat and increase performance are synthetic derivatives of testosterone designed to maximise protein synthesis and minimise masculinising effects.

The anatomical and physiological development of male and female sexuality is comparatively well understood and thus far we can conclude that the Y chromosome is the genetic foundation stone of maleness. Along with the hormones its genes stimulate, testosterone and its metabolites, it produces the anatomic male. But is that it? What about those differences between the sexes that the sociobiologists insist are a consequence of the different ways in which the male and female brains are wired? All those assertions about men – that they are aggressive, combative, violent, abusive, addicted, promiscuous and antisocial – can they be rooted in a tiny little Y-shaped chromosome and its 21 genes?

Testosterone and the Male

At first glance the evidence looks promising in favour of the biologist's argument that testosterone brings about fundamental differences in the way the male brain functions. Research over the past 30 years has shown that it is not only in the area of the internal and external sexual organs that sexual differentiation takes place in the developing embryo. Sexual differentiation also occurs within the central nervous system, including the brain itself. The noted neurophysiologist, Torsten Wiesel, describes it well:

> Genes controlling embryonic development shape the structure of the infant brain; the infant's experience in the world then fine-tunes the pattern of neural connections underlying the brain's function. Such fine-tuning . . . must surely continue through adulthood.[5]

It is now known that the sex hormones regulate the number of brain cells, the growth of the axons and dendrites, which link brain cells via synapses or junctions, and the receptors in the brain on which the sex hormones act. This sexual differentiation of the brain, orchestrated by the sex hormones, occurs during a relatively short developmental period yet it results in permanent changes in the parts of the brain sensitive to these hormones.

Most studies of sexual brain differentiation have been undertaken on laboratory animals and have shown numerous differences between the sexes with regard to hormones acting on brain receptors and involving such behaviours as copulation, scent marking, vocalisation and mate recognition. When, for example, fragments are taken from certain brain centres in newborn male rats and are transplanted into the brains of female rats, male copulatory behaviour occurs in these females in adulthood,[6] while sexual differences have been found in the parts of the brain which govern voice control in songbirds.[7] It has also been shown that exposing the developing brains of female mice and female rhesus monkeys to high levels of circulating male sex hormones makes the females of both species more aggressive.[8] What appears clear from animal studies is that (a) the administration of male sex hormones to genetic females during foetal development results in defeminisation and/or the development of masculine attributes and behaviour and (b) the deprivation of male sex hormones from genetic males during the prenatal period results in demasculinisation and/or the development of feminine attributes and behaviour in adolescence and adulthood.[9]

Such ingenious research findings have led biologists to overreach themselves in explaining human sex differences as the result of sex hormones acting on the developing brain. There are dangers in extrapolating from animals to human beings. The sorts of manipulations applied to rats, hamsters and guinea pigs cannot for obvious ethical, moral and legal reasons be applied to human beings. As a result – and this is a most important caveat – any interpretation of the relationship between hormones acting in the prenatal period and human behavioural development is limited to the making of correlative rather than causal connections.

Nonetheless, researchers have taken very seriously the popular biological theory of sex differences in aggressive behaviour which, on the basis of the animal studies referred to already, suggests that differences in patterns of early exposure to the male sex hormones (androgens) differentially sensitise male and female brains to the activational effects of circulating androgens, making males more likely to be aggressive.[10] The conventional wisdom is that boys play with soldiers and guns, girls with dolls and prams, boys engage in rough-and-tumble play, girls in more ordered and organised games involving domestic and child-bearing fantasies.

So, what happens if, for some reason, females during their embryonic development or their early childhood are exposed to testosterone? Does testosterone make them more aggressive? Does it turn girls into typical boys or does the effect of their chromosomal status and their upbringing as girls offset testosterone effects?

One curious accident of medical treatment has provided an opportunity to assess the impact of testosterone on the developing female. From the 1940s to the 1970s, over half a million human pregnancies were treated with the non-steroidal synthetic oestrogen, diethylbestrol

(DES), the purpose being to prevent spontaneous abortion in pregnant women threatened with the loss of their pregnancy. DES has effects in animals similar to that of male sex hormones. The behaviour of females exposed to DES would, therefore, be expected to show more masculine characteristics. But, while these studies are much quoted by those who believe they clinch the argument in favour of a biological basis for aggression, the findings have actually been contradictory and unconvincing. No consistent alterations have been reported in the gender-role behaviour of women exposed to DES prenatally, although many studies have been undertaken, one of the most quoted being that of Ehrhardt and his colleagues at Columbia University.[11] Thirty women with a history of prenatal DES exposure were contrasted with 30 unexposed women who had been referred to the same clinic for an examination because of an abnormal Pap smear. Gender-role behaviour in childhood, adolescence and adulthood was assessed by means of a semi-structured interview and a number of measures designed to identify stereotypically masculine and feminine behaviour. The results, published in a plethora of papers in distinguished biological and medical journals, were disappointing. All they amounted to was a *suggestion* that women exposed to DES when *in utero* showed less parenting towards their own children in adult life than did controls. (Note that inadequate parenting was assumed to be *typical* male behaviour!)

Nature herself provides another opportunity to study the biological and behavioural effects of the male hormones. There is a condition, termed *congenital adrenal hyperplasia* (CAH) in which the production of abnormally large amounts of male hormones (androgens) can occur in females because of a genetic defect, leading to a situation similar to that experienced *in utero* by foetuses exposed to DES. Women with the defect are chromosomally female (possessing the XX sex chromosomes) but, due to the increased production of androgens because of the congenital defect, suffer a masculinisation of the female genitalia at birth. If untreated, they manifest a masculine physical appearance, a deepening of the voice, an enlarged clitoris and a lack of breast development at puberty. Later still there is a complete absence of menstruation and marked hirsutism. The frequency of the fully developed form in Europe and the United States is estimated at about one in 6,000 live births.

Several early studies appeared to show that CAH girls tended to be more tomboyish in their childhood behaviour than their sisters or unrelated control girls. They tended to be more physically active, to engage in more rough-and-tumble and pursuit play and activities and to be more likely to emphasise careers over child-bearing in their fantasies about their adult lives – all activities and preferences regarded by researchers as indicative of a masculine orientation.[12] In a much-quoted study,[13] Sheri Berenbaum and Melissa Hines observed the play behaviour of girls affected by CAH and compared it with that of their brothers and sisters. Given a choice of trucks and cars and building blocks, of dolls and kitchen furniture, of books and board games, the CAH girls preferred to play with the more stereotypically 'masculine' toys and did so for the same amount of time that the boys did. Both the CAH girls and the healthy boys differed from the healthy girls in their patterns of choice.

Much has been made of this work but it is full of shortcomings. First, the sample of affected girls is small. Secondly, there is the fact, rarely referred to by the researchers, that girls who suffer from congenital adrenal hyperplasia are, for the most part, anatomically and psychologically seriously affected. For the first few years of their lives, and certainly until they have plastic surgery, they have a penis-like clitoris and a scrotum. Then there is the effect of any surgery. There is, too, the question of the parents' attitudes to and expectations of their CAH daughters. It is perfectly possible, as has been persuasively argued by Bleier,[14] that the girls manifesting the so-called 'masculine' behaviour were those most seriously anatomically affected and, as a consequence, most likely to think of themselves as boys and to elicit from others, including their own parents, expectations that they would behave like boys.

Another rare natural experiment involves chromosomal males (XY) who have a partial *androgen insensitivity syndrome* which results from a deficiency in a chemical, 5a-reductase type 2, and makes it impossible for them to respond to normal levels of testosterone. Because the deficiency occurs while the embryo is in the midst of sexual differentiation, testosterone is not able to bring about proper anatomical male development and the result is that these infants are born with genitalia that are incompletely differentiated. Appearing more female than male, they are usually brought up as females.[15] In these instances, the

genotype, that is the actual combination of particular genes inherited which in these cases includes the Y chromosome, conflicts with the **phenotype**, which refers to the observable effects the activity of these genes produces on the individuals. Treatment with high doses of male sex hormones in adulthood appears to improve virilisation and male sexual performance, but many of these chromosomal males seek official reassignment as males and request surgical correction of the somewhat deformed penis and the testes which are often present but hidden.

One of the most celebrated (and studied) groups of androgen insensitivity syndrome patients is to be found in three rural villages in the south-western region of the Dominican Republic. A research team from Cornell University Medical College and the Department of Paediatrics at the National University in the Dominican Republic studied these male pseudohermaphrodites to establish just how important testosterone is to the development of male gender identity.[16] The subjects had plasma testosterone in the high normal range, showed a very impressive response to testosterone and were remarkable models for evaluating the effect of testosterone in determining gender identity. On the basis of detailed retrospective interviewing (by the time the researchers got to see them the 38 individuals had reached adulthood), it was found that 18 had been raised as girls. Anatomically they had presented as females – at birth the scrotum looked like a vagina, there was a rather large clitoris and there were no testes (testes in this condition fail to descend and are to be found within the abdominal cavity). During puberty, when testosterone was at last able to exert its effects, definite masculinisation occurred, the voice deepened, the clitoris grew into a penile size and the testes descended into the scrotum. It was at this time that the parents and the affected 'females' recognised that something was wrong. What was wrong was that the 'females' were in fact males.

Of the 18 raised as girls, 17 promptly changed to a male gender identity. The researchers concluded that, as they rather technically put it, 'where the sex of rearing is contrary to the testosterone-mediated biologic sex, the biologic sex prevails if the normal testosterone-induced activation of puberty is permitted to occur'[17]. In simple English, the effect of testosterone in puberty overrides the effect of rearing the boys as girls in infancy and childhood. These findings serve to illustrate the triumph of testosterone over rearing. The anxieties of some parents, particularly fathers, that their sons are being brought up in 'girlie' ways, with feminine interests, toys and behaviour, can be set at rest!

In these Dominican Republic villages, boys and girls play together until six years of age but then are encouraged to play separately according to gender. The girls help their mothers with household activities, while the boys help their fathers during the planting and harvesting seasons. The boys are encouraged to romp outside the home. The girls are encouraged to stay with their mothers or play in the house. At about 11 years of age, the boys seek entertainment at bars and cockfights. The pseudohermaphrodites had been brought up as girls, helping their mothers, staying at home, avoiding boyish activities and deprived of male camaraderie; yet on reaching puberty they reverted to being males and suffered – so we are told – no obvious ill-effects! The failure of testosterone to work in the early years of their development did not bring about serious physical or psychological difficulties in adolescence or later years, when the testosterone was functioning correctly. This finding is as interesting as the somewhat more obvious one – that testosterone brings about the secondary sex characteristics that characterise male puberty.

What happens if you remove circulating testosterone? Such research as has been done has focused only on the effects on aggressive and sexual behaviour. Studies have been undertaken of convicted sex offenders who have been surgically castrated[18] or have been given chemical agents capable of suppressing testosterone.[19] A number of studies suggest that injections of chemicals which inhibit the secretion of testosterone can reduce the number and intensity of sexual fantasies and episodes of deviant behaviour.[20] Associated claims of reduced reoffending and violence have been made but these rates have not been compared with rates for similar men not so treated. There is some evidence to suggest that recidivism decreases in paedophiliacs following so-called chemical castration; but the use of such an approach is limited by a high refusal and drop-out rate. One would expect, however, that removal of testosterone completely would diminish the sexual drive, and this is discussed below. What we do know is that the great majority of men who sexually abuse and molest women and children do not manifest any consistent, reliable and significant abnormalities in testosterone secretion or levels. Something else is at work in addition to testosterone secretion.

Testosterone, Aggression and Dominance

What about the link between testosterone and aggression? Males have more testosterone in their circulation than females and men are more aggressive.[21] Women do produce testosterone and men do produce oestrogen. The testosterone in women is made in the adrenal cortex and the ovaries. The normal woman produces about 200 micrograms of testosterone and 120 micrograms of oestrogen each day, a testosterone/oestrogen ratio of about 1.6 to 1. The normal male produces about the same amount of oestrogen daily (100 micrograms) but a comparatively huge amount of testosterone – 5,100 micrograms per day – giving a testosterone/oestrogen ratio of 51 to 1. Not only do men have very much higher levels of testosterone than women, they have them at their highest just after puberty and in the early and mid-twenties – when male antisocial activity and aggression is at its peak.[22] Male testosterone levels slowly decrease with age, beginning in the early to middle twenties.[23] Male libido, aggressiveness and antisocial behaviour decline, too, from that same time period.[24] However, before it is automatically assumed that the one causes the other, it is important to note that the actual fall in testosterone levels is small. A man well into his seventies is secreting substantial amounts relative to his body mass.[25]

Testosterone, then, is necessary but not sufficient for normal levels of male sexual desire. Deprived of testosterone, men appear to lose the desire for sex. But the relationship between testosterone and the penis is very complex. Spontaneous erections, such as those that occur in the night (i.e. nocturnal penile tumescence), are highly dependent on the level of circulating testosterone. They occur less or not at all when testosterone levels are low and it has been shown that they occur more frequently when testosterone is injected.[26] In contrast, erections in response to erotic visual stimuli seem to be independent of circulating testosterone![27] The relationship between testosterone and aggression is even more complicated.[28]

With the development of easier and more reliable methods of measuring testosterone, extraordinary claims emanating from research studies have demonstrated varying degrees of imagination and resourcefulness. High levels of testosterone have been reported in violent criminals; in aggressive hockey players; in army veterans with significant histories of marital disruption; in those suffering from drug and alcohol abuse, antisocial behaviour, and difficulties with the law.[29] In one intriguing study, the testosterone levels of four male physicians aged 28 to 38 who were confined on a boat for a two-week cruise holiday were assessed and found to correlate with their dominant and aggressive behaviour as rated by women also on the boat![30]

The controversial and increasing use by athletes of anabolic steroids also offers an opportunity to clarify the links between hormones and aggression. These steroids are similar to testosterone in pharmacological make-up and general effects. Illegal use by male and female athletes to improve their strength, fitness and overall performance is now widespread, and many different steroids and combinations of steroids are in use. Athletes abusing anabolic steroids have been shown to be particularly prone to major disturbances of mood, including severe depression and euphoria and marked irritability and aggression. Harrison Pope and David Katz from McLean Hospital in Boston provide dramatic examples of steroid-induced aggression occurring in a sample of 88 abusing athletes.[31] Because he had been annoyed in a traffic jam, one user, with his fists and a metal bar, seriously damaged three cars while their drivers cowered terrified inside. Another was arrested for causing property damage in a fit of anger at a sports meeting, while another beat and almost killed his dog. Several users reported being expelled from their homes by parents, wives or partners because they had become seriously aggressive. Nearly all of these athletes denied comparable behaviour before they had commenced abusing steroids. A problem with this and other studies, however, is that athletes who abuse anabolic steroids often abuse other drugs too, including alcohol, cocaine, opiates, amphetamines and hallucinogens. Nor is it clear to what extent anabolic steroids cause or exacerbate aggressive and irritable tendencies already well developed in these highly competitive and single-minded individuals. But there is a growing literature supporting the view that anabolic masculinising steroids, particularly when used in very large doses, may cause serious mood disorders – and aggression.

Overall, then, is the case open and shut? Testosterone causes aggression. That is how this body of research is reported and received in the media. Alongside such an interpretation goes the hand-wringing conclusion that attempts to tame and civilise males are doomed by the rampant imperialism of testosterone. It is testosterone-primed aggression that produces the differences in social roles between the sexes and underpins the patriarchy that exists throughout the world. And this being so, we either accept it or somehow pharmacologically eliminate men.

But the reality is much more complicated. What these studies really show is a *correlation* between levels of aggression and levels of testosterone. There is more than one explanation for such a correlation. Yes, indeed, raised levels of testosterone might cause aggression. But, likewise, increased levels of aggressive behaviour might *cause* higher levels of testosterone. And, then again, neither might *cause* the other. And there is little consistency in the findings. For every study that reports a positive correlation between this or that aggressive or antisocial behaviour and testosterone, there is another which fails to find such a link. For example, there are studies of normal boys,[32] delinquent boys[33] and highly aggressive prepubertal boys[34] which have shown no relationship whatsoever between testosterone and the presence or absence of aggressive behaviour. Most important of all, there is no evidence that administering large doses of testosterone to men whose levels are normal makes them any more aggressive or violent than they were before.[35]

Is there any evidence that aggressive behaviour or the anticipation of conflict and competition might result in higher testosterone levels? A major review by Allan Mazur at Syracuse University and Alan Booth of Penn State documents a sizeable body of research which supports such a relationship.[36] For example, it has been shown that testosterone levels rise in athletes shortly before their matches, as if in anticipation.[37] This rise may enable the individual to take risks and improve co-ordination, cognitive performance and concentration. It has also been found that for one or two hours after a match, the testosterone levels of winners are high relative to those of losers.[38] Other studies of non-physical contests show similar findings. For example, testosterone levels rise before chess matches and are higher in winners than in losers afterwards.[39] Even being a passive spectator can produce variations in testosterone. Following the World Cup final in 1994 (in which Brazil defeated Italy after a penalty shoot-out), testosterone levels increased significantly in Brazilian fans who had watched the match on television and decreased in Italian fans![40]

Even more significant research, illustrating the complexity of the role of testosterone in aggressive behaviour, concerns men confronted with a symbolic challenge or insult. It has been shown that people living in the Southern States of the United States are more likely to think it justifiable to kill to protect one's house. Southerners are more likely to take offence at insults and to consider violence an appropriate response to being insulted. And they are much more likely to admit that they would advise their child to fight a bully than to attempt to reason with him.[41] A highly imaginative experiment was conducted in which an experimenter insulted a college student by bumping into him in a narrow hallway and swearing at him. (The students had agreed to participate in the study but were not forewarned or given details.) Northerners tended to ignore the incident. Southerners did not take it so lightly. The testosterone levels of the Southerners surged after the insult, whereas those of the Northerners did not.[42]

Then the researchers added a further twist. Students walking along the passage encountered a massively built character striding menacingly towards them down the middle of the hallway. Southerners who had not just been insulted gave way when the intimidating figure was on average about nine feet away. Those who had just been insulted held the ground until he was about three feet away. It appeared that the Southerners who had just been offended were still in truculent mood, even when they were confronted with someone with a substantial weight advantage. The Northern students' decisions on when to step aside were not affected by whether they had been insulted or not.

Other studies reveal the extent to which social and cultural factors modify and affect any potential relationship between testosterone and aggression. For example, among high-socioeconomic status US army veterans, those with high testosterone levels were no more likely than their peers with normal levels of testosterone to be hard drug users or to have problems with antisocial behaviour.[43] Among those with low socioeconomic status, however, those with high testosterone levels were almost twice as likely as their peers with normal testosterone levels to have such problems. A plausible explanation, suggests Dov Cohen, a leading researcher in this field, is that lower socioeconomic status environments 'are more fraught with dangers and opportunities for trouble and people with higher T [testosterone] fall into those troubles'.[44]

Studies such as these support the argument that aggressive and violent behaviour cannot be explained by simply blaming testosterone. 'Normal' levels of testosterone are indeed necessary for 'normal' levels of aggression, but changing the amount of testosterone in the blood within the normal range does not alter subsequent levels of aggressive behaviour. Administer large doses of testosterone (and they have to be very large) and aggressive behaviour increases, but even this is not as simple as it seems. Robert Sapolsky, in the course of a wise and witty essay, describes an experiment with a group of monkeys. Time was given to let the participating monkeys form the usual hierarchy of dominance and submission. Then one of them was administered a massive injection of testosterone. Sure enough, the testosterone-soaked monkey behaved more aggressively. But he was not indiscriminately aggressive. He remained submissive to the monkeys who had dominated him before he got the extra testosterone, but was insufferably aggressive to the monkeys who were below him in the pecking order. Sapolsky sums up the situation: 'testosterone isn't *causing* aggression, it's *exaggerating* the aggression that's already there.'[45] 'Study after study', he continues,

> has shown that when you examine testosterone levels when males are first placed together in a social group, testosterone levels predict nothing about who is going to be aggressive. The subsequent behavioral differences drive the hormonal changes, rather than the other way around.[46]

There is something wonderfully seductive about arguments that conceive of a multifaceted and complicated set of behaviours we call *aggression* being attributable to the rise and fall of a single hormone, testosterone. It is seductive because it means that instead of having to attend to such complex issues as gun control, adolescent alienation, family breakdown, social deprivation and poverty in an attempt to reduce levels of violence in a given society, we can focus instead on the manipulation of a single hormone or group of hormones by surgical or pharmacological means. Aggression and violence can be turned from political and social problems into biomedical challenges. And it then becomes so much easier, politically speaking, to talk about them! Contrast the clarity of the false statement – testosterone is *the* cause of aggression – with the complexity of the true statement – testosterone and aggressive behaviour are linked in a circular relationship in which aggressive behaviour can result in elevated levels of testosterone and substantial increases in testosterone can lead to increased aggressive behaviour. To construct a tabloid headline out of the first requires little imagination; to do the same with the second calls for ingenuity.

And then there is the problem of what we mean by aggression. For Mazur and Booth, an individual will be said to act *aggressively* if his apparent intent is to inflict physical injury on a member of his species. They distinguish aggression from dominance. An individual is judged to be acting *dominantly* if his apparent intent is to achieve or maintain high status – that is power, influence or valued prerogatives – over a member of his own species.[47] The aggressive correlates of testosterone have been emphasised ever since 1849 when Berthold transplanted the testes of roosters into capons and found that the capons 'crowed lustily, often engaged in battle with each other and the other cockerels, and showed the usual reactions to hens'.[48] Mazur and Booth demonstrate how such a straightfoward linkage of aggression to testosterone, appropriate for many animal species, is too simplistic for human beings. Aggressive behaviour is clearly not one simple behaviour and it is likely that alterations in testosterone may be related only to some aspects of many behaviours.

So what is meant by dominance? Mazur and Booth define it as action intended to enhance status. The words they use to define the core elements include 'powerful, commanding, authoritative, high in control masterful and ascendant'. The action they focus on is competition in which one person gains at the expense of another. At the heart of dominance is the desire to change the views or actions of others and the willingness to engage in behaviour to bring about such a change. The New Zealand social researcher, Valerie Grant, adds the rider that the dominant individual is unwilling to change his own attitudes or behaviour merely (i.e. without explanation) at the instigation of others.[49] Sometimes dominance benefits others, as when a forceful leader helps not just himself but his followers. Altruistic heroes and heroines help others. Any act that produces deference in others can make one dominant. Of course men who wish to dominante may not need to engage in aggressive behaviour to achieve their end. They may end up successful by the use of oratorical prowess, manipulative skill and the simple threat of violence. Now while there is, as we have seen, evidence that circulating testosterone does not cause human aggression[50]

– the intentional infliction of physical injury – it does seem to encourage dominant behaviour intended to achieve or maintain high status. Usually humans express dominance without recourse to aggression. Why men dominate with intent to harm is due to more than just the levels of their testosterone. Ehrenkranz and his colleagues showed in an early study that socially dominant but unaggressive prisoners had relatively high testosterone levels, not significantly different from the testosterone levels of aggressive prisoners, who may well have been dominant too.[51]

It has been suggested that it is dominance rather than aggression that possesses evolutionary advantages for men; it helps them obtain resources in competition with other males. In this respect it is worth noting that women do not find *aggressive* men attractive whereas they are attracted to men who are dominant in *non-aggressive* ways.[52]

Given that women have some circulating testosterone in their blood, can we learn anything about its effects by studying female behaviour? The more incorrigible of the sociobiologists have suggested that, as women occupy more and more of the positions of power formerly exclusive to men, the more like men (i.e the more dominant and aggressive) women will become. An early study purporting to show that testosterone levels rose in women as the status of their occupations increased appeared to bear them out;[53] whereas a later study, undertaken in 1995, of 32 college women found that status (as judged by peer assessments) did not correlate with testosterone levels.[54] However, in the later study, the women's assessment of their own status did correlate with testosterone. Attempts to link testosterone with aggression in women have also produced suggestive but inconsistent results. A study of 84 women in prison and 15 women in college found no overall difference in testosterone levels but women convicted of unprovoked violence did have higher testosterone levels.[55] In another study of female prisoners, no significant relationship was found between testosterone and the extent of criminal violence in which the inmates had engaged, but testosterone levels were significantly related to what the authors termed 'aggressive dominant behavior' while the women were in prison.[56]

There have been attempts, too, to link sexual behaviour in women with testosterone. Women with high levels of testosterone reportedly have more sexual partners and claim to need less commitment from a man before engaging in sex.[57] As for dominance in women, a series of studies by Valerie Grant in Auckland, New Zealand, suggests that women who are more dominant in personality than other women are more likely to conceive sons and differ qualitatively in the way they interact with their newborn sons from the way they interact with their daughters![58] That is to say, dominant women are more likely to conceive sons and then rear them in a manner that ensures they end up dominant! Grant suggests that women, and mothers in particular, play a role in the chain linking testosterone and male dominance:

> These sex-of-infant differences in mothers' behaviors appear to ensure that higher dominance is passed on, via mothers, to sons rather than to daughters, thus both ratifying and perpetuating psychological sex differences in this area.[59]

What about other influences of testosterone on men and masculine behaviour? There was much excitement in the mass media when two American researchers, Alan Booth and James M. Dabbs, produced findings which suggested that men with high levels of testosterone are less likely to marry and more likely to divorce.[60] In their study, men who divorced had elevated testosterone levels before and after divorce. The testosterone levels of men who married during the decade of the study fell as they made the transition from bachelor to married man, and testosterone remained low among stable married men. Much speculation was triggered by this report. The social biologists, enthusiastic supporters of the 'men will be promiscuous rogues because of their testosterone' theory, seized on the link, assuming that the high testosterone made the men unfaithful and less likely to settle to monogamy. But there are other, less simplistic possibilities. Stress can result in high testosterone levels. It has been suggested that for men marital status is less stressful than being single. Single men are more likely than their married counterparts to encounter confrontation and difficulty; they are less stable and secure and lack the social support of a spouse. So, they need to engage in a more watchful, wary and self-protective stance as they negotiate their lives. This is exactly the sort of situation in which testosterone might be expected to rise. Divorce, prefaced and followed as it is by many months and sometimes years of acrimony and bickering, would likewise be expected to be accompanied by persistently high testosterone levels. Mazur and Booth suggest that men in the throes of marital conflict and breakdown will experience rising testosterone levels, 'which in turn encourages further confrontation with their estranged wives'.[61] Another possible explanation is that sexual activity could affect testosterone levels in men – it does in mice![62] – which could explain higher levels in single and divorced men. Laboratory male mice, exposed to new females, with or without physical contact, manifest a rise in testosterone. Following ejaculation, testosterone levels decrease. It is possible, therefore, that the low testosterone levels found in stable, married men are a consequence of a regular sex life, and the high testosterone levels found in single men the result of a persistently frustrated one.

There are some technical objections to simplistic assumptions too. Testosterone measurements, very much more precise now given the relatively recent developments in hormonal radioimmunoassay techniques and salivary analysis, are still far from perfect. Testosterone is secreted not in a steady but in a pulsatile fashion, is clearly sensitive to factors such as sexual activity, temperature, general health, alcohol and drug use, and is often sampled in not strictly comparable ways in many of the studies quoted. The certainty and vehemence with which some commentators assert testosterone's ability to bring about this or that behaviour are certainly not justified when a close look is taken at the research on which such claims are founded.

Has light been cast on the role of testosterone by studying homosexuals or transsexuals? The answer here is no. A biological basis to homosexuality there very well may be,[63] but the issue remains open and provides little to help us establish just how different the brains of men and women are. Male homosexuals are genotypically male and have a Y chromosome. To date no consistent abnormality in testosterone secretion, activity or effects has been demonstrated in studies of homosexual males. A number of questionnaire-based studies have suggested that homosexual men are less aggressive than heterosexual men and closer to women in their score patterns.[64] In a more recent American study, heterosexual and homosexual men described themselves as more aggressive than their female counterparts.[65] While the heterosexual men were more physically aggressive than the homosexual men, no other findings were significant. The finding that male heterosexual orientation is associated with physical aggressiveness might suggest that among males the two traits have the same determinants – that sex and aggression are indeed biologically linked and that timely androgen action masculinises both sexual orientation and physical aggressiveness. (This assumes that the androgen priming of the infant male brain does not occur in male infants who grow up to be gay, but this remains to be established.) On the other hand, the finding is consistent with alternative sociocultural explanations. For example, males who have been socialised to be physically unaggressive might also be likely to develop homosexuality. What this study did show was that neither verbal aggressiveness nor interpersonal competitiveness distinguished between gay and straight men which suggests that sexual orientation develops independently of these. It is conceivable that biological factors might operate in the case of physical aggressiveness, and social ones in the case of verbal aggressiveness and competitiveness.

There is no intrinsic tension within homosexual men concerning their masculine status. Their masculinity is less in a state of crisis and more in a state of siege given that so many heterosexual men, and some women too, view homosexuality as some kind of impaired or weakened manhood. For this reason, gay men do not fall within the remit of my analysis of the precarious state of masculinity and the potential redundancy of phallic power.

What about transsexualism, that condition in which an anatomically normal person believes with an absolute conviction that he or she is a member of the opposite sex? This feeling is usually accompanied by a profound sense of loathing for the individual's own primary and secondary sexual characteristics. Here is a state in which one might have expected to find biological changes in the sex hormones or in the brain to explain it but to date the evidence is lacking.[66] An extraordinary array of investigations has been conducted into the hormonal status of transsexuals with nothing much to show for it at the end.[67] Biological, psychological and social factors appear to play important roles in the determination of the individual transsexual. The case of Joanna/John (see below) illustrates this complexity – an only girl who showed marked 'male' preferences from childhood, she reacted badly to attempts to persuade her to dress and behave 'gender appropriately' and by adolescence was incorrigibly set on 'becoming' a male.

John started out life as Joanna, the youngest of a family of four and the only girl. From the outset, she behaved, in her mother's words, 'like a boy'. She preferred to play with her brothers' guns, railways trains and dumper trucks than with the dolls and dresses that her parents brought

their only darling daughter. She ran, jumped, swam and competed with her three brothers and their male friends. She despised girls and 'girlie things' and showed a robust enthusiasm for dressing in a T-shirt and jeans, which caused repeated trouble at her convent school. With the onset of adolescence came serious trouble. Joanna became highly disturbed, engaging in repeated acts of self-mutilation, assaults against other girls and violence in the family home. She saw a variety of psychiatrists and was prescribed many treatments, with little improvement. Aged 20 she took herself to a gender reassignment clinic insisting that ever since she had any conscious sense of herself she believed she was a male. She was provisionally diagnosed as a transsexual and proceeded to live dressed as a male for two years. Her disturbed behaviour ceased and she obtained a job in a computer firm. At the age of 22 she changed her name to John, took testosterone to suppress her (his) oestrogens and to produce male secondary sexual characteristics and two years later underwent bilateral mastectomy and a hysterectomy. Then surgeons closed the vagina and constructed an artificial penis by means of skin grafts. Once, when asked what, other than anatomy, is the difference between a man and a woman, John replied revealingly, 'A man is active, makes things happen and is strong, a woman is passive, reacts to what happens and is weak. A man makes a life. A woman makes life. I was never cut out to be a woman.' John's answers eloquently reflect the stereotypes of male and female behaviour.

At no stage in his development did John show any hormonal or chromosomal abnormalities. The role of environmental factors in the genesis of his condition cannot be ruled out – he started out as the only girl with three active and energetic brothers and quickly identified with their work and play patterns. While John's mother was kind and gentle but somewhat retiring, his father was a dominant, assertive and exceedingly self-confident man with whom John had a rather tentative relationship. It was his father rather than his mother who found their daughter's decision to seek a sex change well nigh impossible to accept.

What about other behaviours or abilities attributable to the possession or lack of the Y chromosome? Both sexes have been exhaustively studied in childhood, adolescence and adulthood with regard to a variety of psychological and social abilities including sociability; suggestibility; analytic abilities; motivation; self-esteem; verbal, visual and spatial abilities; rote learning and simple repetitive tasks; mathematical ability and aggression.[68] Some consistent findings emerge but none have been linked with specific areas of brain function or with specific sex hormone effects.

Women, in general, appear to have better verbal fluency, perceptual speed, accuracy and ability to recall. They do better on tests that challenge the individual to find words with a specific letter or synonyms for words, are better than men in rapidly identifying matching items and performing certain manual tasks demanding precision, such as putting pegs in different-shaped holes on a test board. Men excel at visual and spatial activities, for example completing a computer simulation of a maze or labyrinth task quicker than women, or manipulating three-dimensional objects. They appear to be more accurate than women in certain motor skills such as guiding or intercepting projectiles, and on tests of mathematical reasoning. It was formerly thought that sex differences in problem-solving tests did not manifest themselves until puberty but there is some evidence that they emerge in childhood and Kimura quotes research which shows that three- and four-year-old boys were better at targeting and mentally rotating figures within a clock face than girls, while prepubescent girls excelled at recalling lists of words.[69] However, and it is a very substantial caveat, these are average results. Many women do as well as or better than many men on tests where on average men excel, and vice versa. It is, as so much is in life, a matter of probabilities.

A number of these test result differences do tantalisingly suggest possible reasons why the sexes have such difficulty in understanding each other. It is tempting to assume, for example, that one of the reasons men resort to physical violence is that their verbal skills are just not up to coping with stress and frustration. But there is a huge gap between the finding of subtle differences in performance on experimental psychological tests and explaining complex psychosocial behaviours such as aggression and violence. There are two larger areas of activity, however, where sex-linked differences are very dogmatically asserted. The first concerns mathematical skills, the second differences in the structure of the brains of men and women.

Men and Mathematics

Many studies of mathematical achievement have consistently found sex differences which favour males.[70] In the United States in the mid-1970s, the National Institute of Education established a grants programme to fund research on the topic of gender differences and mathematical skill which resulted in much valuable research but did not appear to make much difference – males still outstripped females in mathematical abilities. A comprehensive survey of achievement test data in the late 1980s in the US revealed the extent of these sex differences among secondary school and college students. Males scored considerably higher than females on both computer science tests, on all six physics tests, on all four chemistry tests, on both general science tests and on 12 of 16 general quantitative tests. According to Camilla Benbow of Iowa State University, a long-term proponent of sex differences in mathematical ability, it is in junior high or secondary school that the sex difference in mathematics really becomes apparent.[71] Girls excel in computation, boys in tasks which require mathematical reasoning, while no differences are seen in the ability to apply learned concepts or algorithms. Sex differences in mathematics emerge when the curriculum becomes somewhat abstract. In the course of a massive review of the evidence, Benbow considers a variety of social and environmental explanations. Perhaps women have a lower liking for or more negative attitudes towards mathematics than do males. Perhaps they have less confidence in their mathematical ability. What about the fact that men and women stereotype mathematics as a 'masculine' discipline? And surely significant individuals in the growing child's life – parents, teachers, peers – have different expectations of male and female mathematical achievement and encourage males more than females? It is also argued that boys take more mathematics courses than do girls and that girls are less intrinsically motivated than boys.

Benbow is largely dismissive of the social and environmental explanations for the apparent male mathematic superiority. Among the high-ability student population that she and her colleagues studied, no sex differences in attitude towards mathematics were found. Nor did attitudes correlate with either concurrent or subsequent mathematical achievement.[72] Yet evidence from a number of studies supports the argument that girls do have more negative attitudes towards mathematics and that these attitudes appear to correlate with how well or poorly the girls perform on mathematical tests. Ruth Bleier, a fierce critic of the argument that girls are less mathematically talented than boys, points out that mathematically gifted boys

> can confidently expect to use and be rewarded for their skills in math, science and engineering, and will thus be highly motivated to excel, but it has been well documented that, by and large, parents, school counsellors, and teachers have traditionally discouraged even talented girls from

seriously pursuing mathematics and science skills, or, equally damaging, ignoring them.[73]

Perhaps it is really a matter of confidence. After all, confidence has been shown to correlate negatively with anxiety about mathematics and positively with mathematic achievement, the value placed on mathematics and the intention to take optional mathematics courses. Girls are certainly more likely than boys to cite lack of ability as the explanation for why they achieved a poor grade; they are also more likely to cite lack of ability to explain a poor grade than they are to cite superior ability to explain a good grade. There is substantial overlap in the distribution scores of girls and boys and among talented girls and boys the performance on tests of mathematical ability are more alike than different. And, as Bleier herself is at pains to point out, at the same time as Benbow's study asserting male mathematical superiority was being published, 11-year-old Ruth Lawrence got the highest score in the mathematics entrance examination at St Hugh's College, Oxford while Nina Morishge, who received her BA and MA in mathematics at 18 years of age after attending Johns Hopkins University in Baltimore for two years, became one of the youngest recipients ever to receive a Rhodes scholarship to Oxford in the 78-year history of the award.

Male and Female Brains

Supposing, however, for a moment that such differences do exist, where in the human brain might they be located? The recognition that each of the two brain (cerebral) hemispheres represents a relatively complete and independent cognitive system with its own characteristic information-processing style is quite recent. The major research findings only emerged in the 1950s and 1960s although the first evidence for so-called hemispheric specialisation was provided by a number of nineteenth-century physicians, most notably Wernicke and Broca. They drew attention to the fact that damage to the left cerebral hemisphere led to interference with speech and language whereas damage to the right cerebral hemisphere hardly interfered with speech and language at all. Each hemisphere appears to embody a separate representation of reality and of the self. Human behaviour results from the complementary interaction of right and left hemispheres. The left cerebral hemisphere in right-handed people, and in most left-handed people too, which contains the centres that regulate speech and language, is commonly called the **dominant** hemisphere. The right hemisphere is commonly called the **non-dominant** hemisphere.

There have been several reports of a significant sex difference in the incidence of speech loss, or aphasia, following damage to the left hemisphere. Women show much less language impairment than men after sustaining similar degrees of damage following strokes and other forms of brain injury.[74] Other research findings indicate that males are more likely to show hemispheric localisation of verbal, visual and spatial abilities than females, which suggests that females either have a greater degree of shared function between the two hemispheres or that there is a greater degree of exchange and connection between the two hemispheres in females than in males.[75]

Intriguing reports suggest that some of the structures in the brain thought to be responsible for the exchange of information between the two hemispheres do indeed show differences between the sexes. In particular, the cross-sectional surface of the corpus callosum, that part of the brain which forms a link between the two cerebral hemispheres, is larger relative to brain weight in the female brain than in the male,[76] while the shape of the splenium, which is the posterior end of the corpus callosum, is rounder and more bulbous in women. Both of these sex differences have been reported in foetuses and infants as well as in adults, suggesting that they result from genetic or hormonal influences.[77]

But what do such findings amount to? For all the fanfare and razzmatazz concerning gender differences in cerebral lateralisation and brain size the actual extent of the differences seems remarkably modest. Stephen Jay Gould has remarked that in the study of gender differences, measured differences are solemnly reported only when positive and usually without reference to their statistical significance. Rarely are we provided with information concerning how often such differences are found because negative findings (that is to say findings that do not support a difference) are just not published.[78] When differences are found they are usually reported with no reference to the size of the difference: the extent to which it really amounts to much. This is one of the major problems with the current state of research into male and female mathematical ability, cognitive abilities and coping styles. When differences are not found the research receives little or no comment and disappears from sight.

Conclusion

Given the widespread popular assumption about the importance of testosterone, it is somewhat surprising to discover how few and how flimsy are the research findings in support of the theory that increased circulating testosterone increases aggression and dominance in males. Nor is the research adequate on other hormones that are known to influence human behaviour, mood, aggression and dominance, hormones such as serotonin and adrenaline. Testosterone dominates research and public discussion. The reason is simple. Serotonin and noradrenaline are not sex-linked to the extent that testosterone is. Testosterone has become synonymous with maleness, and analysing its effects titillatingly holds out the promise of providing a hormonal justification for male/female difference, for the inevitability of patriarchy and the incorrigibility of human aggression. By concentrating on testosterone, the quintessential *male* hormone, those who most loudly trumpet its alleged causal role in aggression and dominance do so in support of an ideological position.

Viewed from such a perspective, men are puppets of their hormones, blindly driven to assert, compete, fight, dominate and, if needs be, kill. This is the price to be paid for the reward: men will inevitably proliferate in high-status positions of dominance, whereas women, save for a few atypical 'masculine' individuals, will not. And it all makes perfect evolutionary sense, if E.O. Wilson, the father of sociobiology, is to be believed:

> It pays males to be aggressive, lusty, fickle and undiscriminating. In theory, it is more profitable for females to be coy, to hold back until they can identify males with the best genes . . . Human beings obey this biological principle faithfully.[79]

For the sociobiologist, explanations of human behaviour can be located both within neurobiology (or more specifically within the neural networks and receptors of the brain), and within Darwinian evolutionary theory. Within such a schema, sex difference is easily explained and set in unyielding stone. The assertive, aggressive, thrusting, vigorous, urgent male serves evolution best by rushing around promiscuously impregnating as many females as he can, using a variety of strategies varying from manipulation to outright domination. The female, biologically programmed for a more prolonged and demanding investment in the reproduction of the species and receiving no biological advantage by indulging in promiscuity or fecklessness, is predetermined to be cautious, prudent, discriminating and passive.

The belief that men are incorrigibly and intrinsically violent is widespread. For Lionel Tiger there is simply no argument – 'Typical maleness involves physical bravery, speed, the use of violent force' – while psychotherapist Anthony Storr is prepared to make explicit the connection between male dominance and the male propensity for violence: 'It is highly probable that the undoubted superiority of the male sex in intellectual and creative achievement is related to their greater endowment of aggression.[80] The apocalyptic implications of a relentless, biologically driven, testosterone-fuelled male violence have been spelled out by the ethologist Konrad Lorenz who, on the basis of fighting behaviour seen in fish and geese, grimly prophesies that 'intraspecific aggression bred into man a measure of aggression drive for which in the social order of today he finds no adequate outlet'.[81] But, leaving aside the superficial attractiveness of such distinctions, are they true? The simple answer is no. Male aggression and violence are both highly susceptible to factors which are non-biological (i.e. cultural, social and psychological). There is a convincing body of evidence supporting a reciprocal relationship between testosterone and behaviour, and in particular dominant behaviour, in which each affects the other. Testosterone is not necessarily the prime culprit and cause. The research findings of Valerie Grant to the effect that testosterone is linked to dominance rather than to aggression and violence are important, while the research findings that dominant women are more likely to conceive sons and pass on the dominance illustrate the complexity of the interactions of biology, gender and environment.

The message is that men can tame their aggression, can harness and direct their tendency to dominate and can still be men. They are not puppets and products of their hormones. Many men, it is true, believe and are encouraged to believe that their masculinity is related to their aggressiveness. Such men rate highly their competitiveness, their pride, their strength, their independence, their refusal to be pushed around. They see in their willingness, readiness and ability to engage in violence the very essence of what it is to be a man. Their very honour as men is at stake in every challenge, in every act of disrespect. Such men are truly men only if they are prepared to fight like men. If they are correct, then the debate over masculinity and the survival of their species will remain dominated by the need to render men redundant. But if they are wrong, if masculinity and violence are not synonymous, then men can begin to discard their aggressive predilections without imperilling their identity as men.

And if, as I am arguing, testosterone is not the cause of aggression in men but aggravates the aggression that is already there why is this aggression there in the first place? The assumption that because aggression is widespread among men it is therefore biologically rooted in and part and parcel of being a man, serves to protect men (and women too) from the real truth about male violence. The origin of so much of male anger, rage and violence lies within the very way we conceptualise ourselves as men and women and the very way we negotiate the difficulties and obstacles of human love and hate. Attribute the origins to biology, and we must turn to the pharmacologists for a pill to neutralise maleness or the surgeons to root it out. But accept that the origins lie in the interaction of man and society and we must turn to analysis of both for the solutions to our problems and the answer to the question – whither men?

CHAPTER 3

MEN AND VIOLENCE

So the question, 'Are men the prisoners and the products of Y and the fiery hormone testosterone?' can be answered with a firm negative. But if the male predilection to violence is not due to the Y chromosome and testosterone then what is the source of it? There is no argument about men and violence. Men engage in fighting and killing more than women do. Indeed, this is so well known and accepted in our society that it tends to pass without comment. Government think-tanks, international and national commissions, local task forces and clinical workshops sit and solemnly deliberate on the origins of human violence and often the most obvious feature – that it is an activity engaged in almost exclusively by men – receives little attention. I have been at many such conferences. To my shame, I even helped organise one, a conference, put together jointly by the Royal Colleges of Psychiatrists and Physicians in London in 1993, entitled 'Violence in Society'. Many distinguished experts gathered at the Royal College of Physicians to analyse and discuss the issue of human violence with particular reference to its origins, its biology, its social complexity, its possible roots in childhood, the state of research, the role of mental illness, drugs and alcohol and the plight of victims. One speaker even opened his address with the words, 'Women commit less offences than men, a feature so marked that some authors have described it as the most significant feature of recorded crime.'[1] This didn't stop the conference devoting a special session to women and crime – but there was no special session devoted to men and crime.

The Extent of Male Violence

Across a variety of cultures, a man is more than 20 times more likely to kill another man than a woman is to kill a woman, and a man is even more likely to kill a woman than a woman is to kill a man. When a woman does commit homicide, 'she usually kills a man who has repeatedly abused her'.[2]

The toll of male violence is horrendous. Not merely is the male inclination a persistent one but the development of ever more technologically efficient and effective weapons means that man's ability to kill larger and larger numbers of people is escalating exponentially. Modern warfare is usually taken as beginning with the American Civil War, the first major war to rely on machine-made weapons and to involve the railroad, the telegraph, and trench warfare. Whereas at Crécy and Agincourt, the longbow had effectively widened the area between the killer and the killed from an arm's length to over 100 yards, it had not increased the number of people an individual could kill with each arrow. The arrival of the rifle and later the machine-gun increased the target from one to dozens. When 12,000 Confederate soldiers mounted their last great charge at Gettysburg, only 300 made it; the rest were mown down by wave after wave of long-distance Union fire. Since that war, the technology of weaponry has multiplied – the tank, bomber, submarine, recoilless rifle, helicopter gunships, torpedoes, magnetic mines, flame-throwers, napalm, defoliants, gas. Once the most highly developed killing machine was the Japanese sword. Its blade a product of exceedingly sophisticated metallurgy that combined hard and soft steel and provided it with enough strength to avoid shattering, it was a weapon for combat between one man and another.[3] A millennium later, the killing machine was a hydrogen bomb, dropped from a plane with a handful of men as crew, but killing, as it did on 6 August 1945, 80,000 men, women and children and injuring in most horrible ways at least 40,000 more.

Such has been the impact of technology that the spectre of global annihilation is no longer fantasy. Man can now destroy himself as a species. But it is not just man's capacity to kill which raises the spectre of some innate biological predisposition, it is his capacity to inflict terrible suffering with seeming indifference and even delight.

> During the siege of the Srebrenica enclave in Bosnia in July 1995, a middle-aged woman from a village outside the town lost all five of her sons. At a meeting with Dr. Harvey Weinstein, an American psychiatrist and consultant to the voluntary organisation, Physicians for Human Rights, Nura told this terrible story:
>
> Soon after leaving the Dutch compound at Potocari, the bus she was on pulled to a stop at a checkpoint. A Serb militiaman climbed aboard. He was young and hard-faced. She smelled the intensely familiar odour of cigarettes, musty sweat and the faint sweetness of alcohol and with them the stifling heat of the dusty road. Suddenly he pulled the long knife from

> his belt and held it up in the air. He was smiling and his large hands were swollen from the heat. Then, in one motion, he leaned over and pulled the blade across the throat of a baby sleeping in her mother's arms. Blood spattered against the windows and the back of the seat. Screams filled the bus. The man shouted something at the woman and then with his left hand he pushed her head down towards the child's limp body. 'Drink it you Muslim whore', he screamed again and again. 'Drink it'.[4]

This terrible, and sadly too typical story of grotesque human cruelty is but one of millions of violent happenings which suggest that human beings are innately vicious. One of the fathers of sociobiology, the school of thought which insists that human behaviour is primarily to be explained by recourse to biological factors, puts it thus:

> The particular forms of organised violence are not inherited. No genes differentiate the practice of platform torture from pole and stake torture, headhunting from cannibalism, the duel of champions from genocide. Instead, there is an innate predisposition to manufacture the cultural apparatus of aggression in such a way that separates the conscious mind from the raw biological processes that the genes encode. Culture gives a particular form to the aggression.[5]

But human violence is not distributed in a way that would suggest that it is primarily innate. Cultural variations are considerable. Some societies are exceedingly violent, others much less so. Some men rape, and a few repeatedly. But most men do not. Consider murder rates. Colombia's is 15 times that of Costa Rica. Ireland's murder rate – 7 per million in 1994 – is about 7 per cent that of Finland. The US murder rate, one of the highest in the world, is 20 times that of Japan.

As Wilson and others demonstrate, the concepts of aggression and violence are somewhat elastic and can be used interchangeably, and such variation can affect how they are measured and assessed from one culture to another. I understand violence to mean what the Panel on the Understanding and Control of Violent Behavior set up by the US National Academy of Sciences understands it to mean:

> behaviors by individuals that intentionally threaten, attempt or inflict physical harm on others.[6]

When talking about violence we are clearly not just talking about murder. In 1991, there were 25,000 murders in the US but in addition over 6.5 million Americans were the victims of violent crime. The prototype violent crime is aggravated assault – those with weapons causing serious but non-fatal injuries. Such crimes account for nearly 300 of every 1,000 victimisations. Less serious physical assaults account for more than 500 of every 1,000, with robbery accounting for most of the rest. Forcible rapes account for about 20 in every 1,000. The contagion of so much violence is reflected in the extent to which children often witness community and domestic violence, suffer from post-traumatic stress disorder and are, in turn, at an increased rate of becoming violent when they themselves become young adults.

Male violence is endemic. Take the City of Limerick in Ireland, whose overcrowded, insanitary and crime-infested 1930s tenements were vividly recalled in Frank McCourt's best-selling memoir, *Angela's Ashes*. The tenements have since given way to modern public sector housing but the areas remain characterised by low income, high unemployment, dislocated families and environmental fatigue. The Irish media present Limerick as 'Stab City' on account of the high rate of assault involving knives. In the year 1996–7, 100 individuals were tried before the Circuit Court in Limerick, a court which has jurisdiction over the most serious criminal cases with the notable exceptions of murder and manslaughter. Over 50 per cent of the cases concerned serious offences against the person, including stabbings, shootings, grievous bodily assault and sexual assault. Sexual assault, the vast majority of which was against children, constituted 20 per cent. Property offences accounted for 32 per cent and drug offences for 11 per cent. Ninety per cent of the offenders were either unemployed or employed in low-status, low-income jobs, 84 per cent had a criminal record and more than 70 per cent came from the very public sector housing estates that had replaced McCourt's tenements. But the most impressive statistic was the usual one – 96 per cent of the offenders were male. Presenting this data to a joint British/Irish encounter conference on crime, Detective Inspector Dermot Walsh commented:

> Serious crime in Limerick consists of offences against the person and property committed by a hard core of young, unemployed, single males living in run-down, public sector housing estates. Undoubtedly, this would be a typical description of the crime situation in all Irish cities.[7]

Young, single, unemployed males in run-down inner-city areas – it would be a typical description of the crime situation in most cities in

Europe and North America. Everywhere one looks men commit more crimes than women. In England and Wales in 1989, a total of 396,000 convictions or cautions for indictable offences was recorded against men compared to 76,200 for women, a ratio of about 5:1. The rate for crimes of violence against the person was even higher, at 8:1. For every woman serving a sentence for homicide or attempted homicide, there were 27 men, while the ratio amongst those sentenced for other violent offences was 53:1. In England and Wales, nearly half of those appearing before the courts are young – 20 per cent are aged between 11 and 16. One in four young British males has been cautioned or convicted of a standard list criminal offence by his twenty-first birthday. The average age of a British burglar is under 18.

And then there is the violence men direct against women. In the developing world such violence accounts for only about 5 per cent of the total disease burden among women aged between 15 and 44; this is because the burden from maternal and infectious diseases still overwhelms that from other conditions. But in the developed world, where the total disease burden is much smaller, the proportion made up by violence against women is 19 per cent and still rising. Whether she lives in the developed or the developing world, a woman runs a constant, persistent and, in many places, growing risk of being a victim of male violence. Much of this violence occurs in the home. In Britain, one in four women has reported domestic violence.[8] The *World Development Report*, a review in 1993 of data from many industrial and developing countries, revealed that between 20 and 50 per cent of women surveyed had been beaten by their partners and in many instances, the abuse was systematic.[9] In the United States, domestic violence is the leading cause of injury among those of reproductive age. Between 22 and 35 per cent of women who visit emergency rooms do so for this reason. US research also shows that physically abused women are four to five times more likely to require psychiatric treatment than are non-abused women, and five times more likely to commit suicide. They are also more at risk of alcohol abuse, drug dependence, chronic pain and depression.

The risks of being battered or bashed are particularly acute in pregnancy.[10] Between 11 and 41 per cent of antenatal attenders in American studies report a history of domestic violence at some point in the past and between 4 and 17 per cent report domestic violence during the current pregnancy.[11] Several studies have found that women attending accident and emergency departments with physical injuries due to violence in the home are more likely to be pregnant than to be attending with accidental injuries.[12] Women may additionally be subjected to sexual abuse and assault,[13] raising the possibility that conception itself occurs as a result of rape. In this regard, it is worth noting that victims of domestic violence are significantly more likely to describe their pregnancy as unplanned and unwanted than women without such experiences.[14]

Rape and sexual abuse are among the commonest and often the most severe forms of physical abuse by men of women. In one US study, a history of rape or assault was a stronger predictor of how many times a woman sought medical care and of the severity of her health problems than was smoking or other unhealthy habits.[15] In a study conducted by a research colleague of mine, Dr Marese Cheasty, one in every three women attending Irish family doctors reported having been sexually abused at some time in her life.[16] In this study, sexual abuse was defined inclusively, to cover every form from exhibitionism to unwanted penetrative sex. At the other end of the severity continuum, one in 30 women reported having been raped. These were not women recruited because they were an at-risk sample, nor were they attending their doctors for rape counselling or post traumatic stress therapy. Most had never told their doctors their history of abuse. They were attending for the usual sorts of reasons women go to doctors. Cheasty did find that those women who had suffered serious sexual assault at some time in their lives were much more likely to be chronically clinically depressed than women who had not had such an experience.

Her findings replicate those reported elsewhere throughout the world. A study of adolescents in Geneva revealed that one in three girls compared with one in ten boys reports having experienced at least one sexually abusive event.[17] Of the 568 girls who took part in the study, 32 reported abuse involving some form of penetration, compared with only 6 of the 548 boys. Ninety per cent of the abusers were male and 35 per cent came from the victims' peer group. In a presentation to Irish psychologists, Lalor describes a culture of sexual aggression towards teenage girls by teenage boys.[18] One in three female third-level students attending a higher institute of technology reported an unwanted sexual experience before the age of 16 compared with 5.6 per cent of the 71 male respondents. In 80 per cent of cases the child knew the perpetrator. Of the young women reporting abuse, 35 per cent had experiences in which boyfriends forced sex on them despite requests to stop. Only 3 per cent of boys had such experiences. A survey of the teenage magazine, *19*, reported that 22 per cent of young British girls had been forced to have sex against their will yet when British men were asked if they had ever forced a woman to do something she didn't want to do, only 3 per cent admitted they had.[19]

The reporting of physical, including sexual, abuse of children is now a regular occurrence in every developed country and becoming so in the developing world. In the United States, the reported rates have doubled in seven years: 42 of every 100,000 children are abused every year.

Yet many men, and some women too, are reluctant to acknowledge this indictment of masculinity and seek to assure themselves and others that, first, most male violence is perpetrated against other men (which is true) and, secondly, women are just as violent (which is not true).

In the UK in January 1999, the Home Office published a research study entitled *Domestic Violence*[20] to considerable media attention. What received most publicity was the finding that *men* are increasingly the victims of domestic violence. Those most likely to be attacked were in the early thirties, unmarried but living with a woman. The study reported some 6.6 million incidents of assault each year, evenly split between the sexes. In the media coverage that followed publication of the report, considerable column inches were given over to the views of men on the growing assertiveness of women, the narrowing of the violence gap and the dangers men faced in the home at the hands of their partners. What received much less attention was the fact that the same research showed that the *severity* of the violence was very different. Women were twice as likely to be injured and much more likely to suffer repeated attacks. They were also much less likely to be in a financial position to leave such a violent relationship.

There is some evidence that the rise in attacks on men by women may indeed be a 1990s phenomenon. In 1995, just over 4 per cent of men and women said they had been assaulted by a current or former partner in the last year. But 23 per cent of women compared to 15 per cent of men said they had been assaulted by a partner *at some time* in the past. Either women are getting more aggressive, as some men would wish to believe, or they are increasingly fighting back. Young women aged 20 to 24 reported the highest levels of domestic violence in the survey, 28 per cent saying they had been assaulted by a partner at some time and 34 per cent that they had been threatened or assaulted. A carefully conducted epidemiological study of a birth cohort of 21-year-olds in New Zealand does suggest that younger women are becoming more aggressive in the home: 37 per cent of women and 22 per cent of men reported that they had initiated aggressive actions.[21] Severe aggressive acts were initiated by 18.6 per cent of the women but by only 5.7 per cent of the men. Those men who were seriously aggressive were more likely to be deviant on a variety of associated social and psychiatric measures, whereas the highly aggressive women were normal on every other measure. These data challenge conventional assumptions about domestic violence but the results, according to psychologist Charles Snowden, can be explained in terms of social norms and conventions:

> Men are reared to avoid being aggressive towards females and know they are more likely to be prosecuted by the courts if they do act aggressively. Women do not have these constraints and will be held less accountable by society and the legal system.[22]

But there is another explanation. This trend in domestic violence, showing young women becoming as violent as men, may reflect changes in marriage and cohabitation. Marriage, whatever its critics may feel, appears to provide a strong safety factor for women rearing their biological children. Surveys in the US over the period 1970–87 found that 12.6 married women per 1,000 fall victim to violence compared with 43.9 never-married women and 66.5 divorced or separated women.[23] According to information released by the US Department of Health and Human Services, for every married pregnant woman who reported being abused by her husband almost four unmarried pregnant women reported being abused by their partners. Indeed, cohabitation is the strongest predictor of abuse, according to this data: stronger than age, educational status, housing circumstances, access to health care or race.[24] It is ironic that at a time when marriage, accused by many of its critics of institutionalising and facilitating male violence, is in decline domestic violence is rising and is increasingly being committed by both sexes. The growing number of women and men reporting domestic violence reflects the weakening of bonds within domestic relationships.

Blandly reporting rates of domestic violence with the implication that male and female violence are the same is somewhat disingenuous and almost certainly misleading. Yet many do claim that violence is marital and cohabiting relationships is mutual. Much research makes little or no distinction between male and female aggressive behaviour within the domestic situation. But given the very real physical disparities that exist between the average man and woman, such distinctions are important. A woman being punched, slapped and beaten by a physically stronger, heavier and more agile male experiences somewhat different physical and psychological consequences than a man being thumped, having his hair pulled and being scratched by a woman. I have worked in psychiatric settings where violent attacks by patients are not unknown. While attackers can be male or female, there is no comparison between the levels of threat which each represents in terms of anxiety and fear provoked and risk of serious injury. A recent Norwegian review confirms that men with psychiatric disorders are five times as likely to be dangerous as psychiatrically disordered women.[25] Psychiatrically ill women are much more likely than men to injure themselves by means of mutilation or the taking of overdoses.

In the Republic of Ireland, *Irish Times* journalist John Waters has been among the most vociferous in testifying to the amount of violence against men by women. At the first European conference on male victims of domestic violence organised by the voluntary organisation AMEN – abused men – held in Dublin in December 1998, Waters argued that many women are just as violent as men. At the conference, Erin Pizzey, founder of the first refuge for female and child victims of domestic violence in the UK in 1971, declared that of the first 100 women who came to the refuge, 62 were found to be just as violent as the men they had left and that all international research on the subject indicates that domestic assault rates between men and women are about equal. Ms Pizzey, apparently, has felt that the movement she had founded had been, in Water's words, 'high-jacked by extreme man-hating feminists'. In a subsequent article Waters exhorted men to action:

> If I have one public hope for 1999, it is that this will be the year when men finally start to stand up for themselves. I would hope that individually and collectively men would begin to look at the society they are alleged to dominate and ask themselves, where is the evidence of such

> domination in a society which demonises and denigrates them at every turn, which conspires to steal their children at the whim of mothers and institutions, and which seeks to silence, censor and ridicule any serious attempt to bring these facts to light?[26]

Waters's concern is that, in the face of an enormous tide of feeling, those men in violent relationships who are the victims find they are disbelieved or denigrated or simply dismissed. But in common with many men, Waters expresses his concern by linking it with doubts about the arguments concerning the overall abuse and control of women by men. One of the unfortunate consequences of the approach taken by groups such as AMEN is the impression they give that there are men out there who just do not accept that there is a massive problem concerning male violence which dwarfs the issue of violence committed by women. Of course some women can be extremely aggressive and violent towards men and it is important to recognise the fact, but there is substantial evidence that the difference between the sexes in overall levels of violence is genuine and not an artefact. Shortly after John Waters made his impassioned challenge, the National Network of Women's Refuges in Ireland revealed that the number of women fleeing their homes from violent men had increased by 35 per cent to almost 5,000 in 1998. And lest Ireland be regarded as an aberration, international data provided little grounds for comfort. In the 1995 Canadian Violence Against Women Survey, 12,300 women were interviewed by telephone and 63 per cent responded to inquiries concerning their experience of physical and sexual violence since the age of 16. Twenty-nine per cent of those who had ever been married or lived in a common-law relationship reported experiencing violence at the hands of a current or previous partner.[27] A year later the Australian Women's Safety Survey found that 2.6 per cent of women aged 18 or over, currently married or in a cohabiting relationship, had experienced physical assault in the previous year at the hands of their partner, while 23 per cent of women who had ever been married, or had lived in a cohabiting relationship reported experiencing violence at some time during the relationship.[28] In the Netherlands, the first national survey on wife abuse, conducted in 1996, reported an overall prevalence of physical abuse of married women by their spouses of 22.6 per cent. That particular study attempted to distinguish between so-called unilateral violence (committed against a wife by her spouse) and multilateral violence (in which the woman, too, had acted aggressively); 20.8 per cent had experienced unilateral violence and within this group one in five admitted to using defensive violence. Thirteen per cent of women had been injured at some time by a current or previous partner and half of these had sought medical treatment.

> A woman in her forties presented in my clinic. She sported a black eye and a swollen lip and complained that her husband had beaten her up after she had complained about his drinking and his coming home late from his work. When I interviewed her husband, he told of repeated physical assaults by his wife on him, including slapping, kicking, tearing his hair and on one occasion biting. Initially, he expressed bafflement at her behaviour and insisted that he only hit her in retaliation and as part of his attempts to restrain her and defend himself. Careful interviews with their two teenage children revealed an even more complicated and dismal picture. Their father did indeed regularly come home late and drunk and would verbally intimidate and abuse his wife. Particularly frustrating for his wife was the fact, readily apparent in any interview conducted with her and her husband, that he was very much more articulate and verbally skilled than his wife. Eventually she would crack and physically attack him and he would retaliate. It was certainly true that this man was only physically aggressive after his wife attacked him – and that is how it would appear in any survey.
>
> The relationship between inarticulacy and aggression is an intriguing one – often many men explain their ready recourse to physical violence in terms of their sense of frustration at their inability to express their feelings in any other way, including verbal argument and explanation.

There is a truly awesome problem concerning male violence against women, and responding to it by desperately seeking to identify an equivalent amount of female violence against men is a fairly predictable example of male projection and denial. The suggestion that women are as likely to be violent as men has been thoroughly examined, not least by Jukes,[29] who points out that the research is riddled with problems. Distinctions are not made between self-defence and attack, nor is severity calculated. In one major study, often cited by the women-are-as-bad-as-men school, all punches are counted equally so that a 13-stone husband who hits his wife knocking out a tooth is assessed *less* severely than his 9-stone wife hitting him repeatedly in the chest yet leaving no mark at all – because she hits him more frequently than he hits her.

Confronted by a catalogue of male violence it is difficult not to respond with disgust and helplessness. Don Edgar, writing with an

Australian perspective, does not mince his words. He declares of those who beat up women, 'These men are bastards', and argues that they should be exposed and treated as criminals.[30] Adam Jukes agrees, insisting in *Men Who Batter Women* that violence represents 'the unacceptable face of male power over women'. Male violence is at one and the same time a demonstration of how that power has failed and how violence is the ultimate resource available to men who wish to control and dominate women.[31]

Once upon a time, male physical violence may have had a role, in the protection of the species, in deterring attacks, as a means of securing territory and food. In more recent times male violence was still a source of pride and identity. But in today's society it is no longer either necessary or worthy of admiration; it is increasingly seen as the enemy of culture and civilisation. Yet it still exists, destabilising and shaming us in our streets and in our homes, in the school playgrounds and on the football terraces. The real issue is: what are we going to do about it? If male violence is part and parcel of being male, then men are indeed redundant for, whatever the evolutionary purpose such violence once served, it is no longer evident today. But if violence is not an innate and essential part of maleness, then the challenge is how better to understand its roots and remove them.

Origins of Male Violence

'Man is the only species that is a mass murderer,' observed the distinguished ethologist, Nikolai Tinbergen, 'the only misfit in his own society. Why should this be so?'[32] One explanation is that aggression served a necessary evolutionary purpose, that aggression and the violent behaviour it produces are instinctive. In 1955, Lorenz published a paper entitled 'On the killing of members of the same species' in which he declared:

> I believe – and human psychologists, particularly psychoanalysts, should test this – that present-day civilized man suffers from insufficient discharge of his aggressive drive. It is more than probable that the evil effects of the human aggressive drives, explained by Sigmund Freud as the results of a special death wish, simply derive from the fact that in prehistoric times intra-specific selection bred into man a measure of aggression drive for which in the social order of today he finds no adequate outlet.[33]

This paper contains the basic assumptions of the biological basis of male aggression. First, it argues that male aggression needs no outside stimulus to develop but builds up like steam. Secondly, if provided with no outlet male aggression will explode. Thirdly, it has evolved and it is an instinct – here Lorenz draws on Freud's theory of the death instinct to bolster his assertions. It is important to be clear what it is Lorenz is saying. It is that even in a society organised on sound and just principles in which the needs of men and women are addressed, in which issues of property, security, survival and growth are the subject of rational and sensible review and development, aggression and violence will not only occur, they will have to occur. The very hydraulic demands of human aggression for expression are innate – man is driven by an instinctive force to destroy. 'It is the spontaneity of the instinct that makes it so dangerous.'[34] Lorenz's views on aggression – derived, it needs to be remembered, from the study of Brazilian mother-of-pearl fish, East Indian yellow cichlids, spotted wolves and the greylag goose – have been avidly taken up by a bevy of enthusiastic social Darwinians and sociobiologists who appear almost to relish the notion of man as incorrigibly aggressive. The characteristics which enabled man to survive in the earliest days of his existence as nomadic hunter are, they say,[35] speed, courage and the use of force. However, the hunter who became a farmer and later a trader certainly used his mental skills rather than brute strength to survive and prosper. Felicity de Zulueta, whose book *From Pain to Violence* challenges the simplistic view that male aggression is innate, raises the not unreasonable objection that the enthusiasts for this view tend to be men who perceive women as different in terms of their brain processes, and certainly inferior when it comes to the ability to form groups and participate in the economic and political functions of society.[36]

Lorenz's ideas have been immensely influential. They have been endorsed and enhanced by the works of other students of animal behaviour, most notably Desmond Morris, I. Eibl-Eibesfeldt, playwright Robert Ardrey, psychiatrist Anthony Storr and sociobiologist, E.O. Wilson.[37] Some of these follow Lorenz's lead and borrow from Freud's death instinct theories to support their arguments.

In his early writings Freud paid little attention to aggression, preferring to root his biological theories of human behaviour in sexuality. The slaughter of the First World War (three of Freud's sons,

Martin, Oliver and Ernst, served in the Austrian army) and the death of his beloved daughter Sophie in 1919 of the influenza that claimed more victims than did the war itself may well have nudged him to look anew at the issue of violence and death. Biographer Peter Gay, for one, is sympathetic to the possibility.[38]

Whatever the explanation, in 1920 Freud published *Beyond the Pleasure Principle* in which he began to draw a dichotomy between two great instincts: that of Eros or life and that of Thanatos or death. Here he laid down his basic theory of the death instinct:

> If we are to take it as a truth that knows no exception that everything living dies for *internal* reasons – becomes inorganic once again – then we shall be compelled to say that the '*aim of all life is death*' and, looking backwards, that '*inanimate things existed before living ones*' [Freud's italics][39]

Ten years later, in *Civilization and Its Discontents*, Freud describes the origins of his new theory. 'Starting from speculations on the beginning of life and from biological parallels', wrote Freud,

> I drew the conclusion that besides the instinct to preserve living substance and to join it into ever larger units, there must exist another, contrary instinct seeking to dissolve those units and to bring them back to their primaeval, inorganic state. That is to say, as well as Eros there was an instinct of death.[40]

Eros serves to bind individuals, then families, then tribes and nations together into one great unified humanity; Thanatos opposes such an impulse. The instinct of aggression is the derivative and main representative of the death instinct. Freud was dismissive of those who argued that men are gentle creatures who want to be loved and who at the most defend themselves if attacked. On the contrary, he argued, men are creatures with a strong instinctual endowment for aggression. But he was far from sure about his new theory, prefacing his first discussion of it in *Beyond the Pleasure Principle* with the words, 'What follows is speculation, often far-fetched speculation, which the reader will consider or dismiss according to his individual predilection'.[41]

Far-fetched or not, the theory of the death instinct touched a chord. Freud himself spent the next 18 years developing and revising it and became more and more convinced. He saw the death instinct as linked with sexuality in masochism and directed against the outside world in the form of aggression. He also postulated that if human aggression could not find real obstacles in the outside world against which to vent its energies, it might retreat into self-destructiveness.

> It really seems as though it is necessary for us to destroy some other thing or person in order not to destroy ourselves, in order to guard against the impulsion to self-destruction. A sad disclosure it is indeed for the moralist![42]

Like so much of what Freud wrote, his speculations, however well founded or far-fetched, have considerable appeal. Neal Ferguson, pondering the reasons why men fought in the First World War, finds support in Freud's theory for the possibility that many of them did so because they wanted to.[43] He quotes many examples of soldiers who took considerable pleasure in the killing and mayhem, who manifested a marked fascination with death and destruction, and some who appeared to fight for fun or pleasure. For many others it was the greatest adventure of their lives: 'to those intoxicated by violence it could really seem a "lovely war"'.[44]

The major shortcoming of Freud's theory is its insistence that two tendencies – that of the body to decay, degenerate, die and return to its original, inorganic state and that of the instinct to destroy itself and/or others – are one and the same. Can the slow running down of a living organism be equated with destructiveness? And then there is the fact that slow decay and death applies to all organic life and not just human life. It applies to women as much as to men – yet the problem of violence, as we have seen, is largely a problem of men. Interestingly enough, in his letter to Albert Einstein, entitled 'Why War?', Freud did not take the position that war is *caused* by some kind of human destructive instinct. Instead, he took a much more social and cultural view, seeing the cause in realistic conflicts between groups which had always been solved by violence because there were no enforceable international laws. At the end of his letter, he showed an even more fundamental switch in his position. 'We pacifists', he told Einstein, 'have a constitutional intolerance of war', and he wondered whether the process of civilization itself might not be a factor leading to 'a strengthening of the intellect, which is beginning to govern instinctual life, and an internalization of the aggressive impulses.'[45]

I do not think, however, that war can be explained by recourse to testosterone (see Chapter 2). Nor does the thesis that it is caused by some kind of innate hydraulic drive to express aggression stand up to proper scrutiny. We have seen great historical, cultural and social variations in war and violence. The problem with the intransigently biological view of aggression is that what starts out as a theory so easily becomes an ideology which justifies and indeed endorses male violence as the unfortunate price we pay for human progress: bar-room brawls and brutal slayings are the price for the Taj Mahal and *Hamlet*. To question the ideology is to question all sorts of deeply held beliefs concerning issues such as honour, patriotism and loyalty, as well as masculinity.

Erich Fromm, the American psychologist and social philosopher, was someone who accepted that man is violent, the only primate that kills and tortures members of his own species, without any reason, biological or economic; but he believed this to be 'biologically non-adaptive', not genetically programmed and not innate.[46] Fromm drew a distinction between what he termed 'benign-defensive' and 'malignant-destructive' aggression. The benign form, he argued, is a response to vital interests, is genetically programmed, is common to animals and man, is not spontaneous or self-increasing but reactive and defensive. It aims to remove the threat either by destroying it or taking away its source. Fromm's notion of benign aggression approximates to Hannah Arendt's example of justifiable violence, namely Billy Budd, rendered inarticulate on account of his stutter, striking dead the man who bore false witness against him. 'In this sense', writes Arendt, 'rage and the violence that sometimes – not always – goes with it belong among the "natural" *human* emotions'.[47] Biologically non-adaptive, malignant aggression, which includes destructiveness and cruelty, is not a defence against a threat, is not genetically programmed, is characteristic only of man and is biologically harmful because it is socially disruptive. 'Malignant aggression, though not an instinct, is a human potential rooted in the very conditions of human existence.'[48] Such a distinction is helpful. It accepts the evidence that man can be horrendously violent but suggests that the malignant part of man's aggression is not innate and hence not ineradicable. There is still hope.

The distinction is supported by evidence from patterns of human organisation and behaviour over many thousands of years. The factors that provoke or precipitate human aggression include the crowding of strangers in the presence of valued and potentially scarce resources; attachment and co-operation within a group and a tendency to scapegoat outsiders; drastic changes in environmental conditions occurring rapidly; and group loyalties. There is considerable evidence that many aspects of aggression can be learned. The earliest context is that of the mother–infant relationship. In animals, weaning conflict contains many components of later aggressive/submissive interactions.

In recent years there has been a resurgence of interest in the whole issue of attachment theory and the light it casts on the genesis of human aggression. The origins of the theory can be traced back to the British psychoanalyst, Ian Suttie, who in *The Origins of Love and Hate* took issue with Freud's ideas on the death instinct and argued instead that most of the behavioural disorders in early childhood and later life, including seriously disturbed aggressive behaviour, originate in a lack of security and love.[49] This view was taken up and developed by John Bowlby and others in the formulation of attachment theory in all its complexity but Suttie's exposition is refreshingly lucid:

> Instead of an armament of instincts – latent or otherwise – which would lead it to attempt on its own account things impossible to its powers or even undesirable – [the child] is born with a simple attachment-to-mother who is the sole source of food and protection. Instincts of self-preservation such as would be appropriate in an animal which has to fend for itself would be positively destructive to the dependant infant, whose impulses *must* be adapted to its mode of livelihood.

As Professor Sir Michael Rutter's masterful reassessment of Bowlby's original ideas makes clear, it is in the process of growth and development away not merely from the mother but from both parents and family, too, and in the negotiation of separation and the formation of additional and extended peer and other relationships that the growing individual learns to express feelings of love and hate, to cope with possessiveness and rejection, to establish a sense of self-worth or inadequacy, to engage in co-operative relationships or to remain alone.[50] Every society provides guidelines to instil into its young, guidelines which have tended to be useful in the past and which deal with ways of regulating human relationships, of coping with the family and social environment, of taking advantage of opportunities, of learning and managing the processes of survival and reproduction. Such guidelines or customs are learned early in life and are shaped by powerful institutionalised punishments and rewards. A sense of worth usually derives from a sense of belonging to a valued group and that in turn tends to depend on abilities to undertake traditional tasks in that society and engage in mutually supportive interaction. Our very human capacities for attachment, for what Suttie would call love, are linked fundamentally to our capacities for violence. We are prepared to risk our lives and kill our enemies in the defence of those for whom we care.

So we men are killers in adult life because our mothers did not love us when we were infants? Possible, but unlikely. A single factor of biology, the so-called aggressive instinct, cannot alone account for male violence, nor can a single hormone such as testosterone, nor a single psychological or social factor, either. But it is in our earliest relationships as infants and children that the interaction of genes and environment begins to shape our personalities, values and our adult behaviour. We would kill and do kill for a variety of reasons. Violence is easiest to enact when we dehumanise the object of our anger. It is hardly an accident that, in modern nations, most physical violence is committed by low-status males. High-status men are less inclined to act violently because the law and other social institutions provide them with alternative means of enforcing agreements and deterring competitors. Enmeshed with violence are such issues as status, power, control and emotional expression. We know that violence is more likely to occur in areas where life is short, where inequalities are large and visible, where employment prospects are bleak and where families have disintegrated. Poor prospects for employment, marriage and reproduction may make risky tactics such as robbery and violent confrontations more attractive.[51]

For over a decade, psychiatrist Robert Jay Lifton interviewed former Nazi doctors and concentration camp survivors in an effort to understand how perfectly civilised men committed mass murder and perverted the ethics and ideals of medicine. He has suggested that what enabled the Auschwitz doctors to kill was a psychological principle he calls 'doubling', the division of the self into two functioning wholes, so that a part-self acts as an entire self.[52] Lifton identifies five features of this 'doubling'. There is, first, a dialectic between two selves in terms of autonomy and connection. The individual Nazi doctor needed his Auschwitz self to function psychologically in an environment absolutely alien and antithetical to his previous personal standard of ethics. At the same time, he needed to retain his prior self in order to continue functioning as humane doctor, husband, father and friend. Secondly, the process of doubling is inclusive – each self has a coherence which enables it to function in its two distinct worlds. Thirdly, there is a life–death dimension – one self can survive in situations in which the other self or double would be overwhelmed. Fourthly, a major function of doubling is the avoidance of guilt – the second self is the one performing the 'dirty work'. Finally, doubling involves both an unconscious dimension, taking place largely outside conscious awareness, and a significant change in moral consciousness.

Lifton is at pains to point out that doubling is not splitting, a term with multiple meanings that tends to suggest a separation of a portion of the self such that the split-off portion ceases to function or respond. Dissociation or splitting refers to processes such as the denial of feeling or the bland denial of painful experiences or memories. But in doubling there are, as the term suggests, virtually two separate functioning people, almost akin to Robert Louis Stevenson's *Dr Jekyll and Mr Hyde* or Oscar Wilde's *Picture of Dorian Gray*. The character Versilov, in Dostoevsky's *A Raw Youth*, says 'I am split mentally and horribly afraid of it. It is as if you have your own double standing next to you'. Lifton himself draws an analogy with Goethe's *Faust*, in which Faust 'is inwardly divided into a prior self responsible to worldly commitments, including those of love, and a second self characterized by hubris in its quest for the supernatural power of the "higher ancestral places"'.[53]

Lifton's example, of Auschwitz doctors, is the extreme. But consider the average male. From very early on, he is encouraged to deny, certainly downplay a whole aspect of his self which embodies feelings of helplessness, frailty, impotence, a sense of uncertainty and ambiguity, sensitivity and empathy. Little boys don't cry, yet want to. Grown men do feel, but have learned well to disguise their feelings behind a façade of bluff *bonhomie* and anxious jocularity. Men can be turned into killing machines by the deliberate cultivation of a macho 'double', controlled, disciplined, unfeeling, insensitive, aggressive and cold. The terrorist is today's most complete embodiment of the double – a man, almost always a man (though there have been some rare yet spectacular female examples), who has perfected the denial of empathy and the transformation of all human opposition into detached, impersonal objects to be eliminated for the cause.

Men resort to violence when their power is threatened and in jeopardy. While men have so often defined women in terms of sexuality, erotic desire and reproduction and so often defined themselves as multifaceted beings, ironically it is men who operate in the shadow of their own sexuality, fearing it, proving it, forcing it – 'ejaculatory politics', in the words of feminist activist Robin Morgan.[54] Women threaten such male single-mindedness. Their very rootedness in the realities of life, its biology, its relentless practicality, serves to cast doubt on the validity, the worth, the ultimate purpose of masculine desires and ambitions. All that a woman represents – birth, life, domesticity, intimacy, dependence – has to be destroyed. Morgan quotes a passage from *The Catechism of a Revolutionist* written in 1869 by Sergei Nechaev which perfectly captures the dichotomy between 'masculine' pure purpose and 'feminine' contamination:

> All the tender and effeminate emotions of kinship, friendship, love, gratitude, and even honour must be stifled in him by a cold and single-minded passion . . . night and day he must have but one thought, one aim – merciless destruction . . . no place for any romanticism, any sentimentality, rapture or enthusiasm.[55]

What men hate in women is that they represent an embodied reproach to man's idealisation of dead, impersonal things – the revolution, the corporation, the organisation – and abandonment of the personal and the life-giving. Having quoted Che Guevara's observation that revolutionary leaders are not often present to hear their children's first words and that for them there is no life outside the revolution,[56] Robin Morgan remarks ruefully that:

> it's a rare man in any walk of life in any culture who's present to hear his child's first words; that the institution of 'wife' itself, in spirit and legal contract, demands sacrifice to the husband's goal; that friendships, domicile, lifestyle, are determined by his career, work, politics or calling, whether humble or exalted. Guevara is not just describing the revolution. He is describing the institutions of religion, business, war, the State, and the family. He is describing the patriarchy.

In the brutalisation of women, men can call upon that other self that sees women as inferior, less human, as dangerous, subversive, castrating, as the whore who will appeal to their physical needs, the madonna who will appeal to their pity.

> *Explaining* male violence against women quickly slips over into *blaming* women. When Dr Harold Shipman was convicted of killing 15 elderly women patients, one newspaper headlined the case 'The mummy's boy addicted to murder'. It was suggested that because Shipman had, as an adolescent, watched his mother die of cancer, after she had been repeatedly and heavily sedated with injections of morphine, this in some way led him to kill elderly women by morphine injection in his later professional life. Shipman, however, is only one of the most recent in a long line of men who have serially killed women. Peter Sutcliffe, Ted Bundy, Albert de Salvo, Richard Speck, John Christie, Neville Heath and Jack the Ripper are the most notorious serial killers of modern history – and all their victims were women. Dennis Nilsen, who murdered 15 men, and Jeffrey Dahmer, who killed at least 17, are the outstanding exceptions. Serial killing is a crime committed almost exclusively by men against women, and all kinds and classes of women – schoolgirls, young women, single women, married women, lesbians, prostitutes, elderly women – are victims. Any theory which attempts to explain male violence against women needs to take account of misogyny in its most foul and lethal form.

For most men, the process of doubling does not come naturally. It has to be inculcated through systematic indoctrination. The appalling story told by Nura at the beginning of this chapter illustrates the complexity of any contemplation of male violence. The murderous Serb militiaman is himself a product of long, historical, cultural process involving the creation of two cohabiting selves, a man doubtless good and kind and generous to his family, friends and neighbours and a man, devoid of pity, capable of seeing the 'other', the 'stranger', the 'Muslim' as sub-human, a residue of all that is corrupt. But he is also in the midst of a war in which the very intention is to inculcate widespread terror. In *Rape Warfare: The Hidden Genocide in Bosnia-Herzegovina and Croatia*, Beverly Allen insists that the Bosnian Serb military officers 'debated in detail the most effective means of producing terror among Muslim communities'.[57] She quotes from a document allegedly written by the Bosnian Serb army's special services in late 1991 which included experts in psychological warfare:

> Our analysis of the behavior of Muslim Communities demonstrates that the morale, will and bellicose nature of their groups can be undermined only if we aim our action at the point where the religious and social

> structure is most fragile. We refer to the women, especially adolescents, and the children. Decisive intervention on these social figures would spread confusion . . . thus causing first of all fear and then panic, leading to a probable retreat from the territories involved in war activity.

The cold, detached reference to women and children echoes a statement made on 22 August 1939 when Adolf Hitler gave a secret speech to his top military advisers outlining his plans for the German settlement of Poland. 'Our strength', he declared, 'lies in our quickness and in our brutality. Genghis Khan has sent millions of women and children into death knowingly and with a light heart.'[58] Later in the speech, which was reportedly received by the audience, particularly Goering, with enthusiasm, Hitler exhorted them to 'Be hard, be without mercy, act more quickly and brutally than the others. The citizens of Western Europe must tremble with horror.'

Maleness and aggression do not have to go together. Consider again the higher rates of male violence in the Southern United States and the code of masculine horror or *machismo*.[59] Honour, within such a macho culture, is established by the refusal to tolerate any challenge or disrespect and the immediate response with threatened or actual violence to insults and threats to property. Such a code deters theft and bad behaviour but it requires that violence sometimes be employed. This type of culture is to be found around the Mediterranean basin, in most of the New World influenced by Spanish culture, in parts of Africa, central Asia and among the Native American horsemen of the plains. Southerners in America do not favour violence any more than other Americans but their culture values the use of force to protect people and property, to respond to insults and to socialise children.

Nisbett and Cohen see the origins of the culture of honour in the development of organised agriculture, particularly animal husbandry. Animals are easily stolen, so it is imperative for a man who depends on livestock for survival to establish that he is not someone who can be pushed around. The US South, they argue, was settled largely by herdsmen from Scotland and Ireland in the seventeenth and eighteenth centuries when law enforcement was virtually non-existent. Hamburg, in the course of an elegant review of the whole notion of human and animal aggression, provides some supportive evidence. The historical record, he suggests, shows that once human beings developed agriculture, settled in large numbers, accumulated goods and came to rely on exclusive areas for growing food and grazing animals, 'intergroup hostility became common'. Hamburg accepts that aggressive behaviour between individuals and groups has been 'a prominent feature of human experience' for some time and sees it as 'easily learned, practised in play, encouraged by custom, and rewarded by most human societies for at least several thousand years'.[60]

The physical abuse of children represents human beings at their most desperate. The earliest medical descriptions date from the closing decades of the last century. A New York girl named Mary Ellen, discovered savagely beaten by her adoptive parents in the year 1874, is usually cited as the first recorded case. She was removed from her home following a lawsuit brought by the American Society for the Prevention of Cruelty to Animals.[61] Before the middle of the nineteenth century the evidence is thin. By the end of the twentieth century it is overwhelming. This has not stopped us reassuring ourselves that children have always been abused. Demos quotes a physician and author of numerous books and articles writing confidently that 'The neglect and abuse of children has been evidenced since the beginning of time. The natural animalistic instincts of the human race have not changed with the passing of the centuries' and another expert on child behaviour who declares that

> the maltreatment of children has been justified for many centuries by the belief that severe physical punishment was necessary either to maintain discipline, to transmit educational ideas, to please certain gods, or to expel certain spirits.[62]

Such speculation fits neatly with our Whiggish view of history as progression from the bad old days to something infinitely better but Demos is frankly sceptical and after an extensive review of the legal and social historical evidence concludes that there are good reasons to believe that child abuse was *less* common in earlier days. His reasons are of relevance to any discussion of the roots of violence. Premodern society, he reminds his readers, in comparison with today, fully integrated the lives of its constituent members. The traditional village (he gives an example from New England) offered to each person and family a density of human contact that is hard to imagine today:

> The marketplace, the church, the court, the broad spectrum of local routine and custom made a tight web of social experience allowing few possibilities of escape or exclusion. Pre-modern communities had their share of non-conformists, eccentrics and criminals – but no isolates, no

> habitual 'strangers'. The shape of life from day to day expressed the twin principles of mutual support and mutual surveillance. It is just in this regard that the situation of our own abusing parents seems most sadly deficient. Study after study finds them rootless, friendless, virtually unknown even to next-door neighbours.[63]

And what are we to make of violence committed *by* children? In 1968, the murder of two boys aged three and four in Newcastle upon Tyne by 11-year-old Mary Bell was a *cause célèbre*, a savage jolt to the easy assumption that children in general, and girls in particular, were incapable of such dreadful murderousness. Since then we have experienced two decades of a steady increase in violence committed by young boys and male adolescents in the suburbs, small towns and cities of most developed societies, including the beating to death of the toddler James Bulger by two 10-year-old boys in Liverpool in February 1993, the dropping of five-year-old Eric Morse from a 14th-floor window in Chicago by two boys, aged 10 and 11, because he wouldn't steal candy for them, and numerous teenage murders in the US, most notably the casual shooting to death of 12 fellow students and a teacher by 17-year-old Eric Harris and Dylan Klebold at Columbine High School in Denver. It has been argued that chronic, serious, violent juvenile delinquency is increasing and is likely to continue to do so.[64] Referring to work undertaken by the Federal Bureau of Investigation relating to 1993, Wilson and Howell show that juveniles committed 13 per cent of all violent crimes (homicides, rapes, robberies and aggravated assaults) in the US. Juveniles were responsible for 9 per cent of all murder clearances, 14 per cent of forcible rapes, 17 per cent of robberies and 13 per cent of all aggravated assaults. And the overwhelming majority of these juveniles were males. Not merely are many homicides and violent crimes committed by young people. They are committed against young people. Consider the following quote from a review of juvenile violence:

> 'Mom, can I tell you something? I'm worried. All the boys I grew up with are dead . . . What am I supposed to do?' The question was from a thirteen year old boy in New Orleans. His mother suddenly realised that, of a group of six year olds who had started school together seven years earlier, only her son was still living. All the others had met violent deaths.[65]

As Stewart Asquith and his colleagues at the Centre for the Child and Society at the University of Glasgow point out, the value of so much of the work examining the nature and extent of juvenile violence in the United States is that it emphasises the significance of social circumstances 'in providing children with life experiences which put children at risk of becoming serious offenders'.[66]

In the face of this disturbing phenomenon of child and juvenile violence, the social and political reaction threatens to be punitive and emotional. Just consider the call by the then Prime Minister, John Major, in the aftermath of the Bulger murder that 'We must condemn a little more, and understand a little less.' Yet, analysis after analysis of the circumstances surrounding child violence clearly indicates that a greater degree of understanding is the key to breaking the disastrous cycle of human violence. A recent review of the backgrounds of a large sample of children in England and Wales who have killed or committed other serious (usually violent) crimes showed that 72 per cent had experienced abuse of some form and 53 per cent had experienced significant loss (death or loss of contact with someone important).[67] Those who, like Gitta Sereny and Blake Morrison in Britain, have argued against a view of some children as innately wicked, natural-born killers – and for a greater understanding of the factors that lead children to destroy – have encountered considerable hostility.[68] The public debate that follows such an outrage is often more concerned with the simple-minded response of building more prisons and incarcerating more youngsters than with the need to understand and prevent such behaviour and to help young people when such preventive methods fail.

> When I first met James, he was a taciturn, sullen and unco-operative adolescent who had been referred for an assessment after having stabbed his father with a bread knife. The story that emerged revealed a home scarred by persistent rows and arguments between his parents in which, on occasions, his father would beat his mother. James's father regularly humiliated his son whom he saw as a weakling and 'mummy's boy' and James, indeed, did lack confidence and physical courage, being picked on and bullied at school. On the evening of the stabbing, his father accused James's mother of mollycoddling him and in the argument that ensued struck her across the face. James picked up the knife and stabbed him.
>
> His father also came from a dysfunctional family. His own father was a very violent man who served several prison sentences for grievous bodily harm. His mother died of tuberculosis, when James's father was only seven.

There is remarkable consistency within the research field concerning the causes of such violent behaviour in young people, particularly males. One researcher who has explored why some American boys become violent is Dr James Garbarino of Cornell University. In a scholarly review, Garbarino teases out the *mélange* of psychological, social, existential and constitutional factors that precipitate some disturbed boys into violence.[69] And what are the factors that emerge when violent young men are scrutinised? The usual suspects, of course – the lack of at least one loving, reliable and supportive adult figure; living in a drug- and crime-infested neighbourhood; suffering physical or sexual abuse or some other trauma; and lacking any philosophical or religious system of belief to provide meaning and purpose beyond the self. Garbarino is convinced that young people are more angry and violent than ever. His struggle to answer the question, 'Why do human beings hurt each other?' has taken him all over the world, to Yugoslavia and Mozambique, Kuwait and Iraq, Palestine, Israel and Northern Ireland. For a quarter of a century, he has encountered children who have committed and been the victims of terrible acts of destruction. He has listened to their stories. His work and that of others illustrates the appalling hypocrisy of a society that makes children responsible for their actions yet doesn't accept its own responsibility for the well-being of children.

His conclusions? That the aggression and violence of the young cannot be explained by simplistic reference to innate violence and intrinsic wickedness. There are solutions – political, psychological, social and moral solutions to the toxicity of human aggression – but finding and implementing them has not commanded a sufficiently high priority. And, as one reader of Dr Garbarino's book remarked, 'As long as men have wars, so will boys do violence.'

Biology is one factor among many. The child who suffers repeated jolts of stress – such as is experienced in a family characterised by alcohol abuse, violence, repeated separation and emotional rejection – is the child who grows up to develop impulsive anger and aggression. One theory is that the increased outpouring of stress hormones resets the brain's system for regulating fight-or-flight responses, such that they remain on a hair-trigger alert *all the time*. 'The early environment programs the nervous system to make an individual more or less reactive to stress', according to McGill University biologist Michael Meaney.[70] 'If parental care is inadequate or unsupportive, the [brain] may decide that the world stinks – and it better be ready to meet the challenge.'

In other children, repeated exposure to humiliation, bullying, physical or emotional violence can shut down the brain's responsiveness. These develop into the hollow young men whose sensitivity to the needs and experiences of others is non-existent. Their ability to feel, to react, to bond has been destroyed. Such self-esteem as they have is grounded in the extent to which they feel superior to rules and controls and can live by their violence. Most of the available models and scripts for this kind of antisocial and psychopathic individual are male, although the increase in media portrayals of female superheroes, who engage in murder sprees and uninhibited violence, may lead to a growth in the currently tiny proportion of adolescent girls to be found in the catalogue of teenage killers. In general, however, young girls internalise shame, humiliation and ostracism and turn them against themselves in the form of depression, whereas young men turn them outwards in anger and paranoia.

Many aspects of aggression can be learned. Many other aspects can be sublimated, redirected away from physical violence to patterns of structured and ritualised behaviour. The rise of organised sport in the eighteenth and nineteenth centuries may owe something to the need to have identifiable leisure outlets in the industrial cities and towns as an alternative to and an escape from the grim, relentless demands of paid work. But over the past century, as war has become more and more destructive and devoid of chivalry and glory, sport, particularly professional sport, has taken on many of its former trappings – the passion, the shared camaraderie, the opportunities for moments of personal heroism and shared exaltation, the tribalism, the common cause, the will to win and the catastrophe of defeat all expressed in a language of struggle, victory and defeat. We are accustomed to think of the similarities between sport and war when we consider such physically awesome team sports as American football, rugby league and ice hockey. But no sport is immune. In his biography, *Born to Win*, the Australian skipper, John Bertrand, who led the yacht *Australia II* to a pulsating victory over the American yacht, *Liberty*, in the 1985 America's Cup yacht race, describes the extraordinary encounter that pitted against each other not just two crews and two boats but two nations. The contribution of sports psychologist Laurie Hayden in motivating the Australians so that they turned a 3–0 deficit into a 4–3 triumph in the best of seven races was invaluable. Bertrand discovered Hayden when he watched a little-fancied football team, Carlton, coached by Hayden, triumph in the Victoria Football League grand final. 'Just before the Carlton players ran out', wrote Bertrand, 'some of them were seen embracing each other. In other words, they were going to *war* together . . . a matter of life and death' (Bertrand's italics).[71] His remarks capture perfectly the blurring of modern professional sport and martial combat – a collection of tough macho Australians *embrace* each other and then go out to *war* on a football pitch. Bertrand was doing no more than echoing the famous remark of the legendary Liverpool football manager, Bill Shankly, who when asked was football a matter of life and death replied, 'Oh. No. It's much more important than that.'

In sport as in war, winning is everything. Winning sportsmen are aggressive in competition. Losers are not. If Lorenz is right in his assertion that present-day civilised man suffers from 'insufficient discharge of his aggressive drive',[72] then modern professional sport with its language of combat, conquest, male bonding and militarist enthusiasm provides a useful safety valve. Sport has been defined as a specifically human form of non-hostile combat. There is no known sport in which contests are not held and that includes such harmless activities as skiing, ice skating and synchronised swimming and such complex and planned enterprises as mountain climbing, ocean racing and polar expeditions.

According to ethologists, human sporting activity is more akin to serious fighting than is animal play. What is the main function of sport today if not the discharge of aggressive feelings? And, crucially, it is in the playing of sport that modern young man is educated to regulate and control his own aggressive behaviour. Ideals of chivalry and fair play, which have largely departed the theatre of war, are still pursued and cherished on the sports field. Team spirit, disciplined submission to the rules, acceptance of the judgement of referee and umpire, mutual aid in the face of danger – nowhere save in the modern sports arena is there a situation in which all these virtues and ideals are pursued (and contested) with such passion. But as war declines in social value, so has sport become harder, more ruthless, more savage. The line between winning at all costs and just winning has become finer.

Of course sport is not confined to men. More and more women are participating in hitherto male preserves such as football, cricket and even body contact sports such as rugby. But the fact remains that men outnumber women in every sporting activity except bingo, dancing and horse riding.[73] True, a handful of sporting activities do remain relatively free of the smell and sound of war and friendship. According to John Updike, golfers, astronauts and Antarctic explorers are the exceptions, and in his lyrical exposition on the joys of golf, he suggest that golf, like exploration is

> based on a common experience of transcendence;
> fat or thin, scratch or duffer, we have been
> somewhere together where non-golfers never go.[74]

Not all sport involves combat between man and man, Updike reminds us. Beneath the rituals and the formalities, the preoccupation with excellence and the obsession with statistics in a game such as golf lurks combat all right, but combat in which the foe is not humanity but nature; nature in the shape of the anatomy of the perfect swing, the demanding design of a course, the mental strength of the player and the unpredictable variety of the elements. In golf as in the midst of the Arctic wastes it is man against himself, a struggle that transforms male aggression against others into an odyssey of self-control and self-discovery.

The different ways in which young men and women handle stress returns us to the question: why are men so violent? While a simplistic, seductive and reductionist explanation of male violence holds that it is a biological imperative, the very mark of masculinity and the key to human growth and progress, the evidence suggests otherwise. Study after study confirms the multifactorial nature of human violence. Of course, biological factors are there for man is a biological creature. But as research results steadily accumulate, the emphasis increasingly is on the role of social factors such as deprivation, inequality, injustice, overcrowding, poverty and cultural attitudes. A swelling body of research illuminates the role of psychological factors and in particular parent–child relationships and the integrity of the family. Meanwhile in political debate, social planning and popular discussion the serious implications of violence are too often ignored. Many factors which present early in life influence the development of aggressive children –

low family income, harsh or inconsistent parental discipline, family disruption, poor supervision, parental loss.[75] Aggravating factors include low school attainment, high impulsiveness and poor concentration. There is a significant continuity over time between childhood aggression and adult violence. Aggressive children as rated by teachers tend to have later convictions for violence and to be violent as young adults.[76] Violent individuals tend to come from particular kinds of family environments. They are more likely themselves to have been physically abused, to have had alcoholic, drug-abusing or criminal parents, to have had disharmonious parents who are likely to separate or divorce. Physical child abusers are more likely to have had parents who are cold, rejecting and abusive, who use parental love and discipline in inconsistent and unpredictable ways.[77]

In a review entitled 'Causes of violence', the distinguished American forensic psychiatrist, John Monahan, identified among the tangled roots the usual, fashionable suspects – testosterone, head injury, poor nutrition, crime, poverty, unemployment and youth. But he concluded that if research on violence were like stock on Wall Street he would put his money on psychology, or more precisely on

> the developmental processes that we all go through, most of us more or less successfully, but some of us with great difficulty. I mean particularly the family – the filter through which most of the sociological factors, such as parents being unemployed, and many of the biological factors, like poor nutrition, seem to have their effect on a child growing up.[78]

It is within the family that children encounter and assimilate many of the gender stereotypes that will determine much of how they think about themselves and about others. It is when we consider the traits and attitudes necessary for violence and line them up alongside the traits and attitudes which are characteristically thought of as masculine that the link between violence and masculinity becomes clearer – for in truth they are regarded by many, men as well as women, as one and the same. The stereotypical macho man is portrayed as aggressive, rational, controlling, competitive, reticent, taciturn, analytical, single-minded, independent, dominant, invulnerable. Contradiction, uncertainty and ambiguity are anathema to him.[79]

It is only within the past 50 years that such stereotypes have been subjected to serious criticism. As a man, I have inherited a model of the sexes in which masculinity is equated with psychological and physical strength and health, femininity with psychological and physical weakness and illness. The very words we use to describe man and woman are imbued with notions of power and impotence, dominance and submission, health and sickness. As the new century begins, the state of maleness is being portrayed by a variety of commentators as equivalent to a deviant state, a pathology. The very traits which once went to make us the men we think we are and would like to be – logical, disciplined, controlled, rational, aggressive – are now seen as the stigmata of deviance. The very traits which once marked out women as weak and inferior – emotional, spontaneous, intuitive, expressive, compassionate, empathic – are increasingly being seen as the markers of maturity and health.

CHAPTER 4

The Waning Y

A century ago, to be a man meant to be a leader in public life, a patriarch at home. Being a male was the very definition of health and maturity. The stereotype of the successful man did not just embody a succession of positive, virile attributes – strength, power, authority, decisiveness, rationality, calmness, discipline, resourcefulness – it existed in the presence of an opposing cluster of attributes – fragility, weakness, vulnerability, emotionality, impetuousness, dependence, nervousness – the stereotype of the typical woman. Today's male carries around in his head notions of manhood which, while forged over a number of centuries, flowered in the nineteenth century, a century of unparalleled male achievement in science, technology, biology, medicine, exploration and imperial expansion. When we speak of the inheritance of man we do not merely refer to the genes, the biological destiny of maleness but to the social expectations, the cultural notions of what it means to be a male. One of the things it meant less than a hundred years ago was to be strong, aggressive and, if necessary, violent.

Today there is little point or purpose in brutal man if his brutality pulls the temple down. But, in the past, men were more than brutal. Men were in command. Men today are in shock. They still, it is true, dominate the citadels of power, the boardrooms and cabinet rooms of the developed and developing world, they still monopolise the drafting of laws and the implementing of policies, they still bestride the stock markets and banking systems, but like eighteenth-century kings and aristocracy, they can surely hear, if they listen, the tumbrils lumbering up the avenues and the masses calling that their time is up. Men can go on defining themselves in terms of what they do but it has become a great fraud, a confidence trick they persist in playing on themselves. When it comes to work, women can do it too. There is nothing uniquely male about any of it. If work used to define masculinity it does not do so any more. A revolution has occurred.

The high point of male achievement and patriarchal status was the nineteenth century. That too was the time when the line between the definitions of masculinity and femininity was most unambiguously drawn. A key word in the stereotyping of women was *delicate*. It meant easily excited, highly strung, refined, sickly, 'nervous' in some fashion. The word combined the mid-Victorian ideal of female beauty – grace and languor, pallor and vulnerability – with refinement. This refined female spirit, observes Jean Strouse, the biographer of Alice James, sister of the philosopher William and the novelist Henry, 'inhabited a feverish realm of keen perception and subtle response far above the plane of the body'.[1]

Physicians of the time were of the opinion that one-half or more of women suffered from a psychological illness or 'nervousness'.[2] Edward Clark of Harvard Medical School was so pessimistic that he concluded that women would soon be unable to reproduce.[3] But it was not so much that they were women who were sick as that they were sick because they were women. And the doctors were pretty sure what was to blame – a woman's reproductive system. 'Here lay the cause and cure of many of her physical ailments', declared William Dewees, Professor of Midwifery at the University of Pennsylvania, explaining in his standard textbook on female diseases that a woman was subject to twice the sickness that affected man because she possessed a womb that exercised paramount power over her physical and moral system.[4] William Byford, Professor of Gynecology at the University of Chicago, went further and in a monograph on the subject in 1864 declared 'It is almost a pity that a woman has a womb.'[5]

It was, perhaps, understandable that physicians in the nineteenth century should be so preoccupied with the reproductive system, given that pregnancy and childbirth were still exacting a fearful toll in terms of perinatal and maternal mortality. Fewer than one in three women reached the menopause, because of the high rate of maternal morbidity associated with repeated pregnancies.[6] As late as the 1920s, one woman died for every 200 births.[7] (At present in the UK the maternal mortality rate is one maternal death per 33,000 births.) But that was not primarily the ill health to which the doctors referred when discussing the uterus. They were concerned with the very essence of woman herself and, by implication, the essence of man. The female sex, as one physician explained in 1827,

> is far more sensitive and susceptible than the male; and extremely liable to those distressing affections which for want of some better term have been determined nervous, and which consist chiefly in painful affections of the head, heart, side, and indeed of almost every part of the system.[8]

The fragility of the female was due not merely to the uterus but to the intimate and hypothetical link between ovaries, uterus and nervous system. This formed the logical basis for what was termed the 'reflex irritation' model of disease causation so popular at the time. Any imbalance, exhaustion, infection or other disorder of the reproductive system was believed to cause pathological reactions in other parts of the body. Physicians envisaged the body as a closed system possessing only a limited amount of energy. Energy expended in one area, such as during bleeding from the uterus, would not therefore be available to another, such as the brain. The young woman who spent her vital energies in intellectual activities would divert vital strength from the achievement of true womanhood and would become weak, nervous, sickly and possibly sterile. The brain and the reproductive system, at least in women, could not operate efficiently at the same time.

Such views strongly underpinned notions of masculinity and, to an extent, were self-fulfilling. During the second half of the nineteenth century, when small numbers of women were making their presence felt in science, physicians began to express their alarm. 'One shudders to think', wrote one,

> of the conclusions arrived at by female bacteriologists or histologists at the period when their entire system, both physical and mental, is so to speak 'unstrung', to say nothing of the terrible mistakes which a lady surgeon might make under similar conditions.[9]

Rejecting John Stuart Mill's proposal for woman's suffrage in 1867, the *Lancet* observed that a woman's place is in the home because a woman's physical nature

> shows a comparative delicacy, the confirmation of structure and organs is less developed; there is less strength and vigour and less fitness to encounter the obstacles of intercourse with the world.[10]

And so it went on. There can be few more definitive statements of the remorselessly reductionist view of femaleness than that delivered by another prestigious male American physician, the President of the

American Gynecological Society in 1900, George Engelmann. In his presidential address he declared:

> Many a young life is battered and forever crippled in the breakers of puberty; if it crosses these unharmed and is not dashed to pieces on the rock of childbirth, it may still ground on the ever recurring shallows of menstruation, and lastly upon the final bar of the menopause ere protection is found in the unruffled waters of the harbor beyond the reach of sexual storms.[11]

In short, women were to be defined as healthy only when they were no longer sexual beings. Yet this mechanistic and demeaning view of women surfaced again some 80 years later as the feminist revolution got under way. The issue was premenstrual tension. Complicated feelings, behaviours and symptoms were ascribed, on precious little evidence, to the variations in hormones occurring during the menstrual cycle. Ironically, one of the claims made concerned education. On the basis of a number of studies of questionable scientific quality, Dr Katarina Dalton, one of the most redoubtable exponents of the concept of premenstrual syndrome, argued that girls sitting examinations during the premenstrual phase of the cycle did badly.[12] Subsequent studies, better designed, failed to replicate this finding but at the time there was an enormous fuss. Physicians, a century ago, would have understood. They had long argued that women's reproductive functions were simply incompatible with education.[13] Henry Maudsley, one of the most influential British psychiatrists of the time, observed in 1874 apropos of menstruation and its effects on the brain that 'when nature spends in one direction she must economize in another'.[14] There were of course doctors who cautioned against too ready an acceptance of woman as weak and there were, of course, many, many thousands of women who did physically demanding, back-breaking work in the mills and factories and on the farms without anyone worrying very much about the state of their internal organs or the effect on their brains! However, women in the middle and upper classes were confirmed in their subordination by always seeming at a disadvantage as a gender

> whether because of childbirth or because they sought abortions or because they had damaged their health by procuring abortions illegally, or because they were suffering from a 'hysteria' which itself often reflected social deprivation.[15]

These orthodox views on women were exceedingly influential. Educational establishments worried about female entrants. The Regents of the University of Wisconsin explained their concerned in 1877 by explicit reference to the medical arguments, pointing out that 'at stated times, nature makes a great demand upon the energies of womanhood' and that at these times 'great caution must be exercised lest injury be done'.[16] Whichever way women moved they were trapped. Just to be a woman was to be in a state of suspended or latent illness. And to resist the status of womanhood was to be ill, too. The contrast with the masculine state could not have been more striking. Where women were delicate, men were strong. Where women had to conserve energy, because of their reproductive needs, men could express theirs with vigour and relish. This contrast is strikingly captured in an address to the New York Odontological Society in 1879 given by an orthopaedic surgeon, Dr Charles Fayette Taylor. 'Women', he declared,

> are emotional as a class of beings, characterized as a sex with less manifestation of independent thinking, whether from a feebler endowment of reasoning powers, or whether because the intellect is so habitually subordinated to simple feeling, it is not necessary to discuss While education in men makes them self-controlling, steady, deliberate, calculating, thinking out every problem, the intellectual being the preponderant force, the so-called 'higher education' for women seems to produce the contrary effect on them.[17]

Men were calmed by the education they received, women overheated by it. Education would turn girls into 'a bundle of nerves'. What makes Charles Fayette Taylor's views of particular interest is that he was the first of many doctors to treat Alice James, who was indeed, from time to time, 'a bundle of nerves'. In the late 1860s, William James was studying medicine, Henry James was reading literature and writing criticism in his formative years as a novelist. Alice James, in the shadow of her two formidable brothers, struggled to find her role. Could she develop her studies and intellectually blossom or must she accept that she was not made as men? To use her mind productively would involve competition with her intellectually intimidating brothers and a confrontation with her father Henry James Snr who had very decided views on what young women should do. Indeed, in 1853, when his only daughter Alice was five years old, he had written an article in *Putnam's*

Monthly comparing the two sexes in which he declared that according to an 'absolute decree of nature' woman is man's inferior 'in passion, his inferior in intellect, and his inferior in physical strength'.[18]

Not to pursue her studies would mean accepting a role similar to that of the selfless, effortlessly good but rather dull women in the household, her mother and her aunt, and stepping down to their intellectual level (Alice had a reasonably high opinion of her own intellectual endowment).[19] But Alice never had to resolve the conflict because illness intervened. Aged 18, she developed a mysterious malaise, believed to be 'neurasthenia' and was sent for a 'cure' to Dr Taylor. The term neurasthenia had not been invented yet – it was two years later that George M. Beard, a New York physician, applied it to the wide range of unexplained nervous symptoms that were appearing with increasing frequency. Beard listed over 50 such symptoms including fainting fits, menstrual irregularities, headaches, muscle spasms, neuralgia, insomnia, dyspepsia, lack of appetite, vomiting and irascibility.[20] He too subscribed to the notion of the nervous system as a kind of bank account containing a limited amount of energy – too much drawn off and the result was exhaustion and insufficient left to enable the ordinary activity of life to occur. (Contemporary commentators, most notably Professor Simon Wessely at King's College Hospital in London, are struck by a number of similarities between Beard's neurasthenia and today's diagnosis of chronic fatigue syndrome, otherwise known as ME.)[21] Whatever it was, Dr Taylor's exercise therapy did not work nor did the many other therapies suggested by the many other doctors that Alice was to see over the next 25 years. In 1891 Sir Andrew Clark found a palpable mass in one of her breasts, not the origin of her lifelong illness, but enough to cause her to exult that at last something had been found. 'Ever since I have been ill', she wrote in her diary on 31 May 1891,

> I have longed and longed for some palpable disease, no matter how conventionally dreadful a label it might have, but I was always driven back to stagger alone under the monstrous mass of subjective sensations, which that sympathetic being 'the medical man' had no higher inspiration than to assure me I was personally responsible for, washing his hands of me with a graceful complacency under my very nose.[22]

Sir Andrew Clark's grim diagnosis had the effect of 'lifting us out of the formless vague and setting us within the very heart of the sustaining concrete'.[23] She knew the cancer would kill her.

Alice James was in some ways the victim of an age when the lives of women were severely constrained by a stereotype which embedded them in a miasma of delicacy, malaise, weakness and disease. The prevalent cultural values required that women be selfless and ceaselessly effective on behalf of others – 'ministering angels', in the idiom of the time. But Alice James, an exceedingly intelligent and observant woman, managed to be *in*effective. She was self-absorbed and subversively dominant over family members and friends. The illness, in other words, seemed to mock the cultural values and in retrospect can be seen as a form of social protest.

> Despite male beliefs in the inherent superiority of male health, many men are as hypochondriacal, i.e. excessively concerned about the state of their health, as women. A 60-year-old farmer was admitted to hospital complaining of abdominal pain and diarrhoea. He was terrified that he had cancer of the colon, having read about the symptoms on the internet. He was energetically investigated but no evidence of cancer was discovered and he was told he was physically fine. However, he remained extremely anxious, read avidly about bowel cancer and repeatedly sought further examinations and investigations. Eventually he was referred for a psychiatric opinion. A careful exploration revealed that some months before the onset of his symptoms his own father had died after a long battle against lung cancer. Around the same time, his wife had had a scare when a mammogram showed a lump which subsequently proved to be benign. Initially, he insisted that grief following a father's death and worry about a wife's possible cancer were the kind of thing strong men experienced without developing hypochondriacal anxiety. He could not comprehend how feelings, which he regarded as insubstantial and vague ephemera, could cause what he insisted on calling 'real' physical symptoms. The cause of his diarrhoea, abdominal pain and bloating must, therefore, be cancer of the colon. Eventually, he began to accept that there was an important link between the events in his life and the development of his hypochondriasis – and that he was not a weak or deficient man in becoming ill due to such events.

It would be a mistake to imagine that such notions died with the suffragettes and votes for women. The stereotypes of masculinity and femininity that flourished in medicine a century ago reverberate to this day. But now the wheel is beginning to turn. Where once it was femaleness that was equated with pathology now it is masculinity. Men have a variety of serious illnesses which have received far less public and political attention for reasons which many men now argue about. Take the example of breast cancer and prostate cancer. Breast cancer kills some 14,000 women in Britain each year; 10,000 men die from cancer of the prostate. Breast cancer attracted research moneys in excess of £4 million in 1998. Prostate cancer only managed to draw £137,000 in the same year. The discrepancy has provoked many men into blaming women for distorting health budgets and treatment programmes, an astonishing and unlikely explanation given the predominance of men on the major research councils and grant-giving bodies in cancer medicine. Former British MP, Julian Critchley, discovered by chance that he was suffering from prostatic cancer. He attributed male ignorance (and presumably his own) about the disease to the fact that men have, as he put it, 'without protests, allowed ourselves to become the victims of feminist triumphalism that is rampant in our society'.[24]

Furious women journalists responded by asserting that without the feminists' campaigns specific female problems would be as little researched and understood. Critchley is wrong but the feminist critics also miss the point. Women are not to blame for the neglect of male diseases, and there has never been any tendency on the part of the medical establishment to shun research into female conditions or to neglect their diagnosis and treatment. Quite the reverse. Medicine remains as fascinated by women's illness now as it was in the time of Alice James. There are numerous workshops, conferences, seminars, journals, monographs, research reports, think-tanks and task forces devoted to the subject of women's health. There is a particular specialty devoted to women's diseases (gynaecology). The majority of gynaecologists and obstetricians are men, and men continue to be intrigued by women's bodies and what happens to them. The research interest in breast cancer has little to do with feminists. Men are fascinated by women's breasts and medical men are no exception. And, while male-dominated medicine is familiar and comfortable with the linking of women and disease, it is distinctly uncomfortable when it comes to the disease status of men. Men find it much more difficult to talk about illness, to say how they are feeling, to admit they need help. Male physicians are not much better than their non-medical male friends.

When Clare Moynihan, Senior Research Fellow at the Royal Marsden in London, a hospital which specialises in the treatment of cancer, instigated a trial to establish the effectiveness of counselling in men with testicular cancer, only a minority of men showed up.[25] Many of them had been experiencing anxiety, depression or both since receiving treatment for their cancer some one to five years before. Not a single man, however, had sought help, which suggested to Moynihan that 'it was crucial for men to be controlled and silent about their emotional life'. Given some space and time to talk (and a sympathetic woman to listen), the men slowly but with considerable difficulty began to uncover aspects of themselves they admitted they had never before revealed.

> A few men recounted how they recoiled in fear and sadness, sometimes cuddling soft toys, usually in secret. But the concept of 'self control' was clearly demonstrated and a stereotypical masculine identity constantly re-enacted in the face of illness when men described how they wept ('blubbered') in private, far away from their families, and often in their cars where they felt 'enclosed and safe'.[26]

Moynihan goes on to describe the approaches of male doctors to the issue of male patient anxieties. Male clinicians attempted to reduce anxiety by using military and sporting metaphors, for example by referring to infertility (a consequence of treatment) as 'shooting blanks', the loss of a testicle following surgery as 'a plane flying on one engine and landing safely' or 'one cylinder is as good as two'. This kind of language, she suggested, 'reinforces the way in which many men think about their bodies as machines, controllable and controlled'.

But then, for the most part, it is not male bodies men think about, it is women's. The Institute of Cancer Research aimed an awareness campaign at men with an advertisement which, running in tandem with a picture of female breasts, had a copyline which read: 'No wonder male cancer is ignored. These are all you ever think about'.

So controlled, unforthcoming and contained are most men that they are careful when completing surveys and questionnaires which, as a result, are difficult to interpret. The results of many self-report measures are questionable because men, particularly those who present themselves as 'highly masculine', grossly under-report their symptoms.[27] Motives and feelings are concealed when men report on the emotions they think they ought to have according to the stereotypical expectations of masculinity. Moynihan points out that when men are asked to rate personality characteristics on a scale in answer to such questions as: 'How desirable is it for a man to be assertive/yielding?' the expectations that are built into such questionnaires produce limited and static responses, 'only perpetuating the myth of what it means to be masculine and proving that men behave in certain ways'.[28] When researchers asked men and women to score their own 'masculine' and 'feminine' traits, they were somewhat surprised to find that the women and men who scored highly on 'feminine' traits were more likely to make use of health services,[29] and showed greater practical concern regarding their health care[30] – the implication being that it is the unreconstructed, stereotypical macho male who is most at risk when it comes to admitting the presence of ill health and seeking help for it.

A national survey of family planning clinics by the Family Planning Association in Britain has shown that young men are much less likely than women to avail of sexual health service.[31] One of the consequences is a failure of young men to use contraception or to engage in safe sex. Less than 10 per cent of male university students use condoms, while boys are consistently overlooked in the controversies and discussions concerning the tackling of high teenage pregnancy rates.[32] Time and again, boys and men behave as if health and illness, contraception and responsible parenthood are women's issues – and when problems arise they are likely to blame women.

The assumption that maleness and health are the natural opposites of femaleness and illness is itself based on another assumption, namely that testosterone promotes health. Men, said Alice James's doctor, are 'steady, deliberate, calculating, thinking out every problem' and many men heartily concur and thank their testosterone for it. And, being men, they believe that more of the stuff means better. But the evidence is dubious. Maleness does not equate with health and what we are learning about testosterone is testing men's ability to think out every problem to the limit.

Testosterone and Health

In the nineteenth century it might have appeared self-evident that men were a healthier species than women. They lived longer. Being a man at the start of the twenty-first century has no such advantage. In every developed society women are living longer than men, about 10 per cent longer, between five and seven years. In Britain men at every age have higher death rates than women, the clearest and most unequivocal evidence that in terms of mortality men have poorer health than women.[33] And no matter the changes in diagnosis and treatment, the gap persists. While rates of cancer and circulatory diseases, a major cause of mortality in men, fall, other causes of death in men, such as suicide and HIV-related disorders, more than compensate for the improvement. In health terms, men are the weaker sex.

In underdeveloped countries childbirth and its associated complications and demands continue to take a tragic toll. In India, maternal mortality is one for every 170 births, in Sri Lanka one for every 1,500, in African mothers in South Africa one for every 400.[34] Yet, despite such dreadful figures, only in India and Bangladesh do men and women have an equal life expectancy, and that a low one of 60 years. Nepal appears to be unique. Nepalese men live longer than women; but it is a modest difference – a male life expectancy of 54.3 years as against 53.3 years for women.[35]

Interest in testosterone and male health has been somewhat slow to develop – in contrast to researchers' enthusiasm for studying female hormones in the hope of tying them to various examples, real or fallacious, of female pathology and psychopathology. Thirty years ago, doctors, particularly endocrinologists, were very excited by a new toy, the technique of radioimmunoassay, which enabled them to measure hormones with a remarkable degree of precision. However, success in linking oestrogen, progesterone and their metabolites to female morbidity for the most part eluded them, though it wasn't for want of trying.

Now it is the male sex hormones, the androgens, and especially testosterone, which are slowly being identified as the cause of a variety of male health disadvantages. Initially, researchers and clinicians had assumed that since the waning levels of testosterone in men's blood appeared to cause the loss of muscle mass and the decline in sexual vigour and activity that occurred in ageing men, then testosterone was a sort of male life force. Would giving testosterone get the gonads and the man going again? By the mid-1990s there was a vogue for testosterone therapies – in 1996, a cover story in *Newsweek* enthused over the long-term prospects for men's health now that physicians were recommending testosterone supplements for middle-aged and elderly men to enable them to feel more competent, virile and hopeful about their lives. But as research speeded up, the picture proved less optimistic and more complicated.

First, testosterone levels do appear to be linked to what is called 'health risk behaviour'.[36] Higher levels of testosterone are found in the unemployed,[37] in the unmarried (who have been shown to have poorer health than men who are married),[38] in the promiscuous, who are at very much greater risk of sexually transmitted disease, and in those who are abusing alcohol and drugs.[39] In their sample of over 4,400 American men, Alan Booth and his colleagues found that a high level of testosterone increased the odds of behaviour that puts health at risk and was positively related to sexually transmitted diseases and trauma. Even more dramatic is the finding that you can have too much of a good thing. The greatest health benefits are found to accrue to men whose testosterone is neither high nor low but just below the middle range. Men who have high but not very high levels suffer less depression, fewer colds, fewer problems with high blood pressure, heart attacks and obesity. Men with *very* high testosterone levels, on the other hand, not only engage in more risky behaviour; they are also less likely to benefit from the health-enhancing properties of testosterone. Booth and his colleagues estimate that one in ten men falls into this category.

Men, Marriage and Health

We have seen (Chapter 2) that there is evidence linking high testosterone levels and marital breakdown although it is still unclear which is causing which. What is much clearer is the impact that marital breakdown and divorce have on male health.

The first thing that can be unequivocally said about marriage is that it is good for men. In a celebrated study of a group of men who had suffered heart attacks and been admitted to hospitals in Baltimore, Maryland, married men were much more likely to survive than single men.[40] When factors known to increase the risk such as smoking, excessive drinking, older age, obesity and a history of previous heart disease were accounted for, the better survival of the married persisted. Over the following ten years, married men continued to have significantly better survival rates. In another American study, divorced men were found to be twice as likely to die from stroke.[41] Divorced women in the same age group ran a much lower risk. Similar findings have been reported from a more recent analysis of all deaths in Finland from heart disease over a three-year period.[42]

What is it about being single that makes it a risky state for men? Single status includes three distinct groups – men who have never married, those who are divorced and those who are widowed. Being widowed is a particular risk factor for premature death in men. My British psychiatrist colleague, Colin Murray Parkes studied 4,000 widowers aged 55 years or older over a period of nine years. The death rate in these bereaved men was 40 per cent higher than expected and two-thirds of the mortality was due to ischaemic heart disease – the men died literally of broken hearts.[43] Men who remarry after bereavement are less likely to die than those who remain single. Men who never marry are a statistically abnormal lot – given that in most societies about 90 per cent of men do marry. The Baltimore study reported higher mortality for heart disease, a finding also found in a 10-year longitudinal study of middle-aged Dutch men recruited from the general population as part of a heart disease screening programme.[44]

But what is it about being single or divorced that makes it bad for men? Three explanations have been put forward. It has been suggested that healthy men may be more likely to marry than unhealthy men. Alternatively, marriage may bring with it physical and psychological benefits that protect men against disease and death. Or perhaps marriage encourages men to adopt a more healthy lifestyle. There are research findings which provide support for each view. For example, in a prospective study at the beginning of the 1990s of men and women aged 21–24, the group that had not married by the age of 24 contained a higher proportion of problem drinkers at the age of 21.[45] The suggestion in this study was that marriage was being delayed in those with alcohol problems. A different conclusion was supported by findings from a pooled analysis of 12 studies which showed that never being married or becoming single was associated with increased alcohol consumption whereas becoming married was accompanied by a drop in alcohol consumption.[46] A detailed Swedish study has also shown that increased rates of smoking and drinking do help explain why the death rate of middle-aged men in Sweden is twice as high in the divorced population as it is in the married.[47]

Similar findings are reported in cancer research. Several British studies have found that the divorced are at significantly higher risk of cancer than any other marital status group, and divorced men are particularly at risk.[48] In a major study of a representative sample from a data set of some 27,779 cancer cases, a strongly significant relationship between marital status and cancer survival has been found.[49] Being married is associated with an increase in five-year survival that is comparable with being in an age category ten years younger. Even after controlling for the severity of cancer at the time of diagnosis (married people tend to be diagnosed earlier, perhaps due to a spouse's concern), married people have better survival rates than the unmarried, of whom the divorced seem to have the worst survival rate with a risk of 1.27 relative to the married population (1.00).

Marriage makes men not only healthier but happier. Being married has been shown to predict good mental health – and to influence it more than age, race or childhood background. Being married is associated in men with higher scores on measures of satisfaction with home life in particular and life in general, with mental health, and with happiness.[50] But, as David Jewell points out, contrary to popular opinion, male satisfaction with marriage is not bought at the expense of women's health and happiness.[51] A number of studies from the US and Europe have shown lower mortality and psychological distress rates in the married of both sexes compared with single men and women. However, there is one interesting difference: what seems to be important for women's happiness is how good and emotionally satisfying the marriage is, whereas what seems to be important for men is being married at all. Women seem much more concerned about the *quality* of their married lives. Men appear quite content just to be married.

Suicide

Suicide is between two and five times more common in men than in women in Europe, North America, Africa and Latin America. This gender ratio is less pronounced in Asia, being 1.7:1 in Japan and 1.3:1 in India and Hong Kong. In Britain, there are approximately 6,000 suicides each year – one every 85 minutes. The rates of male suicide in all age groups and in most countries have shown a striking increase over the past 30 years, and this is most dramatic in the 15–24 age group. In many parts of the world suicide is now the second commonest cause of death after accident in young men.[52] The ratio of youth to elderly male suicides also varies between societies but, in general, the rate increases with age.[53] However, in recent years the death rate from suicide in young men has started to exceed that in older men.

In most European countries men account for about three-quarters of the people who kill themselves. An equally noteworthy finding is that the suicide rate in women, much lower than in men, remains stable. Could this be because male stereotyping puts a value on emotional control, reticence, stoicism, independence and invulnerability? Women raise the alarm more readily when emotionally distressed or in crisis than do men – cries for help (so-called parasuicide or acts of deliberate self-harm) are very much more common in women than men. Women cry out. Men lash out. Suicide in men is strongly associated with depression,[54] alcohol abuse,[55] and drug abuse.[56] The link with alcohol abuse in young men is important,[57] but the nature of the link remains to be clarified.

Suicide is a very aggressive act even if it is not intended to be so – indeed the motive behind many suicides is to spare survivors trouble and anguish, not to cause it. But the intensity of the pain felt by those left behind, the guilt and the recrimination and self-examination, are terrible. There was a theory, popular for a time, that suicide and homicide might be inversely related, that murderous aggression could be directed outward or inward. Now it is felt that while they are related it is not an either/or relationship. Herbert Hendin, Executive Director of the American Suicide Foundation and Professor of Psychiatry at New York Medical College, writes:

> Suicide and violence show many similarities even when they are not present in the same individual. Hopelessness and desperation are common to both. So are difficulties in dealing with frustration and loss, and in expressing aggression effectively. It is necessary to understand violence to fully understand suicide and necessary to understand suicide to fully understand violence. It is as important to see the suicidal intentions that may be hidden by homicide as to see the homicidal intentions that may be concealed by suicide. Suicide can be used to check homicidal impulses that threaten to overwhelm the individual in ways more frightening than death. Suicidal intentions also may unleash and permit a homicide that would otherwise not take place.[58]

Support for such a view comes from a survey of young men undertaken by the voluntary support group, the Samaritans, in Britain.[59] More than one in three suicidal young men said they would 'smash something up' rather than talk about their feelings, many admitted to picking fights, while 70 per cent said they themselves had experienced violence from an adult and 50 per cent had been in trouble with the police. Suicidal young men were significantly more likely to believe their fathers wanted them to fight their own battles. They resorted to drugs, alcohol and cigarettes to a far greater extent than non-depressed and non-suicidal counterparts. Many reported having an absent father, and having stepfathers was common in the depressed and suicidal. A dual life was described

> in which a front or shell hid an inner turmoil until 'barriers collapse and it all falls apart'. Expectations from the society around them, both their peers and older males, acted as an added pressure. The widely held view was that seeking help placed you in a vulnerable or weak position.[60]

When I saw Sean, a 21-year-old technician, for the first time he had survived a suicide attempt which involved him taking a massive dose of paracetamol and driving his father's car into a lake. A passer-by saw his car leaving the road, rescued him and took him to hospital where he was successfully resuscitated. Sean denied being depressed but admitted his work was going badly; he felt a dismal failure and he contrasted himself with friends who seemed to be doing very much better. He could see little point in going on. When asked why he hadn't sought help, Sean said he wasn't going to pour his troubles over anyone, that a man worth his salt would sort himself out and, anyway, he could not see what anyone else could do.

Sean had two very clear views about seeking help. There was little point in doing so and strong people should be able to sort out their problems without bothering others. He had never confided in an intimate way with anyone in the past – neither his parents, his siblings nor his friends. Not surprisingly, his self-reliance was perceived by all of these as strength. So, when he did try to kill himself the question on everyone's lips was, 'Who would have expected this of Sean? He always seemed so strong.'

The problem with suicide is that it is at one and the same time a declaration that life cannot be controlled and a demonstration of the ultimate in keeping control. The individual who decides that death is preferable to life may have sought advice and help prior to making such a decision. Many male suicides, however, never seek help, overtly at any rate. It is as if many men prefer to die than admit they need help, and prefer to make the ultimate personal decision – that of self-destruction – rather than admit they are not in control. Hopelessness and desperation are common both to killing others and to killing yourself, argues Herbert Hendin. Most men who feel hopeless and desperate find it hard to admit they are in trouble. Even when they force themselves to come for help, they find it difficult to unburden and unbutton so as to enable the helper to help.

Social Support

Men do not just find it difficult to express their feelings, to reach out, to ask for help. They are more isolated, psychologically and socially. They have fewer close personal supports than women do and this lack of an emotional network, when they do reach out, has significant and measurable health implications. Surprisingly, however, there are few reputable studies of the relationship between male friendship (and the lack of it) and health.[61] In their intensive study of adult American men, Daniel Levinson and his colleagues found that friendship was largely noticeable by its absence.[62] They went further and concluded that 'close friendship with a man or woman is rarely experienced by American men'. I don't think this conclusion applies only to American men. In general, men have many amicable and sociable relationships with other men and with women too but most men do not have an intimate male friend of the kind that they recall with affection from boyhood or youth. Many men have had brief, casual relationships with women, almost always involving some degree of sexual intimacy, but most have not had an intimate, non-sexual friendship with a woman. There is some evidence suggesting that homosexual men may have more good, close friends than heterosexual men.[63] This may well be because they have a larger range of personal contacts or an enhanced need for an 'extended family' of friends. Heterosexual men and women are more likely to be involved in family relationships of various kinds and this might account for the smaller number of close friends they may have.

One of the most substantial, consistent and neglected findings in all of medicine is that the presence of close and supportive family and friends protects and buffers us against the impact of disease. What American physician Dean Ornish has termed 'the healing power of intimacy'[64] promotes health more effectively than giving up smoking, monitoring weight, eating a nutritious diet and taking appropriate exercise all added together!

Social support refers to the esteem, involvement, help and affection provided by an individual's support network, usually composed of family, friends and colleagues. When social support is lacking, the impact of biological factors in disease and social stressors such as poverty, poor housing, environmental deprivation and unemployment is intensified. The scientific evidence is every bit as convincing as that which links smoking to lung cancer, but it is largely neglected in medical and political responses to disease. It is not new. Over 40 years ago, research workers at the California Department of Health Services began a study of about 7,000 people living in Alameda County, near San Francisco. During a nine-year follow-up period, they found that individuals who had poor social supports – who were isolated, were not members of a club or community group, whose contacts with family and friends were poorly developed, difficult or non-existent – were between two and three times more likely to die.[65] This finding was not related to such issues as age, ethnic group, smoking, alcohol consumption, over-eating, physical exercise or the use of health services. Nor was gender an issue – women with poor social supports were as likely to die as men. But of course men have poorer social support systems. In another classic study, this time involving over 13,000 people living in North Karelia in Finland, men who were socially isolated had a risk of death some two to three times higher than those who had a greater sense of being socially connected and part of family and community. Again these results were found even when other confounding factors for cardiovascular disease were controlled for, such as cholesterol, blood pressure and smoking.[66]

Indeed the Alameda County study findings showed that individuals who had unhealthy lifestyles, who were overweight, had higher than normal blood pressure, smoked and had high serum cholesterol levels actually lived longer than those with a more healthy lifestyle but who had poor social networks and support. Those with a healthy lifestyle *and* a well-developed and rich social support network lived the longest. In another exercise, 2,800 Dutch men and women aged between 55 and 85 were studied to determine levels of loneliness and the extent to which people perceive themselves as possessing or lacking close emotional support.[67] Those who saw themselves as surrounded by a loving circle of friends 'decreased their likelihood of dying by approximately half' when compared with individuals who reported feeling emotionally isolated. Those with the highest self-reported feelings of loneliness had almost double the death rate of those who believed they were emotionally and socially connected to others.

Perhaps the most fascinating study in this whole area is that of Thomas Oxman and his colleagues at the University of Texas Medical School.[68] They examined the relationship of social support and religious belief to mortality in men and women who had undergone elective open-heart surgery. They asked two main questions. The first concerned regular participation in organised social groups. The second focused on the strength and comfort obtained from religious or spiritual faith – whatever that faith might be. They found that those who lacked regular participation in organised social groups had a risk of dying six months after heart surgery four times that of those who were socially supported and involved. Those who did not draw strength and comfort from their religion were three times more likely to die six months after surgery than those with firm faith. Those who had neither social nor spiritual support were seven times more likely to die within six months of surgery.

These are but a handful of studies from a rich and growing bank. They have been impressively summarised by Ornish, who concludes that

> social support, connection, community, and related ideas – all relate to a common theme. When you feel loved, nurtured, cared for, supported and intimate, you are much more likely to be happier and healthier. You have a much lower risk of getting sick and, if you do, a much greater chance of surviving.[69]

But what about the male bonding that reportedly occurs in the pub, on the sports field and terraces, in clubs and in the workplace? What about the warmth and camaraderie that many young men share, the 'laddishness', that mixture of drinking, brawling, bravado, sexual posturing and social misbehaving in which young men indulge and find friendship and affection? The problem is that intimacy, the letting down of emotional barriers and the expression of innermost thoughts and feelings, is inimical to such bonding. Laddishness includes amongst its characteristics a defiant identification of intimate feeling as something essentially feminine and a projection of it on to women with all their associated and despised connotations of weakness and dependence. Much of what passes for young male bonding is better described as a process of mutual initiation, a rite of passage in which boys and adolescent males, individually and in a group, slowly negotiate a passage to manhood. Making men of little boys involves, in Norman

Mailer's highly relevant words, the winning of small battles. From such a perspective, masculinity is not something given to you, not something you're born with, but something you gain through triumph and achievement. Manhood is problematical, a critical threshold that boys must cross by means of tests and trials. Such trials and tests are defined differently in every society but, according to the American anthropologist David Gilmore, are to be found at all levels of sociocultural development, 'among both warrior peoples and those who have never killed in anger'.[70] All men, young, middle-aged and old, even when in longstanding relationships of affection and comradeship, are locked into such a struggle in every sphere of their lives – as husband, provider, father, lover, warrior. As for those men who fail the test, the effete men, the weaklings, they are held up with derision and scorn to inspire conformity to the ideal of the tried and tested man. Gilmore reminds us of the strength of the idea of manhood acquired through trial and its exemplification in the 'virility school' of American letters which includes such luminaries as Ernest Hemingway, Jack London, William Faulkner, John Dos Passos and Robert Stone. Norman Mailer is currently that school's most articulate exponent. In his *Armies of the Night*, there is the definitive statement of manhood as a Holy Grail to be seized after long and demanding trial – 'Nobody was born a man; you earned manhood provided you were good enough, bold enough'.[71] Mailer's raw, pugnacious concept of masculinity is not restricted to American culture but is to be found in modified or expanded form in many others.[72]

Many of the men I have interviewed over the years – men such as the theatre director Jonathan Miller, comedian Stephen Fry, psychiatrist R.D. Laing, violinist Nigel Kennedy, novelist Anthony Burgess, and mountain climber Chris Bonington – spontaneously described their childhood and adolescence as a time of trial in which their strength and ability to deny feelings (of fear, pain, sadness and loss) marked their status as males. The British public school, with its rites of physical violence and intimidation by older males, was seen to facilitate the development in young boys of the self-reliance and emotional control that marked the adult male. Fathers were more often than not emotionally controlled, aloof, somewhat distant individuals who communicated in a detached and cerebral way with their children. Such a value system was enmeshed within the upper and upper-middle classes in British life and helped create a concept of masculinity characterised by self-reliance, independence, emotional control and a deep suspicion of intimacy.

Many men neglect personal relationships, and are uneasy about intimacy. And the remorseless demands of the workplace take a substantial and corrosive toll of the ability to sustain and cultivate rich social networks characterised by emotional closeness and mutual support. My own experience as a husband, father and doctor testifies to that, as does my experience of working with many professional and businessmen struggling to cope with the demands of their work and personal lives. Traditionally, men at work have found it hard to find the time and energy to devote to friend and family; women too encounter the tyranny of the workplace. Much, rightly, has been made of the role conflict experienced by women torn between the competing demands of the public and private. Less attention, sadly, has been paid to the equivalent dilemma for men – largely because men have neither articulated it nor felt the need to do very much about it. Men have appeared content to devote substantial portions of their lives to competing for the highest occupational positions, oblivious to the cost in terms of health and happiness.

On arriving at the top of their chosen occupation, many men find it is not to their liking or their stay there is short-lived as they are found wanting, suffer from criticism or competition from younger men, are stressed or bored or simply get sacked. More and more middle-aged men are the casualties of what has euphemistically been termed 'downsizing' – in 1996 the Joseph Rowntree Foundation reported that in Britain one in four men over 55, and virtually half of men aged 60 and over, are no longer in work. Redundancy, forced early retirement and the wish to retire early are cutting people off from work.

The change is a dramatic one. Thirty years ago, more than 95 per cent of men aged between 55 and 59 and more than 90 per cent of those between 60 and 64 were still economically active, while one in four worked beyond the age of 65. Available figures make it hard to distinguish between those who have voluntarily retired early and those forced out of work, because many men just won't risk losing face by admitting that they have been fired or rendered redundant, and instead pretend they have taken early retirement. Employers and the labour market discriminate in favour of younger people, and women instead of men.

The psychological problems that attach to men suddenly deprived of work in their fifties are immense. Such men come from a generation in which male identity was bound up with work. Many men gave themselves to corporations and businesses, joining in their teens in lowly positions, leaving at retirement in positions of status and seniority. A man was what he did. But if a man does nothing, or that which previously defined him is removed, he is, to all extents and purposes, no longer a man. He is dead. Clinically, I see many such men. They do not commit suicide. They just slowly wither away. Their spouses watch uncomprehendingly for during their husbands' working careers these wives (many now themselves in their fifties) have developed interests, cultivated friendships, involved themselves in neighbourhood and community and created a multifaceted and intrinsically robust identity. It remains to be seen if a younger generation of women competing successfully with men in the workplace and experiencing their own identity and self-worth primarily through such work will suffer an equivalent loss of self-esteem when they are 'downsized'. Meanwhile, most older spouses who have been working women have avoided near-total identification with a job and maintain a circle of close friends and a clutch of hobbies and interests.

George is a 60-year-old retired managing director who came to see me shortly after retiring from a company he had joined at the age of 15 years as an office boy. He was complaining of depression, memory disturbance and a complete lack of interest. He was spending every morning in bed, had become a virtual recluse, seeing less and less of his golfing friends and venturing out only at night – and then to sit over a drink on his own in his local pub. His wife, who had spent much of their married life at home rearing their four children, was now active in a number of voluntary organisations, played bridge two nights a week and visited houses of architectural interest with a society of which she was treasurer. She found her husband's psychological and social decline both a worry and a stress. Several sessions revealed George to be a depressed and bitter man. He was depressed by his lack of zest which he blamed on the fact that during his time with the company he had never cultivated interests or hobbies outside his work. 'My work was everything to me,' he told me. 'I loved going to work. I hated holidays. I never gave retirement or life without work a moment's thought.' Nor did he ever have to plan his day – on arrival in his office there was a diary on his desk with the events and activities laid out before him. When the company was taken over he lost his job, although he did get a substantial financial payment or 'golden handshake' which guaranteed that he would have no financial worries. He found little consolation, however, in the money. Instead he felt betrayed, let down by a company to which he felt (with some

justification) he had given his life. He also felt somewhat betrayed by his wife and children. He had expected them to be there when he wanted them, providing support and stimulation. Instead they were busy living their own lives. 'I sacrificed my life for them. The least they could do is do the same for me now that I need them.' He resisted attempts to enable him to see how his total commitment to his work during the early years of his marriage when his children were growing up meant that both his wife and children had had to develop their own interests and lives. Efforts to persuade him to use his managerial skills in voluntary and part-time work and to involve himself in joint interests and hobbies with his wife and friends met with limited success. His difficulty getting out of bed in the morning persisted – as he said, 'I never had to plan my day before – it just fell into place.'

Men, Women and Work

If Professor Hendin is right and male suicide rates suggest not merely that men are increasingly depressed but may be increasingly angry too, what have they to be depressed and angry about? Like much aggression, this may well be precipitated, and is certainly aggravated, by territorial invasion – women moving in on men's territory by working outside the home.

Consider the scale of the transformation in the developed world. In the United Kingdom, in 1997 over three-quarters of women aged between 25 and 44 were economically active compared with just over half in 1971. As the proportion of economically active women has increased, the proportion of economically active men has declined. In 1971, 98 per cent of men aged 45 to 54 were economically active; by 1997 this had declined to 91 per cent. While this may not seem a great drop the trend is significant. By 2011 it is estimated that 58 per cent of all women will be economically active compared with 70 per cent of all men.[73] (The reason for the much lower figures is that the proportion of both genders in the retirement age bracket will have risen substantially by 2011.)

In one of the engine rooms of modern society, the world of money, the change is striking. Whereas in 1972 only 1 per cent of the members of the UK Institute of Bankers were women, by 1989 this had grown to 29 per cent. Today 40 per cent of the staff in banking, finance and insurance are women. Critics will argue that in 1988 only 3 per cent of managers and administrators were women but the base was small. The signs of change are there for all to see. In that same year, 1988, 57 per cent of the graduates entering banking and finance were women. Even if there is such a thing as a glass ceiling blocking women from occupying their fair percentage of the top jobs, the number of women becoming eligible for such promotion rises remorselessly every year.

Consider another male bastion, the Civil Service. Women form nearly half of all full-time employees in the non-industrial Civil Service but in 1988, among holders of the top three Civil Service grades (Permanent Secretary, Deputy Secretary, Under Secretary) only 5 per cent were women. So what have men to fear? The same persistent trend as identified in banking: the women are coming. In 1988, 35 per cent of the high-flying administrative trainees were women, compared to 28 per cent in 1986.

What of the two great conservative professions, law and medicine? Thirty years ago, only 30 per cent of medical undergraduates were women. In 1988 the figure was 47 per cent. In 1998, according to the most recent figures available from the Higher Education Statistics Agency (HESA), it was 53 per cent.[74] In 1989 a woman was elected to the Presidency of the Royal College of Physicians, the first time in its 471 years. One in seven hospital consultants and one in five principals in general practice are women. In Ireland the situation is more favourable to women – 25 per cent of hospital consultants are women and one in three general practitioners.

With regard to the legal profession, there would appear to be less reason for men in the UK to be worried. In 1986, only 15 per cent of those holding practising certificates were women, only 7 per cent of partners were women and only 4 per cent of High Court judges (a total of three out of 75). But the same trends are at work. Since 1991 women entrants to the profession have outnumbered men. Once again, the situation for women is more hopeful in Ireland – in 1996 one in three barristers and solicitors was female while over the period 1994–8 over half of solicitors newly registered with the Law Society of Ireland were female. The scale of the rise is again what is so striking: the proportion of Irish barristers who are women has increased almost sixfold over the last 30 years, from 5 per cent in 1968 to 29 per cent in 1997–8.

Similar trends are identifiable in advertising. In 1960 the proportion of women employed in advertising was 38 per cent. By 1989, this had risen to 47 per cent. The increase has been in the professional ranks of agencies. For example, in 1960 over two-thirds of the women employed were in secretarial, clerical or administrative functions; by 1989, only half the women were employed in these jobs, the other half taking up professional roles. The main reason for under-representation of women at the top of advertising is thought to be the fact that there were very few female recruits 15 to 20 years ago when today's crop of top managers was entering the business. Twenty years ago, only 19 per cent of the graduates entering professional jobs were women. Fifteen years ago the number had risen to 23 per cent. Today it is 45 per cent. Marilyn Baxter, Director of Planning at Saatchi and Saatchi and author of a major report on manpower and recruitment, argues that agency CEOs are increasingly of the view that women form the bulk of the best candidates at graduate selection interviews:

> women graduates appear more personable, articulate, mature and self-confident than the male candidates, who are often gauche and apparently incoherent. The women present and sell themselves better.[75]

These steady, upward trends in female employment have tended to be undervalued in the context of the difficulties women have in occupying some of the most senior and powerful positions within the world of work. For all the progress women have made, men still hold most of the levers of power and show little inclination to shift. Such a situation is exemplified by a profession such as education where as early as 1987 women had the majority of teaching posts – 60 per cent – but only 41 per cent of head teachers were women. In secondary schools, men remain four times more likely to become head teachers. The gender disparity is even more noteworthy in universities, where in 1986 only 17 per cent of academic staff and 3 per cent of professors were women.

In 1999, Joyce O'Connor, President of the National College of Ireland, explored the extent of women's penetration of the labour market in the recent phenomenal growth of the Irish economy, and the barriers to their future progress. In her paper, a highly professional summary of the current situation,[76] O'Connor identifies three main changes relating to the role of Irish women in the workforce. First, there has been a massive increase in the number of women working outside the home – from 275,600 in 1971 to 488,000 in 1996. In the same period, the number of men at work hardly altered. Secondly, there has been an increase in the number of married women and mothers working outside the home. In 1971, married women accounted for only 14 per cent of the workforce. By 1996, half of the female workforce was married; one in five of the entire workforce was a married woman. Thirdly, by 1996 the number of couples where both partners were working outside the home was now as numerous as couples where only the man was at work. Not merely are more Irish women in paid work, more are employed in managerial, professional and technical operations, more are self-employed, and the differences in the average earnings of male and female industrial workers has continued to fall. In 1971, the average weekly earnings of women were just under half those of men; by 1997, women's hourly rate had reached more than 75 per cent that of men.[77]

However, the closing of the gap between what men and women are paid for the same job is certainly taking its time. In journalism, broadcasting, the performing arts, the universities, the professions, business and industry, there remain spectacular examples of blatant pay discrimination. A typical media example is the popular British television series *Men Behaving Badly*. The two leading actresses, Caroline Quentin and Leslie Ash, discovered they were being paid £25,000 less per series than their male co-stars Martin Clunes and Neil Morrissey. Sue MacGregor, one of three presenters of BBC Radio 4's flagship news programme *Today* was taken aback to learn that her £100,000 salary was £20,000 less than that paid to her two male colleagues, John Humphrys and James Naughtie.[78] A survey in the *Independent* in November 1999 revealed that male academics in almost every university and college in the UK were being paid more than women – the exceptions being the Glasgow College of Art and King Alfred's College Winchester![79] Some of the worst offenders were the London Business School where the average salary differential in favour of men was just under £20,000 per year and St George's Hospital Medical School, where the male/female gap was £16,000. The problem at the London Business School was compounded by the fact that at the time of the survey there was not a single female professor. Medical schools and universities with their own medical schools manifest considerable differentials between male and female pay because historically such places have been bastions of male domination and privilege and women only now make up the majority of new entrants. It will take time for them to percolate up into positions of real influence – or so the argument goes. In the United States women hold about 40 per cent of all management positions yet only a very few women managers have occupied the top leadership positions in major American companies. These jobs are dominated by men and many organisations appear to prefer to hire or promote men into these positions. A 1990 study of the Fortune 500 and Service 500 companies in the US showed that women accounted for only about 3 per cent of senior managers and just under 6 per cent of corporate directors. At this rate of progress it has been estimated that it will take women about 30 years to achieve parity with men.[80]

Not much for men to get frightened about there! So what, if more women are coming into the workforce in Ireland, the UK, Europe and North America? Why should men worry, seeing the expertise with which they continue to hang on to the jobs that matter, the top jobs with the best pay? Various explanations have been advanced to explain the so-called 'glass ceiling' effect. It has been suggested that women follow different and less effective career paths,[81] that male superiors are unable to deal with employees who do not fit traditional gender roles,[82] that women have different management styles,[83] and that family obligations hinder women.[84]

In 1995, a survey of women in upper level management positions in the United States reported on their assessment of 18 variables known to play a significant role in career advancement, such as a willingness to relocate, communication skills, the ability to balance home and career and so on.[85] The study confirmed what many suspect, namely that for all the talk of the development of a new, more domesticated male and the sharing of family tasks, businesswomen – high flying or not – believe that they are more concerned about children and the care of the home than are businessmen. An obvious impact of this is on occupational mobility: men appear much more willing to uproot and go when corporation or career development demand it. Women, on the whole, want to hang on to their roots, social networks and supports. The US study authors summarise the dilemma of home versus career:

> Exactly what organizations can do about this is unclear. Day care centers and parental leave address some concerns, but they are more a remedy for a symptom than the solution to the problem. Day care and leave help women in taking care of babysitting problems, which is a very real

> balance, but they are not any real help in balancing the demands of home and career. Organizations are still going to have to give serious thought to their expectations for executives. Women are also going to have to wrestle with the same question, 'What are the things that you are willing to do, or willing to give up to make it to the top?'

But of course the question is not one for women alone. Men, too, need to ask about the price they are prepared to pay – are paying every day. And both men and women need to give greater attention to the fact that the question has to be asked with regard to work not just outside the home but within it. Women, and some men, increasingly demand a corporate and professional environment which is more woman-friendly, workplace practices and policies which reflect domestic and family needs, and better childcare services to meet the needs of working parents with children.[86]

But this misses a crucial point implicit in the term used at the beginning of this discussion – 'economically active'. We talk about women who 'work' and women who do not 'work'. Why do we use such discriminatory language in the first place? Practically all adult women work – it is just that a very large proportion of them, the overwhelming proportion in some countries, don't get paid for it! In the words of the United Nations' 1999 *Human Development Report*, the family today 'is a small welfare state'.[87] Women to a far greater extent than men invest time and energy in children; women pay most of the costs of home-making and childcare while other family members, including men, share most of the benefits. What parents do in the home is less transferable outside the family than investments in a career. And what they do in the home is not remunerated. The result, as the UN report makes clear, is that throughout the world families lack 'bargaining power', and one consequence is that public spending on children is modest when compared with spending on them by their parents. Even the elderly, not an over-supported group, receive far more than do children for the simple reason that the elderly have votes and therefore clout. Parents who invest time, energy and love in the next generation of citizens are not directly paid for doing so. Their efforts are constantly demanded, extolled, praised – but they are not economically rewarded.

Parents of course are men as well as women, but throughout the developed world the picture is consistent: men spend more of their time in paid labour, women, including women who work outside the home, spend more of their time in unpaid labour. In Austria, men spend an average of 70 per cent of their time in remunerated work, 30 per cent in unpaid work. In Italy and Spain women spend seven times as many hours in unpaid work as do men. In the Netherlands women spend twice as much time in unpaid work in the home as men.

The situation in the developing world is even worse. Bangladesh is a case in point. It has experienced one of the largest increases in the share of women participating in the paid labour force – from 5 per cent in 1965 to 42 per cent in 1995. But women still work many hours for nothing. A survey of men and women working in formal urban manufacturing activities shows that women spent an average of 31 hours a week in unpaid work – cooking, caring for children, collecting fuel, food and water. Men put in 14 hours of unpaid work, including activities such as house repair. Some men may take comfort from the fact that women still have a long way to go. Women themselves are highly critical of what they see as media hype about female high-flyers and 'the handful of company directors and CEOs who are trotted out again and again as evidence of the gains women have made',[88] given that the average working woman throughout the world, and particularly in the developing world, is still saddled with the burden of household and community work and receives next to nothing for it. It has been estimated that in addition to the $23 trillion in recorded output in 1993, household and community work accounts for a further $16 trillion, of which $11 trillion is contributed by women.[89] In most countries women do more work than men; in Japan 7 per cent more, in Austria 11 per cent and in Italy 28 per cent. Women in developing countries tend to carry an even larger share of the workload – in rural areas 20 per cent higher, in rural Kenya, 35 per cent higher. On these figures, the UN's 1993 estimate that it might take a millennium to achieve economic equality between the sexes appears understandable. Men, I suggest, are growing anxious as women move into their world for the obvious and much-discussed reason that their power is being diluted and their supremacy challenged. But there is another reason, less noted and therefore less discussed. Men are anxious because for so long they believed that intimacy and networking derived from their work.

People do of course derive much from their work but, for the most part, the contract they have with their employers, their colleagues and their work environment is not a contract of intimacy or of emotional investment, nor of mutual affection and regard. Never was this more apparent than during the 1980s and 1990s, a period of driving, entrepreneurial, competitive and ruthless capitalism. But many men are unaware of the extent to which their work fails to deliver, and they are terrified of a life in which work plays a less dominant role.

But the situation is changing. In a provocative exploration of the time demands and the priorities of work, Arlie Hochschild marshals evidence to the effect that, in the US at any rate, a rising number of working women and their partners are clamouring not for more work and better arrangements at home to enable them to work but for more time at home.[90]

Aisling Sykes was 39 when she was sacked from the position of Vice-President at the bank of J.P. Morgan in the City of London in 1998. She had asked the bank for more flexible working hours in order to spend more time with her children, then aged five, four, two and eight months. The bank refused and sacked her. She sued for unfair dismissal. She claimed that her boss compared having children to a lifestyle choice, like playing chess, the tribunal dismissed her claim that the bank's refusal amounted to indirect sexual discrimination. Instead, it ruled that the bank was entitled to make certain demands on an employee as well paid and highly placed as Ms Sykes. She disagreed, observing elsewhere that the ruling amounted to an admission that it is allowable to discriminate against women in the workplace 'as long as you pay them enough'.[91] She felt that because she could afford daycare the bank believed she had no other duty to her children.

As Vice-President, Aisling Sykes worked from 9 a.m. to 6.15 p.m. and again at home from 7.30 p.m. She was also required to manage all-night calls to Tokyo and worked most nights to midnight. She was prepared to do it – 'I'd have the phone on one arm and my new baby on the other' – but the bank, in her opinion, believed that if she was not working at her desk in the office in the morning she was not working. Ms Sykes accepted that having children changed her working style. 'A bank is a very charged place, full of cut and thrust. Before I had children I was one of the boys but afterwards I didn't have time to lunch or go out for drinks, so I got on the wrong side of office politics. I was seen as a trouble-maker as I wanted to do my job in a different way'. Having tried to juggle motherhood and a high-flying job, Sykes eventually admitted defeat, admitting that a woman either has to choose not to have children or be prepared to put the job first no matter what, even if that meant two or three nannies to provide childcare.

Her account of trying to work at the very top and at the same time to be a mother to her young children vividly illustrates the difficulty, some might say the impossibility, of doing both. If a woman was prepared just to see her children at the weekends – like many men – then she could do it. But is this how it must be? And should men accept that, as working hours remorselessly rise, they only see their children at weekends? How remorseless and incorrigible should the demands of work be? The arrival of women at the top of the tree only illuminates how family-unfriendly much of the world of modern work has become.

Such arguments intensified with the arrival of Tony and Cherie Blair's baby. Having made much of the importance of fatherhood to family life, the Prime Minister found himself having to justify why he would not be taking paternity leave on the birth of his son. To compound the embarrassment, Cherie Blair, in the months leading up to her delivery, publicly championed the taking of paternity leave, quoted with approval the fact that the Prime Minister of Finland had twice done so, and opposed government policy by calling for paternity leave to be paid.

Despite a tendency on the part of some media commentators to trivialise the issue in terms of nappy-changing and baby feeds, the issue of the balance of work and family will not go away. Paid paternity leave, extended maternity leave, rights for all parents to flexible working hours, protection of personal time and space are issues which other countries, most notably Sweden, Norway and Denmark, have taken on board and begun to positively respond to without the bottom falling out of their economic worlds. How Britain reconciles the clashing demands of home and work in the post-Blair baby world will decide whether the Blair government is serious in its desire to protect and enhance family life.

Having time together is an absolutely vital precondition for building personal, intimate and supportive relations. Yet virtually all the trends at the heart of modern capitalism are in the opposite direction. For those who are in work, there is less time for anything except work. Men who have dominated the workplace and found their identity there are bound as much as ever; but no longer can they be blind to the cost, in physical, mental and personal terms. The arrival of greater and greater numbers of women in the workplace outside the home can intensify male anxiety, depression, anger and resentment – and indeed appears to be doing just that. But there is another possibility. Men could join with women to reassert and revitalise a system of values in which the personal, the intimate and the social take precedence over the pursuit of power and the generation of wealth.

They might be more willing to do this if they realised that people's satisfaction with their marriages and their families makes by far the greatest contribution to their happiness: much greater than that made by job or money. In two large studies of the quality of life in the United States it was the quality of personal relationships – feelings about one's children, one's spouse and one's marriage – which consistently made a stronger contribution to life satisfaction than what has been termed 'the money index' (feelings about one's family income, standard of living and savings and investments).[92] Commenting on these findings, the Yale University political scientist, Robert E. Lane observes that the main sources of human enjoyment do not pass through the market. He goes on to argue that the main sources of well-being in advanced societies are friendships and a good family life and that once a person moves beyond the poverty level a larger income contributes almost nothing to happiness. He calls for a culture change, a transformation in which governments and political strategists focus less on the pursuit of the aims of the market – more and more monetary growth, productivity, consumerism – and more on the formulation of a strategy

> to create life-frames, scaffolding supporting the microworlds of experience in a manner that protects these little worlds within which people can, mistaken as they may be, grow up without trauma, seek and find education, marry sensibly, enjoy their vocations, find and cherish their friends, achieve local respect, enjoy community life (in the communities that government can facilitate and protect) and pursue their dreams in peace.[93]

There is a role for men to play in such a transformation but whether we play it is yet to be seen. But we had better get the balance between work and personal life sorted out soon. For there are other trends in the construction of personal and family relationship, at the very heart of the generation of human life, which may make the man's contribution to the family by way of the sweat of his brow even less relevant. According to some prophets of the human condition, if men do not engage in a serious revaluation and reconstruction, they will become utterly irrelevant as social beings. Women can do without them in the workplace. Even more significantly, they can do without them in their beds.

CHAPTER 5

The Age of the Amazon

'It could be the dawn of the Age of the Amazon', declared Steve Farrar, science correspondent of the *Sunday Times*, in a piece on the development of a genetic technique which could enable two women to have a child without a man being involved.[1]

American researchers are within two years of creating a healthy mouse that gets all its chromosomes from the female line. The team, led by Dr Rudolf Jaenisch at the Massachusetts Institute of Technology, aim to enable animals to produce young from an unfertilised egg (which can occur naturally in amphibians and reptiles but not in mammals). There is a problem because of the unique way that mammalian DNA functions, where some vital genes inherited from one parent are chemically gagged while those from the opposite sex are able to work as normal. Previous attempts to solve this problem have resulted in grossly abnormal offspring. The Massachusetts team now believe that it is going to be possible to remove all the chemical gags without any harmful effects. The DNA from one treated egg could then be inserted into the nucleus of another, applying the nuclear transfer methods used in cloning to create a viable embryo ready for implantation. While Dr Jaenisch takes both sets of chromosomes from a single mouse mother, it is just as easy or difficult to take them from two separate females. He was quoted in the *Sunday Times* as saying, 'If parthenogenesis works then so will using two eggs – there is no significant difference between them.' But there is more to it than that. What medical technology, driven by men, is creating is a situation where, when it comes to the reproduction of the species, we will be able to do without men altogether. We can forget the Y.

The Road to Reproductive Redundancy

Some date the onset of the sexual revolution from the moment that an effective contraceptive, 'the pill', was launched. Until that time, human beings, and in particular women, were only in partial control of the most momentous decision any of them could take, the decision to create new life. Family planning was the subject of widespread public debate, especially in the United States. For the most part it suffered severe medical condemnation.[2] Male institutions – the law, medicine, politics, the churches – have accepted the very concept of birth regulation with considerable reluctance. From the outset the available methods concentrated on the control of female reproduction, a situation, which (condoms and vasectomy notwithstanding), remains true today. Abortion was a frequently used method of regulating family size. Indeed, the Michigan Board of Health estimated in 1898 that one-third of all the state's pregnancies ended in abortion.[3] By the 1880s, English doctors were warning England's women not to copy the activities of American women. Discussions of birth control in America emphasised the role and motivations of the middle class, the main desire being to limit the numbers of children so as to provide a decent standard of living and education for those already born into an increasingly urban, industrial and bureaucratic society. In Britain there was an anxiety that the entry of women into public life would undermine the country's international standing by causing the birth rate to fall![4] The view that the British needed to breed to keep up the supply of good, keen soldiers for the Empire continued well into the twentieth century.

The concern was understandable. Towards the end of the nineteenth century, with industrialisation and urbanisation well established in Britain, people began to succeed in their attempts to restrict their fertility. Brian Harrison has shown that the control of pregnancy was integral to the emancipation of women; it enabled them to participate to a far greater extent in public life, and it also freed them to have a less anxious sexual life of their own.[5] Women had until then truly been the prisoners of their reproductive system. Now, thanks to medical advances, they were becoming the controllers. Between 1921 and 1931, people were already marrying later, living longer, and having fewer children.[6] However, such methods as were available – the diaphragm, the IUD, spermicidal jelly, creams, foam and tubal ligation – were cosmetically unattractive or unreliable, or extreme. The oral contraceptive, first developed by Gregory Pincus in the early 1950s, was heralded as a breakthrough in female liberation, although since then doubts have surfaced as to whether all the consequences have been beneficial.[7] The pill enabled women to postpone or prevent pregnancy for any reason, in particular to enable them to establish themselves in public positions and careers. In that sense it contributed to the downfall of patriarchy.

In general, men, young men in particular, have shown and continue to show a sizeable amount of indifference to the need to exercise reproductive control. The two main methods of male birth control – vasectomy and condom use – are still disliked by the majority of men. Vasectomy take-up rates are low, especially amongst young men, and condom use is not much better. A recent American survey of sexually active college students showed that only 10 per cent used condoms consistently.[8] Young men are regularly overlooked in discussions as to how best to tackle high teenage pregnancy rates on both sides of the Atlantic, while data from the sexually transmitted disease surveillance programme in the US show an increase in unsafe sex among men who have sex with men.[9]

Male indifference to reproductive control is reflected in the millions of women who, every year, have an unwanted pregnancy. While many such pregnancies are carried to term, others end in an induced abortion. Contrary to common belief, most women seeking abortions are married or live in a stable union and already have several children.[10] They use abortion to limit family size or space their children. Many resort to abortion because of lack of access to modern contraception, or contraceptive failure. For example, many married women in the developing world do not have access to the contraception they require and, often at great risk to their health and safety, resort to abortion.[11] The situation is even worse for unmarried women, particularly adolescents, who rarely have access to family planning information and counselling and frequently are excluded from contraceptive services. But even in developed countries, women pay the price for uncontrolled reproduction. A study in the United States of almost 10,000 women who had abortions found that more than half had been using a contraceptive during the month they became pregnant; the proportion whose pregnancy was attributed to condom failure was 32 per cent.[12] In all parts of the world, particularly in urban areas, an increasing proportion of those having abortions are unmarried adolescents; in some urban centres they represent the majority of those seeking abortion. While there is a plethora of studies relating to the effects of abortion on women's physical and psychological health, there is a striking dearth of studies that have considered male involvement in unwanted pregnancies and abortions and virtually nothing on men's reactions to both.[13] Although men, through the predominantly male institutions of law, medicine and the Church, have manipulated, regulated and controlled women's access to contraception and abortion, they have played a miserly role in the prevention of unwanted pregnancy and the personal control of fertility. Now, as the methods of reproduction control become ever more technical and effective, women are poised to remove male involvement altogether.

In Vitro Fertilisation

While the pill's role in enabling women to avoid unwanted pregnancies has been a crucial one, the fact that it has helped focus attention on the question of whether and when to have a child is arguably of greater long-term significance. Other methods of facilitating pregnancy are also strengthening women's control over their reproduction. Around the same time as researchers were earnestly taking apart the female hormonal system so as to synthesise a hormone that would prevent the ovum being released from the womb, other researchers were as energetically working on ways to persuade, stimulate or somehow shake reluctant ovaries into producing ova in infertile women. In 1978 Patrick Steptoe, a gynaecologist, and R.G. Edwards, an embryologist, developed the procedure known as *in vitro* pre-embryo transfer (IVF-ET) and a real revolution was under way. This procedure enables women who have difficulty conceiving to do so. A number of oocytes (eggs), as healthy and mature as can be obtained, are recovered from the woman's ovary using a needle guided by ultrasound – so-called transvaginal oocyte retrieval. Prior to egg removal, the woman undergoes approximately two weeks of intensive preparation which involves hormonal therapy with so-called 'fertility drugs' – hormones which stimulate ovarian activity so that eggs will grow to their maximum potential. Under local anaesthesia, the mature and healthy eggs are visualised by ultrasound and a needle is guided to the ovary; a number (usually more than one) of oocytes are then retrieved. Male sperm is placed with the eggs when they are ready to be fertilised. The fertilised eggs develop into pre-embryos and, at an appropriate time, are passed through a special catheter into the uterus. If all has gone well, implantation occurs and the pregnancy commences.

IVF is a boon for women with fertility problems even if the procedure is physically demanding, often unsuccessful and occasionally produces multiple pregnancies. But what IVF represents, over and above an effective treatment of failure to conceive, is the technological elimination of the male from the process. The woman's biological involvement in reproduction remains crucial – all that is different is the first few days of conception. The rest remains the same – the nine months of pregnancy, labour, delivery. The male role, never very great to begin with now recedes even further. The man is no longer required to be physically present.

Donor Insemination

The pill put women back in charge of their own reproductive destiny; IVF opened up the possibilities of procreation without the physical involvement of men (masturbation to produce sperm has not exactly the same degree of personal involvement and intimacy as mutual heterosexual intercourse); and AID, or artificial insemination by donor, signalled that fatherhood need no long figure in the equation.

Artificial insemination (the introduction of semen into the female genital tract other than by way of the penis) has a long history, much longer than people imagine. The first recorded case was performed in 1884.[14] By the 1960s, it is estimated, between 5,000 and 7,000 artificially inseminated babies were being born every year.[15] By the end of the 1980s, American estimates were of some 15,000 AID births annually while the British rate at the same time was running at between 2,000 and 2,500 per year.[16]

The procedure was welcomed as a boon to couples desiring a child but unable to produce because of male sterility due to azoospermia (the absence of sperm) or oligospermia (few sperm). It also offered the possibility of conception to those couples where severe rhesus incompatibility meant that any embryo conceived in the orthodox way would be destroyed by the incompatibility of blood types of its mother and father. In relatively rare cases of hereditary diseases such as Huntingdon's disease, where the male carries a doomed gene which causes early dementia, a terrible body tremor and premature death, AID could be helpful in permitting a woman to conceive a child knowing that it would not carry the affected Y chromosome of her partner. But the real impetus behind AID, like so much in modern biological medicine, is the excitement of doing something because it can be done. The 1960s and 1970s saw the technology of AID drastically refined and made elegantly simple and effective.

Artificial insemination by a woman's husband (AIH) raised some qualms but it was generally conceded that since both parties involved in the practice would continue to be the child's parents after conception and delivery these were largely laid to rest. As for AID, the increase in demand for information concerning the practice led to a panel being set up by the British Medical Association under the chairmanship of the obstetrician, Sir John Peel, which recommended that for the small proportion of couples for whom AID would be appropriate the NHS should provide it within specially approved centres.[17] By 1982 the Royal College of Obstetricians and Gynaecologists knew of over 1,000 pregnancies conceived in this way and at least 780 births following AID in Britain.

The general procedure is deceptively straightforward. A suitable male donor is recruited. In addition to being told about the mechanics of the process he is told about the rules. A donor – and every year about 3,000 males in Britain donate sperm – is anonymous. He can place restrictions on who receives his sperm (he can, for example, restrict his donation to married couples). Following the recommendation of the Warnock Committee, set up to examine the social, ethical and legal implications of assisted and artificial reproduction, there is 'a limit of ten children who can be fathered by one donor'.[18] (The Warnock Committee, revealingly, uses the word 'fathering' to describe the process of semen provision involved.)

A sample of semen is inserted into the woman's vagina and placed either just outside the cervix, inside the cervical canal or within the uterus around the time when the woman is most likely to be fertile, that is to say at ovulation. The overall success rate in the most successful centres is in excess of 75 per cent and of those women who do conceive, 95 per cent do so within the first six months of AID treatment. Fresh semen was used in the 1970s but, given the need for testing and retesting in the light of possible transmission of conditions such as AIDS, the use of frozen sperm is becoming more common.

The Warnock Committee recommended that AID should be confined to centres with trained psychological counsellors because of the 'complex emotional decision that couples make when choosing AID', but of course there is no need for 'couples' to be involved at all. It is customary to regard a child as a being whose existence is completely dependent on the wishes of both parents. What is changing – and has already changed – is that we now accept that a child is a being whose existence can be willed by the desire of just one person and whose production is by means that are purely technical and of a highly specialised, impersonal and, in the case of AID, secretive nature. Much of the discussion of parenthood, when it focuses on gender at all, is involved with women. Bioethical debate concerning reproductive choices and artificial methods of reproduction have concentrated on women's choices and role in AID, surrogate motherhood and *in vitro* fertilisation. The male's role is often shadowy, peripheral or, as in the case of AID, anonymous. Artificial methods of reproduction are heavily reliant on anonymous sperm donations. While the laws regulating the relationship between the donor and the recipient vary from country to country, in most cases the donation is shrouded in secrecy. In the case of heterosexual couples, the very fact that donor insemination has taken place is kept from the child, who is deceived into believing that his biological father and his family father are one and the same. In lesbian and single-parent families, the fact of insemination is generally revealed but the sperm donor's identity is kept anonymous. The literature on the moral propriety and ethical basis for AID is growing – though much of it is concerned more with the issue of secrecy than with the issue of fatherhood. There appears to be little need to talk about where fathers fit into all of this. The answer is of course – they don't.

The striking thing is the lack of any seriously informed discussion of reproductive technologies. They appear to develop for no better reason than that the vaguely stated needs of this or that group ought to be met, and we now have the means to meet them: what Petersen and Teichmann refer to as 'the Heraclean myth' that anything that can be handled technically, i.e. by means of medical, psychological or sociological methods, is feasible and therefore producible.[19] But just because we *can* do something is not necessarily a justification for doing it; and never was this principle more relevant than in the area of artificial reproduction.

Artificial insemination by anonymous donor strikes directly at masculinity and fatherhood. Yet the general tenor of the conclusions of the Warnock Committee is surprisingly superficial. For example, a paragraph is devoted to the question of secrecy and anonymity. The committee noted that this amounts to more than a desire for confidentiality and privacy, for often the couple involved

> will deceive their family and friends, and often the child as well. Indeed, couples who achieve pregnancy may come to look on their AID child as a true child of the marriage. However the sense that a secret exists may undermine the whole network of family relationships. AID children may feel obscurely that they are being deceived by their parents, that they are in some way different from their peers, and that the men whom they regard as their fathers are not their real fathers.[20]

But it is not a case of children feeling 'obscurely' that they are being deceived, that they are different from their peers and that their fathers are not their fathers. Where the anonymity of the AID donor is preserved, and such donors are the great majority, *the children are being deceived*. The Warnock Committee members go on to conclude their brief consideration of the issue by blandly deciding that while they agree that it is wrong to deceive children about their origins, 'we regard this as an argument against current attitudes, not against AID in itself'!

One of the voices aired in public opposition to the whole practice of AID in human reproduction is that of Daniel Callahan, a substantial figure in the area of ethics as applied to biology and medicine. He is saddened by the way that professionals have lost a sense of and feel for the way that men, women and children need and best flourish in the company of each other.

> Instead, professionals have done conceptually what society has been doing legally and socially – treating men, women and children as separate and distinguishable, with their own needs and rights. Thus we now speak easily of women's rights and children's rights and (hardly surprising, even if amusing) we have seen the growth of a men's rights movement.[21]

Fatherhood has been steadily devalued in recent years. AID makes a clear statement: if a woman wants a child, it is her right to have one. Nobody else's rights come into it. And, AIDS and a handful of hereditary diseases apart, any old dad will do. What is also revealing about the practice of artificial insemination is the way it has split the act of sperm production from any consequences. The anonymous donor provides the wherewithal to produce a child and that ends his responsibility in the matter. Indeed, even if he were subsequently to try to discover the fate of the child he fathered, he would be prevented by law. He gives sperm as others give blood. But the biological fact remains: a sperm donor whose sperm is successfully used to fertilise an ovum, which proceeds through the usual phases of gestation, is a father. Callahan asks us to imagine the following scenario:

> A father has, through the assorted legal ways society allows fathers to turn over their parental authority to another, legally ceased to act as a father and someone else is caring for the child. But, imagine that the other person fails to adequately act as a father; fails that is, to properly care for and nurture the child. The child then returns to the father and says: 'You are still my father biologically; because of you I exist in this world. I need your help and you are obliged to give it to me.'

Callahan asserts that he has never been able to imagine even one moral reason why a father in that circumstance could disclaim responsibility even if there was someone else available to take care of the child. Neither can I. A father is a father is a father. But in the case of AID he is not. He is a seed provider.

The Warnock Committee appeared to expect a change in public attitudes which would somehow eliminate the need for anonymity. It assumed that public attitudes were the reason for the secrecy, a questionable and largely unsupported assumption. In fact, to judge by the prevalence of anonymity, no relevant change in public attitudes has occurred. As well as secrecy concerning the donor, many parents wish also to keep their child's biological origins secret 'in an attempt to protect both the social father and the child'.[22] Before they even enter the programme, many couples make the decision not to tell the child who might be conceived and born. There is a Dutch study of attitudes of couples whose children were conceived by AID in 1980 and 1996. Couples in 1996 were more likely to inform parents, siblings and friends; but they were no more prepared to inform their children than couples in 1980. What was noticeable, however, was that the 1996 couples wanted much more information about the donor, particularly medical information.[23] In another Dutch study, three-quarters of the AID parents intended not to inform their children about the way in which they were conceived, in contrast to parents who had utilised IVF, none of whom intended to keep the process secret from their children.[24]

It is argued by many researchers that there is no need to fuss about AID. For example, one European study of the impact of assisted reproduction on families reported that none of the children differed from normally conceived children in terms of psychological health and quality of family relationships, and yet none of them had been told about his or her conception.[25] But the oldest child in this study was aged eight! The issue of the right to know about one's biological and genetic identity is not one that ordinarily surfaces much before puberty. The ethical issue is intensified by the growing tendency of parents to tell other people while not telling the child. Pressure to change this emphasis on secrecy has come both from experience gained in the field of adoption and from the general climate concerning freedom of information. The problem, of course, is that adoption and AID are different. In AID the biological identity of one parent is known beyond doubt; there is, as there is not in the case of adoption, an imbalance in the relationship between 'biological' mother, 'social' father and child. Nor is there any genuine comparison with the issue of stepparenting. A child with a stepfather knows that his stepfather is not his father. The stepfather may be better than the child's natural father – kinder, more reliable and less cavalier than the child's father – but he is not the child's natural father – and society does not collude in the pretence that he is.

Robert, Lord Winston, Professor of Fertility Studies at Hammersmith Hospital, has argued that it is wrong to offer IVF to most postmenopausal women because of anxieties about the welfare of the child.[26] Lord Winston is concerned about the fact that such a child would have an elderly mother. However, he seems less concerned about the fact that a child born by means of AID does not know who its father is or even whether he has one.

So why the emphasis on anonymity in AID, if it is not because of hostile public attitudes? Simple. If semen donors were to be identified the whole process would lose much of its impetus. In one Scandinavian study, only 20 per cent of sperm donors were prepared to continue if anonymity were withdrawn.[27] According to the manageress of Dr Louis Hughes's fertility clinic in London's Harley Street, 95 per cent of would-be donors would stop if the anonymity they enjoyed was lifted. She is quoted by *Times* journalist Nick Farley, who had posed as a sperm donor to investigate how they are screened, as declaring, 'It would simply be the end of donor insemination.'[28] Her views are implicitly supported by Professor Michael Hull of the Centre for

Reproductive Medicine in Bristol. 'Why is it generally assumed that genetics define "real" parents?' demanded Hull somewhat irritably in a letter to *The Times*.[29]

> Why does that seem so overridingly important in our culture and others? Why should knowledge of genetic identity be enforced when so many more children are happily unaware that they cannot be their father's child?

It is somewhat surprising that an expert in reproductive medicine can wonder why it might be important for someone to know that the person in his life who appears to be his father is indeed his father. As a psychiatrist, I am interested in psychological and social considerations which Professor Hull might be tempted to dismiss as vague and woolly but I am also concerned about 'hard' medical issues. Consider genetically inherited diseases. Because of donor anonymity, a person born as a result of AID cannot obtain or relay information that might be life-saving.[30] This may also be a problem for donors' offspring when they come to have children of their own, particularly in relation to those recessive conditions which are manifested only when a defective gene is passed from both parents.[31]

The psychological and social implications are, for me, significant ones. Our genetic heritage is a crucial part of our very identities.[32] Advances in medical genetics have strengthened rather than weakened this. Increasing numbers of adopted children have been seeking the identities of their biological parents in order to find out more about who they themselves are.[33]

Studies of the long-term effects on children born through AID have not been done. Hence Professor Hull can without risk of contradiction write of such children being 'happily unaware that they cannot be their father's child'. He likewise seems content to keep them in this state of deception even if it means undervaluing the well-recognised need felt by many adults to know the identity of their biological parents. But why does Hull seem worried? Because if donors knew they would be identified and, worse, if donors were to cease being paid for their donations then the supply of donors would dry up. Hull bemoans the fact that the current debate is 'utilitarian and semantic' when it should be 'elevated empirically and philosophically' to consider such issues as how best to protect past donors' rights and what constitute their 'legitimate expenses'.

The seeming reluctance of experts such as Winston and Hull to confront the child's right to know the most basic of information about her/himself is puzzling. We live at a time when the most awesome knowledge concerning our genetic make-up is being uncovered. Scientific colleagues of Robert Winston and Michael Hull, people such as Richard Dawkins, Steve Jones and Stephen Pinker, regularly inform us of the enormous importance of genes to development, health and behaviour. More than 40,000 internet sites are devoted to geneaology. The facts that DNA testing is now readily available and illegitimacy much more acceptable mean that interest in discovering your own and other people's origins has never been higher. Just when you might expect that there would be a reasonable degree of uniformity over the simple question, 'Do individuals have the right to know about their genetic make-up?' along come eminent scientists telling them: don't be so bothered about that. Just be happy that your parents love you.

Defenders of anonymity in donorship in AID demand evidence to support the case for a change in the law. In a robust response to such complacency, Catherine Bennett wonders what evidence concerning the negative impact advocates of the status quo, such as Robert Winston, would accept.[34] One reason for the lack of evidence is that most children conceived by means of AID do not know; they are deceived by parents who believe that such deception is in their best interests. Many such children grow up in homes permeated by an atmosphere of secrecy and taboo. Some children of AID, although they have their mothers' genes, have a different physical appearance, qualities, talents, interests from other members of the extended family, and may feel they do not fit in.[35] Such differences can be much more difficult to confront if any questions raised are dismissed. Then again, secrets will out. Many children learn about their origins only when their parents separate or divorce. Meanwhile the current awareness of and indeed fascination with genes, largely popularised by the same scientific and medical community so enamoured with assisted reproductive technology, contributes to the anxiety of individuals who want to know more about their own genetic history.[36]

If the issue of children's rights has never been properly faced, neither has the question of the rights and responsibilities of fathers. Tim Hedgley of the National Fertility Association sees no problem: sperm donors have no responsibilities for children born as a result of their donation and they have no rights to them, either. Changing the law so that children would have a right to know about the identity of the donor of the sperm that helped create them 'would give children rights where they could not have balancing responsibilities'.[37] Better by far to deceive them and let them live in blissful ignorance. To tell the whole truth can threaten the mother's desire for absolute independence. The child's need to know details of the father raises for the mother the unwanted prospect of identifying and therefore contacting a man who is by definition unsuitable or unwanted. So instead of the identity of the father in an AID conception being revealed, various ingenious approaches are recommended. For example, the mother is encouraged to focus on the altruism of the biological father and advised to tell her child only the father's first name and place of last residence.[38] This can provide a somewhat terse father story, as in, 'My father's name is Dave . . . he lives in Vermont.'[39]

The arguments for and against secrecy and disclosure have been extensively reviewed.[40] A study of 58 New Zealand couples illustrates the difficulties.[41] Here one couple casts interesting light on what it is that constitutes the essence of fatherhood:

> *Interviewer*: Do you think that you will tell James? *Wife*: I don't know. I have vaguely thought about it, but we haven't really discussed it. *Husband*: What's to tell? *W*: Well, I just don't think there is much to tell. *H*: What's to tell? He can just go and get his birth certificate and it shows me as the father. What is there to tell him that I'm not his father? Who's going to prove that? *W*: I don't think we will tell him. *H*: The way I feel about it is, who in this world can prove that I'm not his father? *W*: No one. *H*: Nobody, it cannot be proven. *W*: What do other couples say to this particular question? *In*: It's too early to say yet what the results will be. So far it's about 50/50. *W*: Well, we haven't given it much thought anyway. *In*: There are some couples where it is impossible for the husband to be the father because he has no sperm count. *H*: That's different because it has been stated unequivocally that I am capable of being the father. I think the reason I say 'What's to tell?' is that I don't think of me not being his father. Telling him about DI [donor insemination] would achieve nothing except give the boy a sense of insecurity. What the hell is the point in that? It would be a different story if he were adopted, that's quite a different thing. I'm saying, 'OK, I'm not your biological father', but in this instance, as far as I'm concerned, I went through the pregnancy, I watched him grow, I was there at his birth, I helped to deliver him – I'm his father. He'll call me Dad, and that's all there is to it. I'll call him son and there's an end of it for me.

Being named on a birth certificate, being present at the birth, being physically able to have a child are here straws clutched at by the husband as justifications for not telling. Up until relatively recently there was nothing that could be told. In the UK, registration of sperm donors only began in 1991. Before that nothing is officially known of the many thousands of men who donated their sperm for cash. The law currently only permits children to discover whether they were born as a result of sperm donation. Later, the authorities may permit children to have access to information currently held on their donor fathers – but it covers less than an A4 page and allows one line for occupation, one for interests and none for academic record. There is a space for an optional brief description 'of yourself as a person' for the donor to fill in, but it may well be blank.

Catherine Bennett quotes Robert Winston as saying that unhappy AID children worry him deeply but he 'can match them with stories of happy families and contented youngsters who feel no sense of loss or deprivation'.[42] But, as she powerfully responds, such a view does not constitute scientific evidence. There are no longitudinal studies of children born by this technique and so we have no idea what young adults will make of the discovery that instead of a long line of ancestors they see 'a syringe and a closed door'. The fact that so many male medical professionals make such decisions with such confidence suggests the very paternalism which experts such as Winston rightly decry in other areas of clinical activity.

Artificial insemination by donor does not cure anyone – not the would-be father who remains sterile nor the woman who receives the sperm and who is healthy anyway. What modern reproductive medicine is treating here is a couple's desire, and increasingly a single woman's desire, to have a child. There is nothing particularly medical about the intervention at all. The procedure requires only a willing donor, a willing woman and a syringe inserted in the vagina. But medicine has adopted the procedure, surrounded it with technical jargon and clinical justifications, and a whole new medical industry has mushroomed. If it has not provoked much of a reaction this is partly due to the dismal public standing of fatherhood. Object to the devaluation of fatherhood implicit in AID, and you risk being told, 'What's so good about fathers? Sure, all they do is what a syringe with a couple of millilitres of sperm can do and then they push off. What's the big deal?' The big deal is that medicine and society are confirming that, on the basis of bad fathers, fatherhood itself can be declared redundant. Such an attitude does more. It confirms paternal irresponsibility by expecting, exploiting and rewarding it. On the world wide web are various sites offering sperm donation for any woman who wants it. You will find them somewhere between 'PIG TRACKS specializing in swine Artificial Insemination equipment and scientific analysis and evaluation of boar sperm cell quality' and 'US Sheep Seedstock and Chickadee Creek Cattle Services'. You will also be encouraged to purchase Marie Sebring's experience of IVF and artificial insemination of a couple who had trouble with infertility. On the net too is the IGO Medical Group of San Diego – a self-styled 'Fertility Institute' – which offers 'office-based egg recovery and transfer', 'embryo cryopreservation' and 'micromanipulation – intracytoplasmic sperm injection and assisted hatching'.

One of the books that seeks to explain AID to the lay public (for it is replete with awesome medical and technical jargon) is *Helping the Stork: The Choices and Challenges of Donor Insemination* [DI].[43] The book aims to inform people how widespread DI is as a means of 'family building' and to help relieve the anxieties of individuals who may be using DI including 'married couples, lesbians and single women'. The authors – Heidi Moss, a clinical social worker counselling infertile couples, and Robert Moss, a professor in the field of genetics and developmental biology – are the parents of two children conceived via donor insemination. The third author, Carol Verloccone Frost, is described as the first clinical social worker at the National Fertility Organisation. All three are keen to tell the world about this new 'wonderfully positive way to build families'. However, it is clear that in their notion of what constitutes families, fathers need not figure. There are sections on 'Becoming a Mom without a Dad' and 'Becoming a Single Mom through DI'. Once being a single mother was an unfortunate consequence of being widowed, divorced, separated or deserted. Now it is quite an acceptable, even a desirable state which can be brought about through the wonders of modern, value-free science.

It is a moral axiom that human beings bear a moral responsibility for those voluntary acts that have an impact on the lives of others. The creation of human life is such a voluntary act. Fathers have a significant moral responsibility for the children they voluntarily create. This is the message which, after all, underpins the vigorous efforts governments throughout the world are making to ensure that fathers who leave their children should continue to take appropriate responsibility for them. What action could be more important than that which creates new life, the burden of which the newly born human being must live with for the rest of his or her life? Callahan argues that 'biological fatherhood carries with it permanent and indispensable duties'. Because it is a biological condition it cannot be abrogated by personal desires, social expediency or legal decisions. Nor can the moral obligations be abrogated unless there are reasons why they cannot be discharged, and certainly not because no one wants them to be discharged. The only difference between the man who impregnates a woman in the course of a sexual liaison and then disappears and the anonymous donor who is required to disappear is that the latter kind of irresponsibility is licensed, legitimised and rewarded.

Why is it deemed so important that the biological father in a broken marriage should continue to take responsibility for the offspring he has sired, when for a few pounds, dollars or shekels a young man with a pair of mature, functioning testes and a penis to match can provide a few millilitres of sperm-packed semen, and then push off, believing he has done the state some service? The child produced from the union of the donor's 23 chromosomes and those of some women he will never see and, if the much endorsed secrecy is preserved, won't ever know, is his biological child whatever science may say. But because the donor is anonymous no one knows who did what and thus there can never be any moral accountability. If the child has a life of misery and suffering, the donor will neither know about it nor be called upon to provide help, fatherly help.

The feminist position on fatherhood and DI is utterly confused. On the one hand, there is the predictable demand that the 'right' of lesbians to 'have' children be protected and advanced. Women must be free of undue coercion and the domination of males. They should not leave their reproductive fate in the hands of feckless men. At the same time, however, the feminists deplore feckless men who leave their women in the lurch. They demand that the whole paraphernalia of government and the law be brought to bear on recalcitrant and neglectful fathers to take long-term responsibility for their moment of impregnation.

The Warnock Committee did consider the issue of single parenthood and DI as follows:

> To judge from the evidence, many believe that the interests of the child dictate that it should be born into a home where there is a loving, stable, heterosexual relationship and that, therefore, the *deliberate* creation of a child for a women who is not a partner in such a relationship is morally wrong.[44]

The committee concluded that as a general rule 'it is better for children to be born into a two-parent family, with both father and mother'. Their somewhat meekly stated view got short shrift from those who viewed the evidence that fathers matter as unconvincing at best and irrelevant at worst. One bioethicist, Carson Strong, in a detailed review of the pros and cons of DI for single women, conceded that there might be disadvantages for the children of such artificial reproduction but since these disadvantages were not 'severe', the argument against lapsed.[45] However, nowhere in her otherwise exhaustive review did she consider in any detail the evidence concerning single versus dual parenthood.

In the abortion debate, men have been written out of the script. The father, in other words, is deemed to have no rights when it comes to information or choice about what happens to the conception. In our acceptance of single-parent procreation and motherhood, for both heterosexual and lesbian women, we have again, in effect, declared that fathers are biologically irrelevant and socially unnecessary. Since this motherhood requires, as a necessary condition, some male sperm, it has not been possible to dispense altogether with males. But given time and more intense biological research, it soon will be.

Cloning

When at a news conference in February 1997, Ian Wilmot of the Roslin Institute, Edinburgh, and his colleagues reported that they had successfully cloned an adult sheep, Dolly, by combining the nucleus of an adult mammary cell with a sheep's egg that had its nucleus removed, there was a massive public reaction. At a ceremony in Paris on Monday, 12 January 1998, 17 European countries signed a protocol added to the European Convention on Human Rights and Biomedicine banning the use of human cloning for reproductive purposes – the first legally binding international agreement to do so. Some months earlier, the 186 member states of the United Nations Educational, Scientific and Cultural Organization (UNESCO) had unanimously passed a declaration calling for a cloning ban, but the declaration had no legal status. There is no explicit or implicit ban on cloning in the UK, Greece or the Netherlands, although in the UK, the Human Embryology and Fertilisation Authority which issues licences for the use of embryos has indicated that it would not issue any licence for research into 'reproductive cloning'. This is understood to mean cloning to produce a foetus or live birth. In Ireland, a country repeatedly exercised by constitutional problems concerning abortion, there is no legislation at all governing the regulation of assisted reproduction and an attempt by Dr Mary Henry, a senator as well as a physician, to introduce a bill to that effect led nowhere.[46] She was reassured by a fellow-senator (male) that she should not be worried because nothing like this would go on in Ireland![47]

In common with virtually every development in artificial reproduction, the principles at the heart of cloning are simple although there remain formidable technical problems in implementing them. To produce a clone of a particular human being, one would have to extract the nucleus from one of the individual's cells and insert it into a human egg cell which has had its original nucleus removed. The resulting hybrid cell would contain the individual's complete DNA code. But it would also have the potential to develop into a mature human organism. To realise this potential, it would have to be subjected to electrical pulses in order to initiate the process of cell division, and then be implemented in a natural or artificial uterus. This process of nuclear transfer parallels the process of ordinary fertilisation. The difference is that, rather than blending the incomplete genetic codes of two gametes, in human terms gametes derived from ovum and sperm, cloning involves the transfer of a complete genetic code from one individual into the germ plasm of an egg cell.

In an examination of the justifiability or otherwise of cloning human beings as a source of tissue for transplantation, Julian Savulescu lists what he sees to be the main arguments for and against human reproductive cloning.[48] Arguments in favour include the freedom to make personal reproductive choices, the freedom of scientific inquiry, the treatment of infertility, the replacement of a loved dead relative, the provision of human cells or tissue in the treatment of a number of serious disorders and the prevention of genetic disease. Arguments against include the fact that cloning is open to abuse, that it violates a person's right to genetic individuality, that it allows eugenic selection, that it uses people as a means, that clones are worse off in terms of well-being, especially psychological well-being and that there are safety concerns, especially an increased risk of serious genetic malformation, cancer or a shortened lifespan.

What is interesting about this list of pros and cons, and it is a fairly typical list, is that one crucial aspect of cloning merits no discussion whatsoever: namely that the cloned offspring has only one genetic parent, that any child of the process is by definition a child of a 'single' parent. Justine Burley and John Harris of the University of Manchester have examined the potential welfare of cloned children, but only in terms of possible harm caused by fearful or prejudicial attitudes people might have towards them, the demands and expectations of parents or genotype donors, and what might happen to a child learning of its origins, for example learning that its genetic donor is a stranger.[49] Burley and Harris provide the following example of the kinds of objections people make to cloning:

> A woman chooses to have a child through cloning. Because she chooses to conceive in this way, she gives the child a bad start in life. Though this will have bad effects throughout the child's life, his or her life will, predictably, be worth living. If this woman had chosen to procreate by alternative means, she would have had a different child, to whom she would have given a better start to life.

What is interesting about this example, and it, too, is fairly typical, is the fact that the father is conspicuous by his absence. Cloning is the virgin birth, twenty-first century style. Women conceive or do not conceive. The person who helps them conceive has become as shadowy and ill-defined as Joseph in the Holy Family.

Dolly provokes the predictable line-up of reactions. On one side there are those who see cloning as a boon with amazing promise. The prestigious *New England Journal of Medicine* argued that any plan to ban research on cloning human cells was 'seriously misguided'.[50] It claimed that applying the cloning technique to certain cells of certain bodily tissue (e.g. cells lining the blood vessels, cells in heart and skeletal muscle, blood cells) 'might revolutionize medical therapeutics' and that the treatment of genetic disorders and of diseases such as diabetes and leukaemia might change dramatically. 'Not a moral threat but an exciting challenge', declared the *British Medical Journal*,[51] in an editorial penned by Professor Winston. He expressed opposition to any precipitate ban on the process being applied to humans, arguing that self-regulation and professional regulation work well. Winston implicitly rejected doubts about cloning as ill-informed, the sort of response you would expect 'in a society which is still scientifically illiterate'. Winston dismissed the doomsday scenario of a cloned human being. The onus for demonstrating the benefits to be anticipated from cloning developments, he declared, 'is on researchers to explain the potential good that can be gained in the laboratory'.

Lord Winston failed to mention that someone who could hardly be accused of scientific illiteracy, a man who had won the Nobel Prize over 40 years earlier for discovering with Francis Crick the structure of the DNA molecule, had expressed the opinion back in 1971 that 'A human being – born of clonal reproduction – most likely will appear on earth in the next twenty to thirty years, and conceivably even sooner.'[52] James Watson was wrong in his timing but his prediction is difficult to dismiss. Reading Watson's article one discovers that some 30 years before Dolly a frog was cloned using much the same technical procedures. That research, led by English zoologist John Gordon, had been directed at discovering whether the process whereby cells continue to divide and differentiate into tissue cells, blood cells, bone cells and so on occurred under the influence of the cell nucleus or other cellular factors. Gordon's clonal frog settled the question by showing that a nucleus taken from a highly specialised cell still retains its capacity for directing the development of a completely normal organism.

As soon as Gordon's work became known back in the early 1970s the public reaction was much as it proved to be with Dolly – one magazine editor commissioned a cover with multiple copies of Ringo Starr, while another provided expanded multiple likenesses of Raquel Welch. Ordinary people were not particularly bothered about the application of cloning techniques to a few cells grown in a laboratory dish. The issue that grabbed the imagination then and has done now, aggravated no doubt by media hype, is the notion of the cloning of whole human beings. What hardly helped in the furore over Dolly was the announcement by a physicist, Richard Seed, that he would clone humans for a fee. Never mind that he had no experience in cloning, was attached to no institution and appeared to have no funding. Watson himself, in his 1971 article and a submission to the Panel on Science and Technology of the US House of Representatives, had suggested that some people may sincerely believe that

> the world desperately needs many copies of the really exceptional people if we are to fight our way out of the ever-increasing computer-mediated complexity that so frequently makes our individual brains inadequate.[53]

However, Watson is not as inclined as Robert Winston is to leave the issue to the scientists, arguing that the matter is too important and that the belief that surrogate mothers and clonal babies are inevitable because science always moves onwards 'represents a form of laissez-faire nonsense dismally reminiscent of the creed that American business, if left to itself, will solve everything'. In response, there were demands that an indefinite moratorium be placed on cloning research and a number of hastily drafted bills were placed before the US Congress.

As ever, supporters identified a veritable well of suffering that cloning might help to ease, implicitly portraying those who had expressed doubts as hard-hearted, insensitive bigots prepared to put high-flown and erroneous theoretical principles before clinical sensitivity and plain human decency. So supporters of the technique illustrated their argument with case histories of people suffering catastrophic disorders due to a single gene and children dying of leukaemia and other diseases because there were no available matching tissues for transplantation. But, as Robert Williamson, Director of the Murdoch Institute at the Royal Children's Hospital in Melbourne, pointed out, 'hard cases make bad ethics in the same way as they make bad law'.[54]

We have become so accustomed to discussing conception in terms of mother and child that the absence of a father is no longer an issue worthy of comment. In 1996, when Mrs Diane Blood, a 30-year-old widow, was refused insemination with sperm obtained from her comatose husband before he died by the Human Fertilisation and Embryology Authority (HFEA), she promptly took her case to the High Court. The HFEA's refusal owed nothing to the consideration that any resultant child would have no father; instead it was based on what might be termed an ethical technicality – Mr Blood had not given his consent for his sperm to be used in this way. The Authority was concerned, understandably, about a precedent regarding the extraction and use of genetic material from dying or dead people. But Mrs Blood pointed out, not unreasonably, that as things stood she would have been entitled to have artificial insemination with sperm from an anonymous dead donor provided that he had signed the consent form, whereas she could not have it with sperm from her beloved late husband because he hadn't. 'Surely', she declared, 'it would be better for a child to know its mother loved its father, it was wanted, it was planned.'[55] I agree with Mrs Blood. But the issue of whether society should *deliberately* produce single-parent families demands discussion too. The Blood case sets a precedent.

Interestingly, the Centre for Reproductive Medicine at the University of Bristol expressed concern about posthumous conception.[56] In a survey of 106 centres in the UK licensed to store embryos or sperm, more than a third were opposed to posthumous use. This substantial minority took the view that it is wrong to assist in the conception of a child after the death of a progenitor. Of course, given the vicissitudes of nature and accidents, many people are born after their father has died, many others never know their father and many more wish they didn't know him. But, deliberately, to set out to create a fatherless family is a different matter.

The Shrinking of Male Sexuality

Men, for the most part, have been worrying more about their allegedly declining sperm count and inability to get erections than the fact that technology and an enthusiastic medical profession are rendering their procreative role ever more marginal. The arrival of sildenafil, known worldwide as Viagra, coincided with reports suggesting that erectile dysfunction, the persistent inability to achieve or maintain an erection sufficient for satisfactory sexual performance (impotence, to the clinically uninitiated), affected up to 30 million men in the United States, between 3 and 9 per cent of the male Swedish population and 10 per cent of adult men in the UK – that is 2.5 million men aged over 18 years of age.[57] The prevalence figures, available to anyone prepared to read the relevant medical literature, surprised pundits while the general response reflected national stereotypes. In the United States, the drug was greeted with a kind of male hysteria – which was even given its own name, *viagramania*. Within three months of its approval in the US in March 1998, 1.7 million new prescriptions for Viagra had been filled.[58] In its first year in Europe, 27 million tablets were dispensed. Since its introduction, nearly 2 million men in the major European countries have sought treatment for erectile dysfunction. In Britain, enthusiasm was tempered by political anxieties concerning the cost. Politicians seemed dazed by awesome financial predictions. Minister of Health, Alan Milburn, told the House of Commons in 1998 that while impotence for some men was indeed a serious and devastating condition, he was determined that National Health Service resources would not be frittered away by its use as a 'recreational drug' rather than for real need.[59] His determination paid off – by October 1999 National Health Service data showed that only £1.72 million was spent on Viagra, accounting for some 32,000 prescriptions and contrasting with the original estimate of £1.2 billion. This suggested to one Irish medical commentator that 'the only part of the body the British male intends on keeping stiff is still his upper lip'.[60]

Despite the fact that Viagra has no effect on sexual desire, men from Sicily to Singapore, Jakarta to Jerusalem, seized upon the little blue pill as the 'sexual rocket fuel', causing the biggest social upheaval since the development of the pill.[61] In fact sildenafil (called Viagra by the man who formulated the impotence drug, Dr Ronald Virag) does not work on male sexual desire but, more prosaically, on the hydraulics of the penis. It has as its central effect the prevention of the breakdown of cyclic guanosine monophosphate, GMP. Actually, to be more accurate, sildenafil blocks an enzyme (PDE5 phosphodiesterase type 5) which breaks down GMP thereby enabling even a small amount of GMP to be effective. Ordinarily GMP, released when the brain sends signals to the penis, relaxes the erectile tissue in the penis and expands the arteries. Blood rushes into the new open spaces and stiffens the penis. A full erection takes place when the veins that usually drain the blood away are squeezed shut so that the blood remains in the engorged penis. In impotent males, the erectile tissue does not expand enough to block the veins because there is not enough GMP. Blood flows out of the penis and the erection withers. In effect, sildenafil acts on the mechanics of male sexual action and not on its psychology.

But the mechanics are not in the best of shape. Prior to Viagra, men were putting their faith and hope in a plethora of pills, potions and gadgets including vacuum-constriction pumps, injections into the penile vascular system of agents to act on GMP and other relevant enzymes, surgical implantation of stiffening rods and surgery to the actual blood vessels. Until Viagra no effective oral therapy was available. American men have been spending upwards of $700 million yearly on their erections while the original estimate of over £1.2 billion which might be spent by the NHS in Britain was based on the assumption that half the men in Britain believed to suffer from genuine sexual impotence would require one or two tablets a week.

Viagramania reminded us that the ability to obtain and sustain an erection defined what it was to be a man – or so many men believed. Prior to the arrival of the drug, most men afflicted by erectile dysfunction did what men do with personal problems – they kept quiet about it. Men who place a particular premium on control are especially threatened when their penis just will not work – hence the extraordinary response when Viagra promised to put them back in the sexual driving seat. The fact that many women are nothing like as perturbed by impotence in men as men believe hardly figures in the discussion of erectile dysfunction. Men's relationship with sex is frequently more with themselves than with their partners; women in such a scenario become little more than extended sex aids to help men gush their seed. If pornography is, as Greer suggests, a flight from women,[62] then men's preoccupation with a sexuality defined by the size, strength and sustainability of their penis is a kind of pornography, a masturbatory sexuality in which notions of mutual pleasure and intimacy are incidental or even alien and threatening. The characteristic of pornography is the satisfaction through fantasy of the hydraulics of male sexuality – excitement, engorgement, erection, ejaculation, exhaustion, ennui. Women often don't enter into it, save as objects. Those men disgusted with the facility with which they can be aroused by women direct their self-hatred at the women who stimulate them. Men unable to masturbate often do the same. Viagra, like all other treatments for erectile dysfunction, tackles the area men most feel at home with – the mechanics. Men equate the penis with masculinity, the cultural stereotype of male sexuality being 'a large, powerful, untiring phallus attached to a very cool male, long on self-control, experienced, competent, and knowledgeable enough to make women crazy with desire'.[63]

'With a dynamic job, a beautiful wife and three children, airline pilot James Williams had everything he had ever wanted', began an article by Rebecca English in the *Express* entitled 'I lost everything after bungled sex operation'.[64] Mr Williams went to a surgeon for help to ease tightening of the skin of his penis which led to pain on intercourse. The surgery went badly wrong. Mr Williams ended up with a gangrenous organ and had to undergo five reconstructive operations before ending up with a penis 'approaching an acceptable state'. He began to suffer from depression and post-traumatic stress disorder; his wife could not cope with him, divorced him and found a new partner; he never flew again, ending up with a desk job, having lost his flying licence due to his mental and physical deterioration. His counsel was reported as declaring: 'There is general agreement that his life has been destroyed. He is a man in effect of no fixed abode, staying with those friends and family who are able to bear his company.'[65] Clearly it was the mental effects on Mr Williams of his ghastly surgical experiences that drove his wife and children away, rather than any changes in sexual function.

Males are preoccupied with a penetrating penis; women don't necessarily share this view whatever men may believe, hope and fear. Women take longer than men to become physiologically aroused and have a broader and more diffuse bodily eroticism. Women take considerable sexual pleasure in being stroked, kissed, massaged, touched, embraced and sexually stimulated other than by direct penetration. Men are penis-centred in a way that women are not clitoris-centred. Men see a penis in front of them. Women see the man behind the penis. The failure of men to see the slow development of so-called erectile 'dysfunction' with age as anything other than dysfunction is a classic case of missed opportunity – men who take time, men who take pleasure in non-penetrative sex, men who are interested in arousing the sensuality of their partners, are actually seen by many women as the real sexual athletes that so many men clearly wish to be. The emphasis on penetrative sex is itself one of the major contributory factors in erectile dysfunction; so anxious are many men to 'perform' that they end up impotent and, worse, bereft of other approaches to mutual sexual behaviour which might give their partners satisfaction and enjoyment.

But male sexual problems do not stop with a faulty erection. Further anxiety surrounds the quality of a man's sperm. Infertile men are much more likely to suffer from psychological distress as expressed in lowered self-esteem, higher anxiety and more physical symptoms of discomfort and ill health.[66] 'It's an internal feeling of inadequacy', one man is quoted as saying of his lack of normal sperm. 'I feel like I'm imperfect, unable to do what other men seem to accomplish effortlessly'.[67] When two papers published in the *British Medical Journal* in early 1996 claimed that sperm counts were falling, they caused pandemonium. One reported a careful analysis of a sample of selected men born in Britain between 1951 and 1973, in whom a progressive deterioration in sperm concentration and total sperm per ejaculate over an 11-year period was found. A smaller study found a significant fall in the sperm counts of sperm donors in Toulouse over a 16-year period.[68] These papers added fuel to the anxiety provoked by a complicated statistical study, reported at the beginning of the 1990s, which suggested that sperm counts in men had fallen between 1940 and 1990 by 50 per cent – from 113 million spermatozoa per millilitre of semen to 66 million.[69] If such a trend were to continue, the male role in reproduction would be in real jeopardy: male fertility starts precipitously to fall when sperm concentrations decline below 50 million per millilitre of semen.[70] Oestrogens and pesticides have been blamed for the reported fall. The Danish Environmental Protection Agency in 1995 released a report which questioned whether there might be links between environmental chemicals that have strong oestrogenic effects and the increasing incidence of testicular cancer and declining sperm counts.[71] Another environmental pollutant that has been blamed is DDT, known to be able to affect testicular function in the foetus. Countries such as Brazil and Mexico used nearly 1,000 tons of DDT in 1992.[72]

The publicity given to these professional studies in the lay press was massive and the possible link with environmental toxins seized upon with alacrity. Subsequent correspondence in the medical journals expressed reservations concerning the actual scientific methodology employed in many of the studies and cast doubt on whether sperm quantity or quality had actually declined. It was pointed out that sperm counts are notoriously variable and subject to many physiological factors including age (they fall as age rises), frequency of ejaculation (they fall with more frequent ejaculations), seasonal changes (they fall in summer, rise in winter), concurrent illness and even differences in the way semen specimens are collected.[73] One commentator noted that the great majority of the men examined in one major study came from Western Europe and the United States, countries where over the past 50 years there had been a major sexual revolution in which 'the taboo on masturbation' had almost completely been lifted.[74] In other words, if sperm quality has been falling it is to cultural explanations and not biological ones we should be looking. Men are worried about their sexual performance despite or perhaps because of a century of sexual liberation. Critics have focused on the mixed blessing that is the so-called sexual revolution for women. On the one hand, more women have enjoyed more active and positive sexual lives, and men, too, have been drawn into this guilt-free and pleasurable culture. On the other hand, greater sexual awareness and sophistication on the part of women, coupled with a perceived heightened expectation on the part of men that they need to provide their lovers with 'successful' and 'satisfying' sex, have constituted for many men a heavy burden. Men joke a great deal about sex but reveal little. There is a taboo on public exhibition of the penis. Men seek constant reassurance concerning its performance and are ready, indeed eager for their partners to tell them that such factors as the size and shape of the penis are not relevant to satisfying penetrative sex. The more men define themselves in terms of their sexual prowess, the more likely they are to experience a profound jolt to their self-esteem. At the beginning of the twenty-first century, men need to realise that there is more to successful sexuality than a fully engorged, rapacious penis.

Conclusion

It is a measure of how far men have been separated from the process of procreation that Robin Baker can write the following and be taken seriously:

> The jewel in the reproductive crown is the chance completely to sever sex from procreation. Sex can become purely recreational and reproduction can become purely clinical, the product of in-vitro fertilisation (IVF). Already more than half a million people – the oldest now 21 – owe their origins to a petri dish rather than parental union and like the first swallows they are the harbingers of a new summer.[75]

The extraordinary developments in assisted reproduction have been implemented at a remarkable speed, which has made attempts critically to assess and even question their implementation seem half-hearted and half-baked. Further developments in technology may render some of these issues redundant – better methods of stimulating poor egg production and correcting faulty or low-quality sperm may mean less recourse to such methods as AID. But what this current debate reveals only too clearly is the extent to which the rights of biological fathers to take up their responsibilities and the rights of children to know the identity of their fathers have been disregarded in favour of the overriding importance of adult human beings, sometimes in a couple relationship, sometimes not, being enabled to exercise their 'rights' to have a child at whatever cost. At least Baker is honest and indicates what he really thinks of childhood, family relationships and nurturing. Parenthood is to be replaced by a petri dish. If you think this is unlikely, just pause for a moment. Fatherhood already has been.

CHAPTER 6

Farewell to the Family Man

The increasing redundancy of male violence, the growing irrelevance of men to reproduction and the expanding self-confidence and assertiveness of women all constitute mighty blows to male confidence. But there is another revolutionary change that men are still grappling to come to terms with. The decline of the traditional nuclear family represents one of the less recognised but arguably the most significant of all the threats to phallic superiority. The death of the patriarch is not just an important structural change in the long evolution of social and family relationships. The decline of the two-parent family and the rise in the number of families headed by women create the very antithesis of the patriarchal family. Where once the family was dominated by an adult male, now in more and more families there is no longer an adult male to be seen.

We have become so accustomed to the gendering of the public and private spheres – of men earning their reputation and deriving their self-esteem from the public, of women confined and assessed within the private – that we may be in danger of underestimating the relationship between masculinity and domesticity. Much of the self-esteem which men possess, perhaps most of it, has derived from the reputation *outside* the home, earned in making a living, engaging in a profession, changing the world. Historical scholarship, sociological research, psychological theorising, all have contributed to the notion that until recently the public sphere has belonged to men, the private to women. The underlying assumption is that what makes a man is what he does. And yet, of course, the division between public and private has never been an absolute one: a man's duty to his family has also been an elemental part of his masculinity and self-reliance. The man who was not master in his own house earned the derision of his peers. The extent to which his personal life and his most intimate relationships were disciplined or chaotic affected the way he was perceived and judged in the wider social context. Political thinkers have long argued that the authority relationships within the family are a microcosm of the state.[1]

To this day, for example, we are still arguing about the relevance of a male politician's private life to his public performance.

The origins of the modern family are customarily rooted in the late fourteenth and early fifteenth centuries with the emergence of the child as an identifiable person in his or her own right and not, as in the Middle Ages, thought of, spoken to, dressed and treated as a miniature adult.[2] Lawrence Stone, in his monumental work, *The Family, Sex and Marriage 1500–1800*,[3] identified a number of overlapping stages in which although the relationship between society and the family subtly altered, that of the male head hardly changed. Originally marriage among the upper and middle classes was primarily a means of tying together two kinship groups and, from the perspective of society, a convenient way of channelling sexual desire and ensuring a stable production and rearing of children. Children lacked a single mothering figure and their supposedly sinful will was crushed by brute force at an early age. Within such a family model, men were powerful and autocratic and their position did not alter as, in the late sixteenth and early seventeenth centuries, this family type began to give way to one that Stone has termed the 'restricted patriarchal nuclear family'. Passive obedience to the husband and father in the home mirrored and was the model for obedience and submission to an increasingly powerful and centralised state. The boundary between the nuclear family and the more extended system of relations and friends became more clearly demarcated. As both the neighbourhood and the kin as units of influence began to decline throughout the seventeenth century, so the 'closed domesticated nuclear family' evolved. Husbands and wives personally selected each other rather than obeying parental wishes and their prime motives were now long-term personal affection rather than economic or status advantage for the lineage as a whole. More and more time, energy, love and money were devoted by both parents to the upbringing of children. The home became a more private place. Externally it was closed off from prying neighbours.

And thus the four key features of the modern family – intensified emotional bonding of the nuclear core (mother, father, children) at the expense of neighbours and kin, a strong sense of individual autonomy and the right to personal freedom in the pursuit of happiness, a weakening of the association of sexual pleasure with sin and guilt, and a growing desire for physical privacy – evolved over several centuries and were all well established by 1750 in the key middle and upper sectors of English society. The nineteenth century and the early part of the twentieth saw much wider social diffusion of all of these. And as the family evolved, the power of the patriarch within it consolidated.

However, fatherhood, as historian John Demos observed, 'has a very long history but virtually no historians'.[4] The prominent part that men have played has been the public and official part. Yet by the late seventeenth century the father was taking on a broad range of what would now be termed domestic and private responsibilities. He was a pedagogue to his children, imparting the rudiments of reading and writing. He played a pivotal role in the courtship and marital arrangements of his offspring, approving or ruling out a proposed match and allotting portions of property to secure the couple's future. Men were expected and indeed required to overrule women in the domestic sphere, for it was accepted that here as in other areas of life men had received from their maker a superior endowment of reason. Fathers were there to discipline: all children, after all, were seen as having come into the world 'stained' by sin, and with their powerful passions and impulses and impaired reason, they required moral and physical control. Fathers were regarded as better placed to understand the young and provide them with the very best of models of good behaviour and decent character. 'Once infants were past the age of breast-feeding', writes Demos, 'their fathers came strongly into view; and girl children, no less than boys, required moral supervision from a man'.[5] A picture emerges from the records of the time of an active and involved role for a middle-class father, a role which did not involve a major split between his public and domestic identities. Social and cultural traditions meant that all adult men expected to become fathers, and many were fathers many times over. It has been estimated that an average couple would produce eight children surviving past infancy, and often a man was over 60 before his youngest child had married and left home, which meant that fathering lasted into old age.

The Home/Work Split

'The most important of all the effects on the family group of modernisation', according to Peter Laslett, one of the great historians of the family, 'has undoubtedly been the physical removal from the household of the father and other earners for all of every working day'.[6] Such a removal began insidiously enough – as late as 1850 most men still worked at home or lived close by their place of employment.[7] By the latter half of the nineteenth century, the growth of what continues to be a particular problem of modern family life – the separation of home from work and, with it, the beginnings of the isolation and diminution of fatherhood – was well under way. Initially, the private role of the father became somewhat more attractive, certainly when compared with public life. It has been convincingly argued that the nineteenth century was the first in which significant numbers of men of education and means began to experience work as alienating because of the polluted environment in which they had to do it and the dehumanised personal relationships which characterised it.[8] The technological and economic progress of the industrial revolution was brought at an appalling cost and one consequence, the separation of the place of work from the place of residence, led to the home becoming in men's eyes a refuge, of psychological and emotional support. 'Domesticity', writes Tosh, 'supposedly allowed workhorses and calculating machines to become men again, by exposing them to human rhythms and human affections.'[9]

The problem, however, was that while the nineteenth-century patriarch might regularly retreat to his home for rest and emotional sustenance, he could no longer hope to exercise unquestioned authority within it. For one thing, he was only at home for relatively short periods. Apart from his workplace, there were the alternative attractions of all-male clubs, all-male sports and the mushrooming array of associations and committees which helped divert men from their domestic responsibilities. The work of the Victorian middle-class male – what he did during the day – was now distant from his home and invisible to its occupants. On both sides of the Atlantic, the power within the home began to shift from father to mother.[10] In the first half of the century, fathers were given the largest share of blame or credit for how the children turned out, more frequently corresponded with their adolescent and adult children and played the central role in guiding or fully controlling their marital choices. But by the end of the century the mother's role in the domestic framework had become pre-eminent. As early as 1847, a New York court had declared that 'all other things being equal, the mother is the most proper person to be entrusted with the custody of the child' and by the end of the century the law, at one with common opinion, 'affirmed maternal preeminence in childrearing'.[11] Between 1880 and 1910 there was a dramatic reduction in the number of women in employment *outside* the home, despite the fact that the demand for female employment actually increased during this period. Large numbers of women began focusing their energies on full-time domestic work within their own families. Orthodox feminist analyses portray these late nineteenth-century wives as victims of controlling and domineering patriarchs. Joanna Bourke, a historian who has suggested that this view is too simplistic, points out that there were important economic forces attracting women into full-time work within the home.[12] With rising prosperity the productivity of domestic labour expanded dramatically. Increased consumption within the family required increased production. Bourke suggests that as a middle-class family starts to eat meat and a wider range of foods, to live in larger houses with separate kitchens, to experience dramatically lower infant mortality and to invest in education, then a full-time housewife is required. Children became more important for female members of the household than for male since women tended to marry younger and outlive their husbands. With improvements in nutrition, health care, education and living standards, maternal mortality was falling dramatically. Accordingly, women were more liable than men to be dependent on their children in their old age. The consequences of this trend, negative as well as positive, were only to be fully realised a century later.

By the end of the nineteenth century, then, the mother had become the primary parent, a role she has occupied ever since. The gendering of public and private in upper- and middle-class families was largely complete, the female sphere being the home, the male sphere the public world. Of course the distinction was not absolute. Hundreds of thousands of young women, and children too, worked in the factories, potteries and mills, in the sweatshops and in traditional 'female' occupations including laundering, childcare and domestic service. Many men worked within the home – one thinks of such occupations as bookbinding, carpentry, baking and weaving. But the great majority of men were increasingly drawn away from their families and into work located away from home. The workplace and the home became very different, each with its own atmosphere, values, modes of activity, relationships, shortcomings and satisfactions. While there is much argument about the extent to which late Victorian males were domesticated, there is no argument about the fact that the wrenching apart of home and work had a massive impact on fatherhood. Key elements in being a father dwindled away – father as teacher, father as moral overseer, father as companion, father as adviser. Instead, a new role emerged – father as breadwinner. Before the latter part of the eighteenth century, breadwinning was embedded in a large matrix within which public and private work were inextricably intertwined. With the industrial revolution, work in the factory and the office became differentiated. 'Now', writes Demos, 'being fully a father meant being separated from one's children for a considerable part of every working day'.[13]

By the twentieth century, changes in the role of the father had spread to the home itself. Within it, the father retained a degree of status as formal head but he had in effect lost to his wife the roles of child adviser, moral guide and decision maker. The belief began to take root that men were biologically designed to play little or no part in the nurturing of children. Such a belief, Adrienne Burgess persuasively suggests, still lies behind the reluctance of many women to involve their men more deeply in child-rearing and the reluctance of many men to push themselves forward; it is 'as if such investment might be a waste of time'.[14] Men began to look outside the home for the status and meaning of their masculinity. By the 1960s, fatherhood as a social role had shrunk and paternal authority had become reduced to two tasks – head of the family and breadwinner.[15] It shrank even further in the 1970s, as David Yankelovich describes, quoting from a public attitudes study of the time:

> Until the late 1960s, being a real man meant being a good provider for the family. No other conception of what it means to be a real man came even close. Concepts of sexual potency, or physical strength, or strength of character (manliness) or even being handy around the house were relegated to the bottom of the list of traits associated with masculinity. By the late 1970s, however, the definition of a real man as a good provider had slipped from its number one spot (86 percent in 1968) to the number three position, at 67 percent. It has continued to erode.[16]

During the 1980s and 1990s efforts were made to resuscitate the male role within the family with the emergence of the so-called 'new man'. Such a man embodied traditional 'feminine' virtues – gentleness, a lack of aggression, sensitivity and a willingness – nay a desire – to play a much greater domestic role. New men were expected to participate in household tasks – cleaning, laundering, cooking, and taking turns to stay home from work to care for newborn and sick children. Many men did indeed discover new sides to themselves, new needs, new desires. But the structure of society and particularly of work remained impervious to demands for family-friendly policies that would enable the more personal and domestic aspects of being a male to flourish. So some chose to 'drop out' and turn their backs on career while the remainder, the majority, for all the enthusiasm and talk about the emergence of this 'new man', remained incorrigibly 'old'. At the same time, changes were occurring in the structure and solidity of the family which were beginning to imperil the very role of males as fathers and family men.

Divorce and Men

One of the most remarkable changes in personal life in the developed world in the twentieth century was the increase in divorce. Between 1970 and 1996 the number of divorces almost doubled, by which time the United Kingdom had the second highest divorce rate in the European Union, at 2.9 per 1,000 population, exceeded only by Belgium.

The Divorce Reform Act 1969, which came into force in 1971, introduced a new ground for divorce, that of irretrievable breakdown of the marriage. In 1995 the marriage figure was the lowest recorded since 1926; whilst about 8 per cent of births in 1996, or one in every 12 children born, were registered by just the mother, almost three-quarters more than the proportion in 1971. In England and Wales in 1995 there were 155,000 divorces, affecting just over 160,000 children – twice as many as in 1971. Thirty per cent of these children were aged five years or under while 70 per cent were 10 years old or under.

But, whatever their ages, the majority of these children ended up *losing regular contact with their natural fathers*. Nine out of ten fathers involved in divorce leave the family home to become non-resident. Fifty per cent of these fathers see their children just once a week and only one in 20 obtains full custody. For a growing number of children in the developed world, Father was no longer even a shadowy figure, playing a walk-on role in the portrait of family life; he had become a memory, in many instances airbrushed right out of the family picture.

It has been said that families are valued so tremendously that most people will have at least two of them![17] In many American cities, the family has virtually collapsed. Among households with children in deprived inner-city neighbourhoods, fewer than one in 10 has a father in residence. Important economic and social changes have seriously weakened the link between parenthood and partnership, particularly for men. It has become much more common for women to raise children without men and for men to escape or be ejected from the nurturing role, responsibilities and burdens of fatherhood.

The phenomenon of the fatherless family did not happen overnight. It began slowly in the early 1960s, picked up speed towards the end of that decade and then exploded during the 1970s and 1980s. In 1961, 38 per cent of all households in Britain were 'traditional', comprising a couple with dependent children, but by early 1998 this had decreased to 23 per cent. Over this period, the proportion of households consisting of a lone parent (usually the mother) with dependent children trebled to 7 per cent.[18]

The conventional wisdom has been to see divorce as a regrettable but unavoidable evil, a sad but necessary solution to the problem of intractable marital breakdown and an opportunity to begin again for adults whose relationships have unhappily failed. It was assumed that for the children divorce is a lesser evil than witnessing their parents trapped in a miserable marriage. Any adverse consequences of divorce, such as the loss of a father, are viewed as less significant than the consequences of warring parents staying 'for the sake of the children'. Indeed, the argument goes, since many of the fathers are deadbeat and uninterested, the impact of divorce on the children is likely to be temporary. And many fathers leave anyway, divorce or no divorce.

In the face of the remorseless, seemingly incorrigible rise in divorce in Western societies, psychologists, psychiatrists, family therapists, politicians and social commentators have been caught up in the tide. Many of the experts have been affected by the trend. When, in early 1998, an analysis of more than 200 British research studies appeared to indicate that poor outcomes for children of divorced parents 'are far from inevitable', some welcomed this as evidence that divorce might actually be harmless. The *Daily Telegraph* headline simply declared 'MAJORITY OF CHILDREN "GET OVER DIVORCE"'[19] while *The Times* headline read 'DIVORCE MAY OFFER CHILDREN OF WARRING PARENTS BEST FUTURE'.[20] Dr Jan Pryor of the University of Auckland, one of the authors of the report, was quoted in the article as saying, 'In Western countries separation and divorce is here to stay. It is foolish to put too much energy to try to stop people separating.' Yet, the analysis by Pryor and Bryan Rodgers, her co-author, actually confirmed that children of divorced parents are significantly at risk of a wide variety of health problems, educational difficulties and behavioural disturbances.

A few months later, the same newspapers were wrestling with the results of a three-year project by the Mental Health Foundation in London which identified marital conflict and divorce as major factors in the mental ill health of children in Britain.[21] There is a very considerable body of research which challenges complacency about marital and family breakdown and testifies to both the short-term and the long-lasting impact on children.

One of the earliest comprehensive reviews of the impact of divorce on children in Britain concluded that 'marital separation is a process with profound consequences for children' and the authors noted that the most common reactions of affected children included sadness and depression and anger directed at one or both parents.[22] In younger children, clinging to parents and regressive reactions such as bed-wetting were frequently seen, while older children reportedly withdrew somewhat from the home and sought relationships elsewhere. Butler and Golding's analysis of the Medical Research Council's National Survey of Health and Development 1980 birth cohort confirmed this tendency towards 'regressive' reactions.[23] Children whose parents divorced before they were five years old were 50–100 per cent more likely to bedwet, soil or throw temper tantrums. Similar evidence emerged from the 1946 birth cohort study, where bedwetting amongst children who had experienced parental divorce before the age of six was more than twice the rate of those whose parents had not divorced.[24] In addition, children of divorced parents were 50 per cent more likely to be admitted to hospital,[25] and, according to data from the second National Health Interview Survey on Child Health in the US, two to three times more likely to have been suspended or expelled from school and three times as likely to be in need of treatment for emotional or behavioural problems.[26] A meta-analysis of some 50 studies showed that the prevalence of juvenile delinquency in homes broken by separation or divorce is 10–15 per cent higher than in intact homes.[27]

Nor do the effects appear to be temporary or short term. In the 1946 cohort study, subjects were interviewed, tested or examined throughout childhood, at 21 years, 26 years, 31 years and, in 1982, at 36 years. The findings revealed a disturbing fact: the experience of divorce as a child often has adverse effects on health, behaviour and economic status even 30 years afterwards. Those whose parents divorce when they are less than five years old are particularly vulnerable.[28] Children of divorce persistently fare worse in terms of educational attainment and behavioural measures too. Analysing data from the first four sweeps of the 1958 National Child Development Study, whose respondents were aged 7, 11, 16 and 23 respectively, Elliott and Richards in 1991 noted that children whose parents divorced between sweeps of the study were already scoring lower on a range of measures in the sweep *prior* to the parents' divorce than were children whose parents remained married.[29] These authors suggested that factors apart from divorce itself may be at work, including parental conflict, social class, and the age of the children at the time of their parents' break-up. Within a period of some 40 years, divorce has gone from being a regrettable, sad, relatively unusual phenomenon to being 'such a common event that it must be considered to be a normal part of family experience'.[30] This has occurred despite the wealth of evidence that there are significant adverse outcomes, in the short and medium term, affecting children's physical and psychological health, education and behaviour, and in the longer term when adolescents' chances of leaving school without qualifications, their risks of pregnancy, out-of-wedlock births and of early, brief marital relationships are greater than those of children whose families remain intact.[31] These effects have been shown to extend into adult life, and particularly to relate to men. In the most extensive study of the effects of divorce, conducted by sociologists Sara McLanahan and Gary Sandefur in the US, young men from disrupted families were found to be more idle and inactive in their mid-twenties than those from two-parent families. 'Growing up with only one parent', they note, 'has a lingering effect on young men's chances of finding and keeping a job'.[32] There are also secondary effects across the generations on the children of children whose parents have separated.

A number of post-war material developments have been identified as putting extreme pressure on the moral consensus which favoured marriage and the family. These include rapid economic development, the expansion of educational provisions, the advent of freely available and very effective birth control and a reduction in the stigma associated with single parenthood and births outside marriage. These developments ruptured the marital 'package deal' – of having sex, having children, marrying and living together. These activities became disconnected behaviours about which separate and explicit decisions could be made.[33]

A significant factor contributing to the decline of fatherhood has been more ready acceptance of divorce and single motherhood. My own country, Ireland, provides an interesting example. Up to the early 1960s, to become pregnant out of wedlock was a disgrace, both socially and personally. Yet within 30 years, one in six of all births in Ireland was to an unmarried woman.[34] By the late 1990s the figure had reached one in four (similar to that found in most other European countries). In Ireland, as elsewhere, the ideology of the 1960s – with its greater emphasis on personal choice, self-fulfilment and self-expression and its lower valuation of personal sacrifice, family commitment and self-denial – raised individual expectations of marriage, and reduced individual tolerance of bad marriages. More and more marriages began to crumble such that by 1995, when a constitutional amendment in favour of the provision of a highly restrictive form of divorce was proposed, it was estimated that there were between 70,000 and 80,000 broken marriages in the country. Women in Ireland were no longer prepared to accept that they had to remain trapped within what they saw as unbearable marriages.

But perhaps the most important factor in the explosion of divorce that occurred in many developed countries after 1960 was a shift in ideology concerning the very nature and function of the family. So quickly did divorce become accepted as a fact of everyday, normal life that to caution against an over-enthusiastic acceptance of it was a risky business. 'Liberals' who wished to raise concerns – about the children who suffered economic hardship or emotional dislocation from divorce and the slow disappearance of their biological fathers – risked being bracketed with 'conservatives' intent on endorsing 'family values' who were overtly hostile to single mothers and exceedingly keen to reassert the traditional stereotype of women in the home, men in the public arena. One of the first to take the risk and get badly burned was Daniel P. Moynihan, better known now, perhaps, as a venerable senior senator for New York in the US Senate, but in 1965 Assistant Secretary of Labor. Moynihan was worried about certain financial implications. In 1965 he issued a report on the African-American family, which concluded that single motherhood was a growing problem in poor urban communities and if left unchecked could undermine much of the progress that had been achieved in the early 1960s by the Civil Rights movement. Moynihan blamed the increasing number of female-headed families on rising male unemployment, which in effect made black men unmarriageable, and he called on the federal government to be more proactive in the generation of jobs for black men.[35] There was uproar. Moynihan's arguments for more federal support for jobs was lost in a welter of acrimony, and accusations that he was blaming *women* for problems not under their control.

Critics of those arguments, such as myself, who point to the substantial evidence testifying to the problems associated with single parenthood insist that many children emerge from single-parent homes with distinction (which is true) while many other children from intact homes display a myriad difficulties (which is true too). What is ignored in such generalisations, however, is the fact that the issue is not about certainties (it never is) but about *probabilities*. Not every single-parent family has problems, and not every two-parent family is a haven of harmony and health. But the odds, the probabilities, strongly favour the family with two parents. Not to say so for fear of alienating this or that lobby is a form of moral cowardice. (The hostility provoked by any reference to the research findings on the adverse impact of single parenting remains intense – in a millennial discussion programme on Channel 4 television at the beginning of 2000, chaired by Jon Snow and devoted to an examination of the future of the family, the psychologist Oliver James made a measured reference to the data and was howled down for his pains.)

In their analysis of four national surveys, Sara McLanahan and Gary Sandefur set out to establish the impact of divorce on children, whether or not any damage was purely economic in nature and remediable by a higher income, and whether children were 'better off' living with two married parents, even if the parents did not get on, or whether they would lead happier lives in a single-parent or stepfamily household. Neither author had a particular axe to grind, as can quickly be appreciated if one takes the trouble to read their work. After an exhaustive and painstaking review of the evidence, they quite bluntly conclude that

> Children who grow up in a household with only one biological parent are worse off, on average, than children who grow up in a household with both their biological parents, regardless of the parents' race or educational background, regardless of whether the parents are married when the child is born and regardless of whether the resident parent remarries.[36]

But is divorce damaging because it results in economic hardship? Does divorce cause financial difficulties, as critics of divorce often argue, or are marriages that end in divorce more disadvantaged to begin with? To try and tease out the economic issues, McLanahan and Sandefur looked at a sample of African-American and white children who, at the age of 12, were living with their parents. Using information on the status of these children five years later, they divided them into two groups – those whose parents had remained married, and those whose parents had separated or divorced in the intervening five years. They then compared the income of these children at 12 and at 17. They found that there were income difficulties between the black and white families and between black families where the parents remained married and those where they separated and divorced. They also found that regardless of race or income level, the financial loss caused by divorce *per se* was considerable (Table 1, overleaf).

Table 1 Median family income for children at ages 12 and 17 in stable and unstable families by race and by mothers' education (in 1992 dollars).

Race, education and family type	*Age 12*	*Age 17*
All		
Stable families	$59,741	$64,789
Unstable families	$55,864	$33,509
Whites		
Stable families	$61,559	$66,696
Unstable families	$62,367	$36,662
Blacks		
Stable families	$39,040	$40,934
Unstable families	$28,197	$18,894
Less than high school education		
Stable families	$42,659	$45,512
Unstable families	$44,293	$27,821
High school education		
Stable families	$61,858	$65,798
Unstable families	$60,725	$37,290
Some college education		
Stable families	$80,191	$91,766
Unstable families	$73,833	$38,082

S. McLanahan and G. Sandefur, *Growing Up with a Single Parent: What Hurts, What Helps*, Harvard University Press, Cambridge, Mass., 1994, p. 87.

These findings confirm substantial differences in income by race – both groups of white families earned more than either group of black families. In black families, those that broke up were earning much less than those which remained intact, providing support for the argument that financial pressure is a factor in family breakdown. In white families, financial stress *prior* to divorce did not seem to be a significant factor – those families that did eventually break up were actually earning slightly more than those which remained intact. But what is most interesting to note is the finding that, regardless of race, the adolescents whose parents broke up experienced a substantial loss of income as a direct consequence of divorce, whereas those whose parents stayed together experienced a steady gain in family income over the five-year period studied. Divorce, concluded McLanahan and Sandefur, *does* cause financial hardship, and the hardship persists.

One major factor contributing to the rise of the single mother and the decline of the father in the family is the fall in men's earning power relative to women.[37] There is still a gender gap in earnings – women to this day earn less than men (a subject of much discussion and argument: see Chapter 4). Nevertheless, the gap has been narrowing at a remorseless rate since the 1960s. In 1959, for example, full-time working women aged between 25 and 34 years earned 59 per cent of men's earnings in the US. In 1980, they earned 65 per cent, in 1990 74 per cent. In two decades, the economic advantages associated with marriage had declined by 15 per cent. The narrowing of the gender gap was different for different groups. Between 1970 and 1990, working women's earnings hardly changed while men's declined. Semi-skilled and unskilled men became poorer. Their marriage prospects plummeted as they increasingly experienced difficulty in finding work and fulfilling the breadwinner role as husbands and fathers. The situation was different for university-educated men and women. Between 1980 and 1990 the earnings of college-educated women in the US grew by 17 per cent while those of college-educated men grew by 5 per cent. While the economic benefits which these men were bringing to marriage were declining, there was still a greater financial incentive to marry and remain married than for working-class men and women. Supporting such a thesis is the fact that divorce rates in the US (and in the UK) are higher for working-class married couples than for university-educated couples.

There is a widespread assumption that the children of warring parents suffer whether those parents divorce or stay together. In so far as divorce adds to the suffering, so one argument goes, it is on account of the financial disadvantages that accompany it. If government and society did something to ensure proper financial support for single parents and stepfamilies then, so the argument goes, the adverse consequences of divorce would diminish considerably. In favour of such an argument is the fact that, once divorce occurs, the likelihood that a child in Britain or the US will be living in poverty doubles. Even when they work full time, most single mothers remain near or below the poverty line.

However, the McLanahan and Sandefur study has seriously challenged the assumption that lack of money fully explains the negative impact of divorce. For example, they found that despite the fact that the income level of stepfamilies was well above that of single-parent families, and close to that of intact families, living in a stepfamily was no better than living in a single-parent family in terms of outcomes. The rates of high-school drop-out and teen births, for example, were the same. Economic advantage is not enough to offset the many psychological and social disadvantages of family break-up. McLanahan and Sandefur conclude that

> stepfathers are less likely to be committed to the child's welfare than biological fathers and they are less likely to be a check on the mother's behavior. Rather than assisting with the responsibilities of parenting, stepfathers sometimes compete with the child for the mother's time, adding to the mother's and the child's level of stress.[38]

But can we be absolutely sure that it is not just a question of money, that financial hardship is not the reason why children who live apart from one of their parents are more likely to drop out of school, become idle, fall pregnant before reaching their twenties, have poor mental and physical health and contract brittle personal relationships? After all, a careful analysis of the results of the four national surveys in the US does suggest that family income differences accounted for about 40 per cent of the difference in school performance and academic achievement between children from one-parent and two-parent families. But income did *not* account for as high a proportion when comparing differences in behavioural problems between children from one-parent and two-parent families. Nor is income an important factor in explaining the disadvantages associated with stepfamilies. Parenting practices account for over half the difference in school drop-out, for all the differences in idleness among boys, and for much of the difference in risk of early child-bearing among girls.

Besides economic security, children need parents who are able and willing to spend time with them; to help them read and do their homework; listen to them, console and support them. They need parents able and willing to monitor and supervise their social activities outside school. 'We suspect', say McLanahan and Sandefur, 'that parental involvement and supervision are weaker in one-parent families than in two-parent families', and they go on to show that their suspicions are well founded. Parents in one-parent families are, in general, less involved with their children than parents in two-parent families. The uncomfortable fact remains that children who grow up with only one parent are at greater risk of a disadvantaged life in terms of education, employment, personal relationships and their own parenting skills, and that this is true for the children of the divorced well-offs as well as those of the divorced poor. But does the *cause* of single parenthood matter? After all, children lose a parent not just through divorce, which may be avoidable, but through death, which most often is not.

By the age of 15, about one in six children in the US born in 1879 had experienced the death of a father. Indeed at the turn of the century middle-aged widowed men outnumbered middle-aged divorced men by more than 20 to 1.[39] To historian Stephanie Coontz, people, such as myself, who worry about fatherlessness are historically ignorant. She argues – and her point has been taken up with relief by many intent on making us all feel better about divorce – that today divorce does to the family what yesterday death did: it removes the father. The result is that 'about the same number of children spend their youth in single-parent households today as at the turn of the century'.[40] In fact, because of extended families living under one roof, fewer than 10 per cent of all children lived in one-parent homes in 1900, compared with 27 per cent in 1992. Nor can death and divorce be so simply equated. Comparisons have been made between children born to unmarried parents, children with divorced or separated parents, and children with widowed parents. Findings from the US National Survey of Families and Households showed that children born to an unmarried mother were more likely to drop out of high school than those whose parents divorce. Both sets of children were at a significantly higher risk of educational impairment than those who lost a parent through death.[41] Indeed, the risk of dropping out of high school was the same for children who lived with a widowed parent and for those who lived with both their parents. A similar pattern emerged with regard to teenage motherhood.

It is not surprising that the death of a parent may be less disastrous for a child than loss through divorce. Death is involuntary; divorce is willingly entered into by at least one of the parents. This distinction is not lost on children. The death of a parent is usually recognised as a severe blow and results in an outpouring of emotion in support of the child from the other family members and in a process of grieving in which the lost parent is remembered with sympathy, pride and affection. The widowed parent shares in the child's loss; together they can maintain an idealised picture of the dead parent and can, even through death, build a sense of connectedness. The loss of a parent through divorce is a complete contrast. The child's perspective and that of the parent with whom he/she lives are almost always utterly different. The parent wishes to move on; the child is torn between competing loyalties. The parent is preoccupied by the faults of the wife/husband. The child clings to the strengths of the mother/father. Society does not extend to a child who has lost a parent through divorce the sympathy, understanding and support available to bereaved children. And, as Barbara Dafoe Whitehead observes bluntly, 'a living parent who remains remote or absent can be a source of continued torment in a way that a parent who dies is not'.[42]

> When I first saw David he was a 14-year-old whose father walked out of the family home two years previously and went to live with his secretary. David was truanting, abusing drugs and had twice been in conflict with the law over aggressive episodes. On one occasion he stole and wrecked a car. On another, he smashed an empty beer bottle on another youth's head. David's anger with his father was immense – he refused to see him, abused him verbally and on one occasion slashed the tyres of his car. His mother endured bouts of aggression too – David oscillating between demonstrations of physical affection and intense criticism, the latter consisting of blame of his mother for having caused his father's departure.
>
> Contrast David's emotional turmoil with that of Matthew, who also lost his father when he was 12 – his father dying suddenly and without warning of a coronary. While Matthew experienced periods of great sadness and loss, his memories of his father were warm and positive. His family's periodic reminiscences of their life with their father have strengthened his relationship with his mother and his brothers and sisters. A decade on, he relates well to his peers and shows few emotional scars of the bereavement. Over the years, David, however, has remained intensely ambivalent about his father with whom he has almost entirely lost contact. His relationship with his mother has improved but on occasion he still accuses her of having driven his father away. His relationships with women are fraught with difficulties which relate in the main to his tendency to interpret any criticism or disagreement as tantamount to rejection.

It has been estimated that lack of income and loss of income associated with divorce are responsible for about half the disadvantages of living in a single-parent family, but insufficient parental involvement, lack of stability and supervision, and continuing difficulties between the now-divorced parents are responsible for most of the remaining disadvantage. Money, as McLanahan and Sandefur show, is not the sole deficit created by family disruption; creating a second family through remarriage, while it may increase overall income, itself causes new strains and leads to greater residential mobility which often undermines children's links with neighbours and friends.

It might be thought that having a sympathetic stepparent could do much to alleviate some of the stresses associated with divorce and living in a single-parent post-divorce family. A number of studies and commentators have failed to establish such a reassuring outcome. In fact, the findings are bleak. Conflict between parents and children remains high in unmarried families. Stepfathers remain disengaged and become more so in the face of persistent antisocial behaviour on the part of their stepchildren. Sibling relationships are generally worse and relationships between children of two previously separate families brought together in remarried families are more often than not negative and improve only slightly over time.[43] Factors that aggravate the stepfamily situation include continued conflict between the biological parents, less acceptance of parental authority, copying of inter-parental discord witnessed before divorce and disengagement by mothers and stepfathers, with a decrease in parental monitoring of adolescents. One British psychiatrist who specialises in adolescent disorders is particularly candid in his detailed summary of the results of research concerning divorce, stepparenting and children:

> A number of naïve assumptions about the effect of remarriage are not confirmed and in general terms it does nothing for the psychological health of adolescents in the medium term . . . Divorce seems to have an adverse impact of its own on adolescent psychological functioning.[44]

In the majority of cases it is women who file for divorce, women who seek full custody of the children and women who are granted custody. Three-quarters of divorce decrees are granted to wives. The most common reason for women to be granted divorce is the unreasonable behaviour of their husbands, which is cited by petitioning wives of all ages. (The commonest reason for men to be granted divorce is the adultery of their wives.)[45] In the controversial Exeter study of family breakdown, 57 out of the 76 divorces examined were initiated by the wives.[46] It is understandable that this should be so. Over the past 40 years women have grown economically more independent of men. They appear better able now to support themselves outside marriage,[47] although, as McLanahan and Sandefur have shown, this may not be the case in practice. They can exercise more choice about whom they marry, and they are much freer to withdraw from a marital relationship if it proves unsatisfactory, unfulfilling, unstimulating, abusive or downright violent.

Women demand divorce and, as numerous surveys have shown, greater numbers of divorced women than men declare that their lives are happier after divorce – in one study, 80 per cent of the divorced women as against only 50 per cent of the divorced men felt they were better out of their marriages.[48] Some of the men's doubts are due to the fact that for many of them divorce does not just mean separation from the wives with whom they found it impossible to live; it means separation, often of a final kind, from children about whom they have no complaint at all.

Because of the children, divorced parents often have to stay in contact with each other even when what they desire is to terminate all communication. In these cases the main reason for continuing contact between ex-husband and ex-wife is shared parenting responsibilities, rather than friendly feelings towards one another.[49] The legal and social expectations that divorced parents will maintain a civil, polite and constructive relationship for the sake of the children require a great deal of two adult people who could not tolerate living together for the sake of those same children. The post-divorce state requires parents to renegotiate boundaries between them and between them and their children. Emery and Dillon state the issue unequivocally:

> Parents do not divorce their children and because of this they cannot fully divorce each other. Thus former spouses must define their relationships on new terms. If they are to become successful co-parents, the central task is to disentangle ongoing parenting roles from the spousal roles which have ended.[50]

The problem is that such disentangling rarely occurs. What much more frequently happens is that one of the parents, usually the father, is disentangled or disentangles himself not merely from his role as spouse but as parent too. One of the most thorough studies of the father's role after separation and divorce is that of Judith A. Seltzer.[51] Her study involved 1,350 cases in the United States' National Study of Families in Households and concentrated on three aspects of father's roles after divorce – social contact, economic support and involvement in decisions in the child's life. Nearly 30 per cent of children had not seen their father at all in the previous year, while only a quarter saw their father at least once a week. Children whose parents were not married were less likely to have contact with their fathers than those whose fathers and mothers had been married. Fathers who had been married to the mother of their children were more likely to make support payments, as were fathers who contacted their children regularly. However, there was less correlation between contact and involvement in decisions concerning their children in that less than half (47.6 per cent) of fathers who saw their children frequently had frequent discussions with their mother. With the passage of time, such influence as the fathers retained in decision making declined even further. Seltzer reported that two out of three previously married respondents who had been separated for two years or less reported that fathers had some influence in decisions affecting the children. Among those who had been separated for ten years or more, only one in three reported some paternal influence.

One family with whom I worked rather tellingly displayed the truth that while parents may divorce each other they do not divorce their children and the battles go on. When Edward split up from his wife Eileen he agreed she would have full custody but obtained generous visiting rights. However, one of the problems that had contributed to the deterioration in their marriage was they disagreed on how best to bring up children. Edward had somewhat inflexible views on such matters as punctuality, cleanliness, homework and the use of leisure time. Eileen had a more relaxed and permissive approach. The battles which had disfigured the home when he was present became less frequent (because he was physically present for less time) but more virulent and combative when he was there. The children expressed reluctance to go and visit him, which he interpreted as evidence that his former wife was poisoning their minds against him. They also quickly learned how to manipulate and deceive him, much to the distress of their mother. Eventually, Edward started to visit less – whereupon Eileen found that her ability to discipline and control the children had evaporated. She had for so long taken their side and argued their corner that when the time came for her to draw the line and set limits she found she had little effect. It was at this somewhat late stage that she, or rather her teenage son Mark, came for help.

A father's contact with his children after divorce is positively related to his provision of economic support, but economic support is not sufficient to ensure deep involvement in children's lives.[52] Seltzer concludes her report with an observation confirmed by other reports:

> For most children who are born outside of marriage or whose parents divorce, the father role is defined as much by omission as commission.[53]

In a 1991 survey of lone parents conducted in Britain, only 57 per cent of former partners maintained contact with their children.[54] Indeed, a measure of the degree of separation of fathers from their children following divorce is revealed by the fact that Seltzer's study of paternal involvement had to rely on the reports of *mothers*: the data from mothers living with their children were more reliable than any information that could be squeezed out of fathers now living elsewhere. 'It is a major research problem', observes One Plus One, the marriage and partnership research charity in London, 'that such men are difficult to access, or reluctant to participate in such research'.[55]

Another study, ranging over three years and involving 136 children aged between 9 and 12, found that boys living in stepfamilies who maintained contact with their biological fathers had better psychological adjustment and fewer classroom problems than those who kept little contact.[56] However, only half of children in stepfamilies maintained regular contact with their biological fathers, compared with two-thirds of those living in a single-parent family, but economic hardship in the latter families more than offset the advantages conferred by greater contact.

Among the less publicised consequences of the rise in divorce is what David Blankenhorn, one of America's most pugnacious advocates of paternal rights, has termed 'the visiting father'.[57] The visiting father is a shadowy, displaced figure trying to avoid becoming an ex-father, who stops but does not stay, who is no longer a man of the house but a visitor who comes and goes. He tries hard, he cares, he stays in touch. He represents a large coalition of men. Of the approximately 10 million father-absent homes in the US in 1990, just over half the fathers had visiting privileges and about one in 14 had joint custody. Blankenhorn estimates that in 1990 there were between 4 and 6 million fathers who did not live with their children but who visited them on a regular or occasional basis. The public and political consensus favours visiting fathers, encourages them, approves of them. Those who insist that divorce need not be a disaster for children are fond of the idea that divorced fathers who stay in touch and provide financial support can prevent most if not all of the unwanted consequences of marital and family break-up. The problem is that in the majority of cases the whole idea of visiting fathers is a fantasy, for the very good reason that most marriages that end do so in bitterness, guilt, pain and a welter of accusations. Father leaves and the children stay with their mother. However, the defenders of divorce still cling to the notion that if the process could be made more civilised, if with mediation and counselling a shared approach to the ongoing care and education of the children could be agreed between the warring parties, then much of the damage of divorce could be avoided.

Much hope has been placed in the encouragement of post divorce arrangements whereby both parents share responsibility for major decisions about their children, including those relating to health, education, religious instruction and even place of residence – so-called *joint custody*. Such an approach, theoretically of great appeal, demands that the parents put aside argument and acrimony and bend their collective will to the interests of their children. The rationale for joint custody emerged from concern for children. It was a deliberate attempt to prevent the total loss of one of the parents, usually the father, from the family home. Joint custody, too, reflected a growing view that women are not ordained by nature to be any better as parents than men. Some men express the wish to remain in close contact with their children; some women express the wish to work outside the home; some share the childcare arrangements.

Recent research, however, confirms that joint custody arrangements are fraught with problems. Each parent is required to organise routines and schedules to coincide with the other's needs. Joint custody involves an extraordinary degree of co-operation and communication between couples who have been so disaffected with each other that they have been prepared at great cost to terminate a significant social and personal contact. The wars that lead to divorce rarely end with it.

In one study, children of divorced parents who were in single and equal custody arrangements were compared.[58] The amount of positive love, affection and support between parents and children was assessed, as was the level of disagreement between parents concerning custody. It was found that high levels of parental disagreement were associated with high levels of disagreement between parents and children, regardless of custody type. Children in equal custody arrangements were actually *less* supportive of their parents than those in single custody arrangements. One of the most challenging and controversial was the 15-year study of 60 divorcing parents and their 131 children reported by Judith Wallerstein and Sandra Blakeslee in the United States.[59] This study showed that, contrary to popular assumptions, divorce is not a short-term crisis but a chronic rupture, with a radical and profound effect on the continuing lives of all concerned. Two years after divorce, children raised in the joint custody households desired by the parents (and not ordered by the courts) were no better adjusted than children brought up in sole custody homes. Joint custody does not minimise the negative impact of divorce in the post-divorce years, despite the fact that fathers in joint custody arrangements are seen to be more committed to their children.

These findings will be seized on, indeed already have been, by those who see them as vindicating the acceptability of granting a parent, usually the mother, sole custody. If it makes no difference to the outcome whether the child sees his or her father regularly or not, then why bother? But that is to miss the point. Divorce in the majority of cases removes the father, whatever the custodial arrangements. The father visits his children and his children visit him. But, as Blankenhorn makes plain,

> Visitation unfathers men. This phenomenon gradually strangles the father–child relationship. Indeed, the ultimate result of such not-like-a-father visiting is nothing less than the ending of fatherhood. Faced with the inherent falseness of their situation, many of these fathers, as Frank Furstenberg and Andrew Cherlin report, 'start feeling like strangers to their children, like impostors'.[60]

Furstenberg and Cherlin's survey of the consequences for children when parents split up concluded that joint legal custody, which was intended to increase fathers' visits, boost child-support payments and reduce conflict between the parents, has done none of these things.

Perhaps it is not divorce that causes the problems, but conflict between the parents, conflict which predates divorce and is the cause of the divorce in the first place? If there is constant conflict, then divorce disperses a destructive marital and family atmosphere, allowing the adult parties to start again and the children to have another opportunity to develop in a less stressful situation. Such an argument has been dubbed 'divorce for the sake of the children' and it derives much support from a number of studies. For example, reviewing American research into the impact of divorce on children in the 1980s, Demo and Adcock observed that 'many studies report that children's adjustment to divorce is facilitated under conditions of low parental conflict both prior and subsequent to divorce',[61] while Gable and his colleagues conclude that 'marital and interpersonal relations pre- and post-divorce, rather than the break-up of the family, may be more informative in accounting for children's behaviour problems and adjustment difficulties'.[62]

In a recent US study of 100 divorcing families with school-age children, Abigail Stewart and her colleagues argue that popular images of divorce are stigmatising, unjustifiably negative and ignore the positive effects on family members and family relationships after divorce.[63] They argue that divorce is not so much an event as a process of family transformation and that children followed up over a period of some 18 months had 'adjusted' to parental separation and divorce. This longitudinal study, funded by the National Institute for Mental Health (NIMH) in the US, suggests that many families do find healthy ways 'to make the transition from a one-household to a two-household family' and that society should be working to make divorce not just a 'painful last resort for the unhappily married' but 'a potentially growth-promoting opportunity'. However, their results, hailed as the perfect antidote to the doomsday discourse on divorce, derive from studying divorced mothers in the main (few fathers participated) and are based on an assessment and follow-up of the children which was relatively short (18 months at its longest).

In Britain there has been only a handful of studies that have looked at parental conflict, divorce and outcomes for children. The controversial Exeter study, conducted by Monica Cockett and John Tripp, compared children in intact families and children whose parents had divorced. The children of divorce were classed according to their current situation: single-parent families, stepparent families and 'redisrupted families', meaning families where the custodial parent had experienced at least one further relationship breakdown after the original divorce. The intact families were divided into 'high conflict' and 'low conflict' groups. The poorest outcomes were observed for children in the 'redisrupted' group. The best-outcome children were in low-conflict intact families. Most controversial was the claim that children in high-conflict but intact families had better outcomes than children who had experienced divorce, for it appeared to suggest that it is the loss of a parent and separation and divorce itself which create the worst outcomes for children rather than the presence of conflict. A barrage of criticism has been directed at the Exeter study's methodology, yet the findings are consistent with studies which have found that adults who have been divorced more than once have poorer mental and physical health than those who have been through one divorce.[64] Both the Exeter study and the NIMH study suffer from the fact that they had no pre-divorce measures of the psychological and social functioning of the adults and children they surveyed, an important limitation in studies such as these and one not easy to overcome.

The Exeter study did confront the crucial question: is it better for the children of unhappy, bitter, quarrelling parents if they divorce or remain married 'for the sake of the children'? Its findings suggest that staying together may well be the best option – for the children. The McLanahan and Sandefur analysis in general agreed, although it did provide evidence suggesting that where there is severe, highly visible and continuing conflict between the parents characterised by verbal abuse and/or physical violence, it may be better for the children if their parents separate. But when it comes to what might be classed as less grievous, explicit and physical dissension such as emotional disaffection, boredom, lack of mutual affection, incompatibility, or decline in sexual interest – some of the commonest reasons for filing for divorce – 'the child would probably be better off if the parents resolved their differences and the family remained together, even if the long-term relationship between the parents was less than perfect'.[65] Since most estimates suggest that only some 10–15 per cent of marriages ending in divorce involve a serious amount of violence, a substantial number of marriages that currently end in divorce warrant greater attempts at salvage. But given the growing disillusion of so many women with the idea of being married in the first place, and the incorrigible tendency of so many men following divorce to lose contact with their children and/or fail adequately to support them, who is going to make such attempts?

I have spent some time considering the issue of separation and divorce and its impact on children in a book on men because the issue has a particular relevance for men. There is persuasive evidence that the role of the father is especially vulnerable to marital disruption. Whereas children who do not live with their mothers are almost as likely as children who do to report a good relationship with their mother, the same is not true in the case of fathers. American evidence suggests that boys not living with their father are twice as likely to report a poor relationship with him than those who do live with their fathers.[66] More than half of all children who do not live with their fathers report they do not get the affection they need. Fathers who, though divorced, remain committed to their children struggle to visit regularly yet, contrary to what one might expect, frequency of visiting does not appear to reduce children's sense of being rejected. Indeed, many divorced and separated men, because they make special efforts, can end up spending *more* time with their children than many fathers who are part of intact families spend with theirs. What matters to children, as the Wallerstein and Blakeslee study in the US shows, is not the quantity of time fathers spend with them, but the quality:

> Where the father is regarded as moral and competent and the boy feels wanted and accepted by his father, then the boy's psychological health is likely to be good. The psychological adjustment of teenage boys within divorced families is greatly eased by the perception that 'my dad is a man, my dad cares for me, encourages me, respects me.'[67]

But where do fathers go who leave or are ejected from their families? What happens to those absent dads? Many remarry or enter into cohabiting relationships and many of these establish new families. Some escape, freed of responsibilities and duties which for one reason or another they cannot meet. Others drift away, embittered by what they see as a hostile culture which favours mothers over fathers in such matters as custody, maintenance, visiting rights and parental choices for their children. And the law, to an extent that depends on differing jurisdictions, does not make things easy for fathers.

Fathers and the Law

Married parents have the same legal powers and legal duties in respect of their children. However, where parents are unmarried, although the mother's position is unchanged, the unmarried father has duties but no powers. He does not have the power, for example, to decide where his child should live or go to school or whether his child should or should not have medical treatment. In 1989 the Children's Act was introduced in the UK. It aimed to emphasise to parents, particularly fathers, that children are their responsibility. The legal term *parental responsibility* was coined. This enabled unmarried fathers to obtain rights concerning their children equal to those possessed by married fathers. However, unmarried fathers have to get the permission of the mother and make a formal agreement with her, a parental responsibility agreement (PRA) or they can apply to court and, if successful, are granted a parental responsibility order (PRO). However since the Act was introduced there have been few such applications by unmarried fathers. Pickford points out that, for example, in 1996 there were 232,553 births to unmarried parents but only 3,000 parental responsibility agreements and 5,587 parental responsibility orders.[68] It would appear that there is no great desire on the part of unmarried men to exercise parental responsibility for the children they have fathered.

The claims of men to have their paternal role and responsibilities taken seriously seems weakened, too, by the meagre financial contribution which so many separated and divorced men make for their children. Given the inexorable increase in the number of fathers, married and unmarried, living apart from their children and the financial difficulties experienced by so many of the mothers and children in these fractured families, governments everywhere regard with alarm the prospect of having to step in and make up the monetary shortfall. Instead, they have embarked on desperate measures to compel men to honour their economic responsibilities as fathers. In the UK the Child Support Act was introduced in 1991 and financial liability for children was switched from the courts to a new Child Support Agency (CSA), charged with pursuing negligent fathers. In the United States, federal child support legislation was passed in 1984 and 1988 which mandate state guidelines for minimum family and child support levels and better mechanisms for collecting support payments. The results, however, have been depressing. The CSA has had enormous and well-publicised problems in achieving the improvement in the level of payment of child maintenance it was set up to provide. Its analysis of compliance in 1996 showed that only just over 25 per cent of non-resident parents for whom there had been a full child support assessment by the Agency were paying the full amount demanded, a further third were paying a part of the amount and the remainder, some 40 per cent were paying nothing at all.[69] The proportion of lone mothers who report receiving child support regularly from the father of their children has not increased since the establishment of the CSA, and was around a third or less in both 1989 and 1994.[70] Fathers, however, tell it differently: almost six in ten of the non-resident fathers in a 1996 survey claimed they *were* currently making child support payments and just over 75 per cent said they had done so at some point.[71] (But then it might be objected that erring fathers would say that, wouldn't they?)

These findings have been used to argue that unmarried fathers and divorced fathers are feckless, and indifferent to the children they have bred; and to reinforce the stereotypical notion of mothers as naturally caring and nurturing, fathers as uncommitted emotionally and unreliable financially. But there are other more prosaic explanations. Ros Pickford has shown that many unmarried fathers are unaware of their legal position.[72] A majority in her study believed that married and cohabiting fathers had the same legal status. All the unmarried fathers in this particular study were concerned about the lack of information provided during the process of separation, and demanded that information about their duties and rights should be given to all fathers at an appropriate time and place. Seventy per cent found the process of applying for PROs very difficult and time-consuming. Many also reported that applying for such orders exacerbated confrontations with the mother, who had sometimes become inflexible on discovering that the father had no rights. A common complaint was of court bias in favour of the mother, 'whose views and objections were perceived as carrying more weight than those of the father'.

The poor payment of child maintenance is not a simple case of male indifference, either. No doubt a lack of interest by fathers in their children operates in some instances, perhaps many, possibly most. But there are other explanations. Many non-resident fathers are unemployed or poorly paid or have further calls on their finances as a result of the formation of second families. The financial problems are exacerbated if their new partner already has children living with her. One assumption that underlies the Child Support Act 1991 is that stepchildren will receive the support of their biological father and that the stepfather's priority is to make financial provision for any children he has himself fathered in the family from whom he is now living apart. However, non-resident fathers have clearly felt that the Act has not sufficiently taken into account the financial needs of their second families.[73] Then again, losing contact with children and failure to pay child support can have a circular relationship – half of the non-resident fathers in the 1996 survey said they would be less likely to pay the full amount of maintenance assessed if they lost contact with their children.

Conclusion

At the heart of the argument concerning the presence or absence of fathers is an assumption that fathers don't matter. Many fathers have brought such a judgement upon themselves. Many others, however, suffer because of a stereotype which classifies them as useless, uncaring and irresponsible. It has been argued, most notably by David Popenoe,[74] that the two major contributory factors to the steady disappearance of the father from today's family are the exponentially rising divorce rate and the growth in births to single mothers. In the US, the UK and much of Western Europe, the chances of a first marriage surviving is about 50/50, while births outside marriage are running at between 25 and 30 per cent of all births. In my own country, Ireland, single-parent families as a percentage of all families with children under the age of 15 years increased from 7 per cent in 1981 to 11 per cent in 1991, to 18 per cent in 1996 – increases in the main due to marital breakdown and births outside marriage.[75] Fatherlessness caused by non-marital births is, in many societies, almost equal to that caused by divorce. In divorce situations, the children have had some experience of and contact with a father; for the majority of children born out of wedlock, there is no father available from the outset. There has also been a devaluing of the role of the father in our culture. Up to 30 years ago, it was well nigh universally accepted that children needed a father as much as a mother. The fact that many men did not wish to be fathers, that many fathers were deficient in various ways, destructive and damaging in others, and that many fathers refused to acknowledge their fatherhood and accept its responsibilities in no way invalidated the conviction that a father was important to his children. Not so now, when the notion of a family without a father is becoming widely accepted and even promulgated. Yet the evidence that there is a substantial price to be paid for divorce and the loss of the father, and that it is being paid by many of today's children, is massive and cannot be ignored. There is evidence, powerful and persuasive, that two parents, a father and a mother, are better than one and that society would be well advised to do all in its power to protect and support parents and help them stay together.

But the uncomfortable facts, uncomfortable for men at any rate, remain. Most divorces are sought and are welcomed by women. Many men avoid paying maintenance. Many more are noteworthy for indifference rather than commitment to their responsibilities as fathers. Men who begin their post-divorce lives with a strong commitment to support their children fail over time, as contact with their children weakens and/or they acquire a second partner and a new family.

Are the critics of fatherhood right? Perhaps the father is more of a menace than a help. Perhaps we would be better off acknowledging that the role of the father is, like so many other male roles, redundant, and that today's mother, with the help of sperm donation, a decent welfare system, appropriate alterations to the work situation and the generous support of her sisters, can expect to do perfectly well on her own. If men still have a role as fathers then it is time they explained *what* it is. And it is time they fulfilled this role. What is it that fathers do, what is it that fathers are? What do they bring to society that society cannot do without?

These are not just questions for men as individuals. They are questions for those man-made and man-dominated institutions that so influence and shape all our lives: the cabinet rooms, banks, boardrooms and businesses, the political structures and professions, the unions, clubs and guilds where policies are elaborated and implemented.

Peter Jones, a hospital manager who works flexitime to be available for his children in the evening, musingly puts forward his own answer:

> I want to be there for them . . . I made a conscious decision that I won't work myself to death and ignore the children really, that's a conscious decision to do that . . . I don't think it's how many hours you put in – it's what you do when you're there . . .[76]

So what is it fathers do – when they are there?

CHAPTER 7

MAN THE FATHER

Everyone needs a caring and involved father. Such a statement might appear self-evident. In fact it has not been so easy to prove. The conclusive research is only now being done. In contrast, social science and family studies research literature bulges with studies demonstrating the importance and impact of the *mother* on the child's psychological and even physical development. Such research includes videotaped studies of mother/baby interactions, exploration of the development of infant vocalisation, assessments of the relationship between maternal involvement and reading skills and calculations of the impact of maternal disorder and stress on the development and health of children. Such a preoccupation with the role and significance of the mother is not, of course, without its hazards. Just as she is credited with the major role in the positive development of her offspring she, and not the father, is blamed whenever things do not work out so well. Indeed, the growth of the behavioural sciences has been accompanied by what one researcher has termed 'mother-blaming'.[1] In a review of clinical journal articles from 1970, 1976 and 1982 in which the cause of someone's emotional problems was discussed, Caplan and McCorquodale concluded that:

> the overwhelming picture in all journals for more than 63 items (such as whether mother's pathology or father's affected the family; whether only mother or only father was involved in treatment; number of words used to describe mother compared to number used to describe father) was one of mother blaming.[2]

These authors documented over 70 mental health problems that have been blamed on mothers, including schizophrenia, anorexia nervosa, depression, enuresis, suicidal behaviour, truancy, autism and alcohol abuse. In contrast, such research as has been done has persuaded some influential commentators to argue that fathers do not matter at all. The problem, however, lies with the paucity of the research. For example, in 1997, when the academic journal *Demography* proposed devoting a special edition to 'Men in Families', the guest editor, Suzanna M. Bianchi, remarked that 'the question we discussed at some length was whether there was enough high-quality social demographic work on men to constitute a special issue'.[3] It is hardly surprising that some enthusiastic biologists have concluded that fathers contribute little except their semen to the survival of the species.

For over 40 years there has been much discussion, debate and dissension concerning the concept of 'maternal deprivation' and, in particular, its effects on the child's physical, psychological and social development. In so far as 'paternal deprivation' is discussed at all, it is usually in terms of the financial consequences for the family. The psychological worth or otherwise of a father often receives little consideration.

From the outset, psychological discussions of parenting have been heavily influenced by psychoanalysis. One of Freud's central tenets was that the relationship between mother and child established the style and pattern of adult relationships. About this, as about so much else, he was emphatic:

> The relationship to the mother is unique, without parallel, laid down unalterably for a whole life-time, as the first and strongest love-object, and as the prototype of all later love relations.[4]

Freud may well have been influenced by his own experience. His mother, doting and domineering, appears to have been besotted with her eldest child, her 'golden Sigi', as she was fond of calling him. Later he was to remark 'that if a man has been his mother's undisputed darling he retains throughout life the triumphant feeling, the confidence in success, which not seldom brings actual success with it.'[5] Freud had more ambivalent views of his father, Jacob. One crucial childhood memory involved a story his father had told him when Freud was about 10 or 11 years old. Apparently, Jacob described how, when he was a young man out walking, a Christian knocked off his cap and shouted 'Jew, off the sidewalk'. Freud asked his father what he had done in response and was shocked when Jacob replied 'I stepped into the road and picked up my cap.' Freud was scornful of his father's submissiveness and lack of heroic qualities and stung by the spectacle of the cowardly Jew grovelling to a bullying Gentile.[6]

Whatever the reason, mothers attracted more of Freud's consideration than fathers and were more central to his theories concerning the importance of a child's earliest years in the formation of the adult personality. He did acknowledge the role of the father in negotiating and influencing the mother–child relationship into a triangular relationship. He did reflect on the role played by the father in helping the maturing adolescent let go of the mother. But he was much more interested in and exercised by the attachment between mother and child and its primary influence on adult development. One British psychoanalyst, strongly influenced by Freud and likewise convinced of the significance of the earliest years for the healthy development of the infant and child, was John Bowlby. The hypothesis that children should not be 'deprived' of contact with the mother during the critical period of infancy and early childhood when the primary attachment relationship is being formed was first proposed by him in a 1951 report to the World Health Organization.[7] The report originally arose out of a WHO request for an assessment of the mental health consequences for 'children who are orphaned or separated from their families for other reasons and need care in foster homes, institutions or other types of group care'.[8] He proposed that maternal love and commitment are as vital to the healthy development of the child as are vitamins and proteins for physical health. He went further and, *à la* Freud, declared:

> the prolonged deprivation of the young child of maternal care may have grave and far-reaching effects on his character and so on the whole of his future life.[9]

Bowlby derived support for these arguments from observations of children separated from parents when placed for short stays in a hospital or institution, children in long-term orphanages and foundling homes, young rhesus monkeys separated from their mothers and raised in isolation, and from studies which linked adolescent delinquency and behaviour problems to some form of separation in childhood. In subsequent writings Bowlby modified his argument to take into account the influence of other figures in a child's life, but the emphasis on the crucial role of the mother remained. In so far as fathers figured at all it was mainly in supportive roles. Bowlby did accept that as the children grew older their father would become more involved, but given the demands of work the father could not be expected to exercise an influence comparable to that of the mother. Robert Karen, who has written one of the most readable and dispassionate accounts of Bowlby and his work, observes:

> To Bowlby, a nonstop worker himself, whose work *was* his life, and whose rare displays of temper were occasioned by the intrusions of his children, it perhaps seemed inconceivable that a father could be more intimately involved, so that his presence, too, would be a source of security.[10]

Bowlby's single-minded preoccupation with the mother's role exposed him to fierce criticism by many commentators who feared his argument would be used (and it was) to combat women's increasing independence, to militate against their occupational mobility outside the home and to discourage the use of such supportive childcare facilities as crèches and nursery schools.[11] Less controversial however, indeed almost ignored, was Bowlby's neglect of the father's role. Up to 30 years ago, parenting in the social science and psychological literature meant mothering, and studies either frankly used the term 'mothering' or, as one reviewer commented, 'one quickly learned that all the subjects were women, though the title referred to parents'.[12] But while, slowly, the balance has been shifting within the worlds of research and academia, the neglect of fathering has fuelled the growing assumption that fathers do not really matter and that the fact they have been neglected simply reflects the assumption that they are largely irrelevant to child-rearing and child development.

Irish journalist, Kathryn Holmquist, reviewing one of the more polemical contributions along these lines, *Baby Wars: Parenthood and Family Strife* by Robin Baker and Elizabeth Oram,[13] was forced to ask:

> When the male's financial input is stripped away, what can he offer? Research shows that lone mothers can do very well on their own, provided they have the financial resources. To encourage well-being among lone mothers, we would have to reorganise the Irish workplace to be more family-friendly so that more lone mothers could earn good incomes . . . But considering the stigma against lone motherhood here, any such thinking seems a long way off in the Republic. Even more crucially, men are the dominant policy-makers and they are unlikely to make themselves redundant by encouraging working women to have successful families on their own.[14]

Holmquist is a talented and usually informed journalist yet she makes the common error of supposing that all the negative consequences of single parenthood are due to financial difficulties and would be solved by getting rid of men and getting more women out to work. As for the 'stigma' in Ireland against single parenthood to which she refers, it is certainly not strong enough to prevent the country from having one of the highest single parenthood rates in Europe, higher than Belgium, the Netherlands, Germany, Luxembourg, Switzerland, Italy, Spain, Portugal and Greece!

Yet while it may seem obvious to many that fathers do matter – children in single-mother homes, as we saw in the previous chapter, are in general at a singular disadvantage – researchers have been much more interested in clarifying the potential confounding role of problems such as poverty, bad schools, persistent post-divorce conflict and the lack of a family backup system, than in establishing just what it is about *fathers* that makes them important or redundant. One major problem is that the most common source of information about fathers is mothers, partly because fathers are so difficult to find! Whether rich or poor, married or unmarried, more than 40 per cent of men who don't live with their children don't even mention they are fathers in national surveys. National household and population surveys, the main source of information on families, rarely include men who don't live at home. Frequently they neglect to study the men who do. It was not until 1995 that a US President, Bill Clinton, issued an executive order which started to give fathers equal weight in research and policy initiatives. Only now is the US Department of Health and Human Services looking at ways to strengthen poor fathers' visitation rights and the role fathers might play in child education programmes. In the year 2000, for the first time, men are included in the National Survey of Family Growth.

Those who believe there is a role for the father usually have firm views of what he should be. Religious groups argue that he should be a leader. Others suggest he be a 'male mom'. Fathers are expected to play sport and provide discipline for their sons, be caring and available for their daughters, negotiate the difficult tension between making money and being around. Is it what a father *does* that is important? Is it what he *says*? Is it the money he has in his wallet? Is it simply that he is there? Whatever role fathers should assume, they will be doing so in a world that has fundamentally changed. The changes that have occurred in domestic life, personal relationships, the structure of the family, the demands of work, the notion of breadwinning and the role of women mean that the role of father has to be redefined too. As one long-term analyst of paternal roles has put it:

> Men can become participant fathers, as many are increasingly doing, or they can give up the idea of family life and do their best in the outside world. Either way the notion of being the boss at home is over, probably for ever.[15]

Most unmarried and divorced fathers have left after the first years of their child's life. Are they insensitive and callous, inadequate in taking responsibility, incapable of expressing feelings and preferring, as Kraemer suggests, to take their chances, in the outside world? Or are they shut out and rendered redundant by angry mothers, women who are now confident that they can do it on their own? Because men have traditionally been classed as breadwinners, researchers have tended to concentrate on the father's pay packet and not his heart. Contrasting assumptions on parenthood include the devoted and dedicated mother, the deadbeat and deficient dad.

The media present fathers 'as either "heroes" or "villains" with little serious debate about fatherhood'.[16] The villains are the growing number of fathers living apart from their children. Between 1 and 6 and 1 in 7 fathers are not living with any or all of their dependent children.[17] Approximately 8 per cent of all birth certificates in Britain (22 per cent of unmarried births) do not reveal the identity of the father – 51,000 births in 1996.[18] At present there is a prevailing sense that men are ineffective as fathers, and a growing tendency to portray men as disinclined to take on the responsibilities of fatherhood. But why, at the beginning of the twenty-first century, are so many men removing themselves or allowing themselves to be removed from their children's lives?[19]

Fatherhood is the commonest experience of adult men. More than 90 per cent of adult males in Britain marry and over 90 per cent of these couples have one or more children in the home. How these fathers behave in the home, how they express their feelings for their families, how they promote the development of their children varies considerably. And, despite assumptions to the contrary, evidence is growing to support the instinctive feeling that there is indeed a role for the father and, like that of the mother, it is a role with both positive and negative possibilities.

Effects of Paternal Deprivation

It has been suggested, most notably by the German psychoanalyst Misterlich,[20] that the difficulty fathers have in sharing with their children the nature of their work creates a vacuum in the child's psyche which is filled by hostile fantasies of the father as bad and his work as evil. The result is widespread 'paternal deprivation' or 'father hunger', characterised by a profound yearning for a good or at least a good enough father. A variety of problems have been blamed on such 'paternal deprivation'. Children growing up without fathers are more likely to fail at school or drop out,[21] have emotional or behavioural problems necessitating psychiatric intervention,[22] and develop drug and alcohol problems.[23] Adolescent males who attempt suicide appear more likely to come from homes where the father is absent.[24] Other studies have found a statistically significant incidence of separation and divorce among parents of adolescents who attempt suicide as compared with control groups.[25] Boys growing up without fathers reportedly experience difficulties in the areas of sex-role and gender identity, school performance, social skills and the control of aggression.[26] A second consequence of life without a father is that children, especially sons, grow up without direct access to him and view him by necessity through their mother's eyes. This experience effectively alienates them from their own sense of themselves as men. And it effectively ruptures the natural transmission of the role model of being a resident father such that many boys and young men now 'face their future with progressively reducing social pressures or social training to become responsible and competent fathers'.[27]

The yearning of a lost son for an absent father is a widespread if not a universal theme in the world's literature and religions. The dominant image in Christianity is Jesus, who never had a human father, never becomes a father and dies on the cross lamenting his abandonment by the most powerful father of all. Shakespeare's *Hamlet*, Homer's *Odyssey*, Joyce's *Ulysses*, the story of Joseph in the Bible all involve the fate of a son separated from his father. However, it is not the story of the absent father so much as the violent one that has had the most powerful influence on modern psychology. In the legend of Oedipus, Laius, the father of the infant Oedipus, orders his son killed and Oedipus is left on a hillside to die. He is found by a shepherdess, who raises him. Later, as a youth, he encounters an old man who refuses to move out of his way as each tries to cross a narrow bridge. Oedipus kills the old man who, unknown to him, is his father, Laius. Oedipus ends up saving the city of Thebes by answering the riddle of the Sphinx and marries the Queen who, again unknown to him, is his mother.

Freud, in his creation of the so-called Oedipus complex, claimed the myth revealed the unconscious desire of every son to kill his father and marry his mother. It has, however, been pointed out that the story of Oedipus is possibly darker than even Freud's interpretation would have it. It is, after all, a story of gross paternal aggression and abuse. The tragedy starts with a father, Laius, ordering his own son to be killed and tells of the intense, potentially destructive conflict between the generations – the young Oedipus and the old Laius competing to cross the bridge. But the story of Laius himself is relevant. Like Hamlet, Laius was a son displaced by his uncle. Laius took refuge with the neighbouring King Pelops and ended up sexually abusing the King's young son. In turn, King Pelops cursed Laius predicting, correctly, that he would be killed by his own son. Subsequently, Laius became King of Thebes and conceived Oedipus unwillingly (his wife got him drunk and seduced him). He then commanded her to kill the child by exposure and she initially complied but later relented. Woven into this tragic myth are many of today's most elemental preoccupations and anxieties – child abuse, paternal violence colluded with and participated in by mothers, jealousy and revenge within the family and the sexual humiliation of women by men.

In the main narrative text of the Bible there are plenty of fathers but precious few good ones. Adam, Noah, Isaac, Jacob, Abraham, Moses, Saul, David and even Solomon have been judged failures in some important aspect of their fathering. In apparent contrast, there is the New Testament God the Father. But this father embodies many of the strains and contradictions which in more human form bedevil struggling-to-be-good-enough parents. On the one hand, this heavenly father is loving, nurturing, forgiving, the provider of daily bread and the forgiver of sins. But on the other hand he is a fierce and omnipotent judge who remorselessly separates the goats from the sheep, elevates those who have behaved to the highest realms of heaven, damns those who have transgressed to the deepest recesses of an infernal hell.

Henry Abramovitch, in a rich examination of the archetypal images of the father,[28] emphasises the extent to which the themes of death and continuity, separation and reconciliation, rejection and confirmation are enmeshed in the father–child relationship. In the story of Jacob and Joseph, for example, Jacob believes his son, Joseph, is lost for ever and lapses into protracted grief. Joseph succeeds in a foreign land but is cut off from his father. When finally they meet, they embrace. Joseph weeps 'for a good while' and Jacob declares, 'Now I can die, having seen for myself that you are alive.'

Today's fathers carry in their heads the memories and recollections of their own fathers and their experience of being fathered. But they also have expectations concerning their own need to be a just father, a wise father, an accessible and involved father, a loving father, a stern father, a good father. And they struggle, some attempting to be a father like their own father, some struggling to be quite the opposite – and all around them rages the argument of what actually constitutes a good father and whether it makes all that much difference what kind of father they are.

What the Father Offers

Reviews in the 1980s concerning the amount of involvement of fathers in the lives of their children suggested the effects were minimal.[29] However, more recent research strongly suggests that preschool children whose fathers are substantially engaged with and accessible to them (i.e. performing 40 per cent of the care within the family) are more competent, more empathic, more self-confident and less stereotyped in terms of gender roles.[30] The evidence indicates that such positive effects begin early. For example, the degree of positive paternal involvement in the month following birth is strongly associated with the infant's cognitive functioning at one year.[31] Research has also shown significant positive relationships between positive father engagement and intelligence, academic achievement and social maturity at ages six and seven.[32] Such involvement is significantly related to a cluster of outcomes, including self-control, self-esteem, life skills and social competence in both children and adolescents. Most striking is the finding that a more actively involved father leads not to more but to less gender-role stereotyping behaviour in the children. That is to say, children and adolescents with positively involved fathers hold *less* traditional views as adolescents about gender stereotypes, dual-earner parents and about the parental sharing of childcare.[33]

But how can the effect of the mother's involvement be separated out from that of the father? Is it not possible that those fathers who seem very positively engaged in the care of their children are married to or living with exceedingly committed and involved mothers? A careful analysis of the American National Survey of Family Health results – which controlled for the positive involvement of the mother as well as ethnic background, income and social class – has shown that for both boys and girls, a high positive involvement of fathers is significantly related to such social skills as getting along with others, carrying out responsibilities and doing what parents ask.[34] In addition, boys have fewer behavioural problems while girls are more self-directed – i.e. more willing to try new things, be active and socially involved. This analysis confirms that a father's positive involvement with his children has beneficial effects independent of any effect of the mother's own involvement.

In the late 1930s, Sheldon and Eleanor Glueck of the Harvard Law School commenced a cross-sectional study of 500 delinquent and 500 non-delinquent boys. The Gluecks followed their subjects for 25 years and during that time social workers, doctors, criminologists, psychoanalysts and social psychologists all recorded their contrasting views of the 1,000 inner-city youths.[35] Then psychiatrist George Vaillant took over and followed these men for a second generation, including their experience and behaviour as parents.[36] In 1982, Professor John Snarey became involved in the longitudinal study and he has focused particularly on the children, the sons and daughters, of the original sample of men. This unique study, now of four generations, provides an unrivalled insight into the nature and state of fathering at the present time.[37] Snarey writes of 'generative fathers', meaning fathers who contribute to and renew the cycle of the generations through the care they provide as birth fathers (biological generativity), as child-rearing fathers (parental generativity) and as cultural fathers (societal generativity). The concepts draw heavily on Erik Erikson's model of human personality development. Erikson, the first Professor of Human Development at Harvard University, views generativity as the primary developmental task of adulthood. Generativity versus stagnation is the seventh in a sequence of eight stages of personality development in Erikson's theoretical model. In his scheme, each stage of development ends with a turning point or crisis, a crucial period of potential and vulnerability. The first two psychosocial turning points, trust versus mistrust and autonomy versus doubt, are believed to occur during the first two years of life. Initiative versus guilt occurs during early childhood; industry versus inferiority during later childhood; identity versus identity confusion during adolescence; and intimacy versus isolation during the early adult years. Then comes the psychosocial task of generativity versus stagnation during the middle adulthood years before the final stage is reached characterised by the crisis of integrity versus despair.[38] The psychosocial task of adulthood – attainment of a favourable balance of generativity over stagnation – involves achieving 'a reasonable surplus of procreation, productivity and creativity over a pervading mood of personal depletion or self-absorption'.[39]

Generativity means any caring, outwards-directed activity that contributes to the generation of new or more mature individuals, ideas, products or works of art. John Kotre has taken up the concept of generativity and expanded it into four categories.[40] First, there is *biological generativity*, which includes the begetting, bearing and nurturing of offspring. Then there is *parental generativity*, which involves child-rearing activities that care for, promote and initiate children into the family. The third category, *technical generativity*, involves the teaching of skills, the passing on of knowledge and experience. Finally, there is *cultural generativity* which involves mentoring – the creation, renovation and conservation of a symbol system passed on from parent to child, adolescent and young adult. Erikson's model echoes Freud's and Tolstoy's assumption that the two main functions of the adult human being are to love and to work. Erikson goes further and argues that the degree to which a man's external life is characterised by mature love – the caring for others – and mature work – creativity and productivity – is critically correlated with the maturity level of his personal development.

Drawing on Erikson's theories, Heath followed up a group of men from their entrance into college through the onset of the middle adult life.[41] He found that fatherhood promoted men's self-understanding, their willingness to understand and empathise with others and their ability to comprehend and express their own feelings. Those men who enjoyed being fathers were also more likely to have

> volunteered to serve others or been elected to a leadership position in their communities or professions within the preceding ten years . . .

> Enjoying being a parent – one of the more demanding and selfless roles an adult assumes – reflects and nurtures an other-centred and giving character. With such a character, it is not that big a step to want to give to our larger family – our community.[42]

The wives of the men studied by Heath, when they entered midlife, were asked to recall their own parenting. Those wives who had successful work careers, in contrast to those who were less successful, recalled that when they were children their fathers had held high expectations of them, had strongly encouraged them academically and urged their participation in sport. Their fathers clearly valued them, actively participated in their education and opened up the outside world. In addition, their fathers provided valuable advice:

> They talked to their daughters about how to get a job, prepare for an interview, dress appropriately, get along with men and their bosses, deal with male ways of being critical and supportive, read the financial pages, ask for a raise, invest their money for income and capital gain, make alliances.[43]

Snarey comments that in Eriksonian terminology these fathers had provided all three types of parental generativity – support of intellectual-academic, social-emotional and physical-athletic development. Like the men studied by Heath, they themselves had also benefited from the demands and responsibilities of being parents. Fatherhood has a dramatic impact on men. Contrary to many men's fears (and some women's too), putting their families first does not harm male careers. Fatherhood enhances the ability of men to understand themselves as adults and sympathetically to care for other adults. The effect of active fathering on fathers has recently received scrutiny. Analysing patterns over four decades of male life, Snarey found that men who took an active role in the home were, by the time their children were grown, better managers, community leaders and role models. He found, too, that the amount and quality of their care for their children's social and emotional development during childhood and adolescence actually predicted the fathers' later marital stability and contentment. The more fathers participated in the rearing of their children during early adulthood, the more likely these fathers were to be happily married at midlife.

George Vaillant's 35-year study of college men also found that satisfaction with the paternal role was significantly and positively associated with other forms of caring and involvement outside the family home. Vaillant found that those men who in Erikson's terms had become most generative – that is to say were the most truly responsible for other adults, enjoyed their work and helped others to grow – were also the men who had best mastered intimacy at an earlier period and maintained stable first marriages.[44]

These findings flatly contradict the popular assumption that career achievement and involvement with children necessarily conflict. In fact, there is impressive research testifying to the fact that adult men with the poorest professional and occupational achievement also manifest poorly developed generative traits.

> Michael is a married man in his fifties with four children. He has worked his way up to a senior management position in an oil company he joined shortly after his marriage. For the first ten years of marriage, during which his children were born, Michael devoted long hours to his work, leaving early and coming home late. He also worked most weekends. Some of his work time was spent on social and leisure activities related to his work, such as golf, corporate entertaining and conferences. However, on his promotion to a post responsible for personnel and human relations matters, he slowly began to acknowledge how little time he was spending with his family and how much pressure and tension he was feeling as he tried to cope with the demands of work and home. Many colleagues he was seeing in his professional position were presenting with stress related to the same issue. He decided to change his own lifestyle. He started to reorganise his time, spending less hours at work but working the hours he did spend there more efficiently. He cut down on golf and virtually eliminated after-work hospitality. He stopped attending weekend conferences altogether. His own health improved spectacularly – the irritability, tension, sleep disturbance and heavy drinking for which he had initially consulted a psychiatrist gradually ceased. His end-of-year personal assessment was the most positive he had received in his years at the company. It particularly praised him for his high level of involvement, his sensitivity to employee dissatisfactions and his effectiveness in ensuring a work atmosphere congenial to effective working. His wife also commented that he was not merely a visible father in the home – but a more patient, responsive and considerate one.

These findings also support the controversial assertion that family life is a civilising force for men. Sociologist David Popenoe puts it bluntly: 'Whenever large numbers of young, unattached males are concentrated in one place, the probability of social disorder greatly increases.'[45] David Blankenhorn, President of the Institute for American Values, is no less convinced: 'Across societies, married fatherhood is the single most reliable and relied upon prescription for socializing males.'[46] Someone who agrees but does not share the enthusiasm for the consequences is Gore Vidal who, in a feisty article on sexual politics, argues that in societies where it is necessary to force people to do work that they don't want to do marriage at an early age is encouraged 'on the sensible grounds that if a married man is fired, his wife and children are going to starve too. That grim knowledge makes for docility.'[47] Vidal's waspish comment is a variant on Cyril Connolly's depiction of the pram in the hallway as the enemy of promise. However, confronted as we are by the nature and extent of male violence, not everyone is as dismissive of social docility as Vidal. Others have argued that poorly fathered young men, and young men reluctant to involve themselves in a relationship of commitment and intimacy, become so vulnerable to and incompetent with women that they end up avoiding them, brutalising them or both. Disconnected young men are most likely to prove their manhood in crime and by violating those who represent outwardly the shameful, hated, feared feminine part of themselves.[48] In Britain, A.H. Halsey has been one of the most vocal in warning of the emergence of a new male who is

> weakly socialized and weakly socially controlled so far as the responsibilities of spousehood and fatherhood are concerned . . . he no longer feels the pressure his father and grandfather and previous generations of males felt to be a responsible adult in a functioning community.[49]

There is some persuasive evidence in support of the view that men who are deprived of a father's influence are more likely to engage in what has been termed 'overcompensatory masculine behaviors', which is jargon for crimes against property, child abuse and family violence.[50] Such a protest masculinity, characterised by exaggerated attempts to prove manliness, is seen to arise from a basic fear of being feminine that flourishes in the absence of male models. Men from homes where there is a weak or absent father do not have the role model of a stable, long-lasting family in which every member contributes by working for the integrity and stability of the family as a whole. Young men from such a shifting and unpredictable background can see no great reproductive advantage to be gained by carefully choosing a suitable mate and postponing reproduction. Instead, they struggle with their peers in short-term sexual competition, exhibiting in the process aggressive, exhibitionist and exploitative behaviours.

The absence from the home of a strong adult male figure has particular implications for mothers with growing, physically aggressive and assertive sons. Psychiatrists, psychologists and social workers are well versed, through their professional work, in the tensions in adolescent males when a mother has to step, as it were, into a departed father's shoes. In an article on a highly publicised case in Britain which involved the murder of a single mother by her 18-year-old son, Lisa Jardine, Professor of Renaissance Studies at the University of London, protested that often the deserted mothers find themselves blamed for the aggressive behaviour which many adolescent sons in this situation go on to display.[51] Professor Jardine points out that boys who live with a lone mother are far more likely than girls to resort to violence. Studies show that sons of absent fathers develop difficulty in controlling aggressive and impulsive behaviour.[52] Among the reports of growing domestic violence (including violence against women perpetrated by their male partners) there is an increasing number of incidents in which the mother is beaten up by her son. If the son is over 18 then he can be treated as an adult and a barring order obtained against him. But if he is not technically an adult, such an abusive young male is exceedingly difficult to manage, legally as well as physically. Lisa Jardine deplored the fact that the murder of a mother by her son had led to a media witch-hunt in which alleged maternal deficiencies were in some rather murky way blamed for the killing. Professor Jardine's more temperate and thoughtful analysis reflects the growing realisation of the importance of paternal discipline, example and control in the successful socialising of the growing adolescent male and the impact on single mothers of the absence of an adult male.

Fathers, Sons and Daughters

There is strong suggestive evidence that a father's influence on and contribution to a daughter's development is strongest and most crucial during her adolescence, whereas his influence on a son's development occurs earlier. The early years of development of a boy require him to start to separate from his mother and identify with his father – his same-sex parent – as part of his gender maturation. Like girls, boys start out with a close physical and domestic relationship with their mothers. But at some point every son has to redefine himself and prepare for the extra-domestic role as man and father, in large part among men. Access to a father's warm, close guidance promotes this growth. A father's support for his son's physical, athletic, intellectual and emotional development facilitates the transition from childhood to adolescence and indeed later enables and encourages him, as a young adult, to turn to his father for advice. David Guttmann talks of a 'crucial baptism' whereby a son redefines himself from being the son of his mother to being the son of his father.[53] Sons of fathers who are physically and/or psychologically absent cannot make this transition. Sons of such fathers do not separate from their mothers in the psychological sense. True, they leave home, find girlfriends or wives, but because they have not truly developed a sense of mature masculinity they bring their dependence on the mother and their identification as sons rather than grown and independent men into their relationships and marriages and turn their partners into surrogate mothers.[54]

> When Mary and James came to me their mutual complaints centred on Mary's view of her husband. She felt he expected her to behave just like his mother. Before the arrival of their three children, Mary did indeed look after James's every domestic need but once the children arrived she began to expect that he would help with the shopping, would take the children to school and assist with such domestic chores as washing up and leaving out the garbage. James responded badly to such expectations. Having coped rather badly with the arrival of each of the children (he had a brief affair after the first and was ill after each of the others), he continued to resent the attention she gave them. There were constant arguments about and with the children. During several exploratory sessions it emerged that James had a very strong idea of what his wife should be; in essence, a successor to his mother, who had devoted herself entirely to his needs and those of his two brothers. His father, a busy publisher, had spent the greater part of his life outside the home and had played no part in the upbringing of his children. James did not find it easy to see his wife in relation to her children as he saw his mother in relation to him. In marrying Mary, James had simply transferred his dependence on his mother on to her.

A daughter's primary identification, in contrast, remains with her mother during childhood. The father's affection and support do not detach a daughter from her identification with her mother, but his provision of safe, secure excitement during infancy and childhood can contribute to her sense of trust and autonomy. It is in adolescence that a father plays a more crucial role in his daughter's development, as she begins to achieve a significant degree of separation from her mother. Such a view is supported by Hetherington's early research, which indicates that the negative effect of a father's absence did not impinge on daughters until they had reached adolescence.[55]

Fathers in general promote their daughters' developing autonomy by inviting them to participate in non-traditional areas of mastery with them, such as active physical play. Mothers can of course be athletic, but when this care comes from the father it also appears to promote the daughter's ability to launch out of the mother–daughter orbit into the outside world. Earlier research work had suggested that a father's willingness to involve himself in a daughter's growing sense of her own potential is influential. One key researcher, L. Tessman, has summarised it thus:

> More salient than a distant pride in her achievement is his willingness to involve himself in the process . . . Women who emphasize their father's contribution to their enthusiasm in work usually stress . . . his treatment of her as an interesting person in her own right . . . his trust in her developing autonomous capacities during joint endeavours, his own capacity for excitement or enthusiasm about discovery in work or play.[56]

Tessman studied high-achieving women students from Massachusetts Institute of Technology. The typical father was described by his daughter as encouraging, stimulating, involving her in joint endeavours, showing trust in her growing abilities and as a playful and enjoyable companion.[57]

Fathers can promote their son's later educational or occupational development by providing in childhood high levels of care for their social, emotional, physical and intellectual growth. Commonly this is seen when fathers share their sons' sporting activities and encourage their sons' sense of industry and autonomy. By tracking the boys of the 1930s through manhood and parenthood, and their children in turn, the Gluecks, Vaillant and Snarey have been able to cast considerable light on the issue of paternal influence. Their research showed that men learn how to and how not to become fathers from the fathering they themselves received. For example, those fathers whose boyhood relationships with their own fathers had been distant or non-demonstrative were more likely to provide their own adolescent children with an above-average level of emotional and social support and involvement. Those fathers whose own fathers had used physical punishment or the threat of it were likely to counterbalance this in their own fathering. Snarey describes what happens thus:

> The intergenerational flow of successful fathering appears to follow two primary patterns: a) modelling, in which a man replicates the strengths of the fathering he himself received, and b) reworking, in which a man rectifies the limitations of the fathering he himself received.[58]

Not all such modelling and reworking are positive. Some men replicate the aggressiveness and violence of their fathers by indulging in a pattern of punitive discipline and autocratic control within their own families. Some rework the effects of an absent father in their adolescence by becoming more intolerant of anything smacking of dissent or disagreement on the part of their partners and children. But what is reassuring in Snarey's work is the finding that many men do *not* go on to reproduce the pathological faults and behaviour of their fathers but learn to develop less harsh and more appropriate means of family discipline and communication.

Fathers and Involvement

Two perspectives on the issue of how much or how little time modern men devote to their domestic roles and responsibilities have been identified.[59] The first, which regards the principle of *fairness* as primary, takes as axiomatic the contention that men are under-involved in the home and leave the bulk of responsibility to their partners. Such a perspective stresses the need to persuade men to take more responsibility within the home and to share on a broadly equal basis the various tasks and demands. The *developmental* perspective emphasises the qualities and experience men need if they are to make a successful transition into parenthood. Women are seen to have a certain 'biological advantage' over men in this transition because of the fact that pregnancy and giving birth provide a remarkable opportunity for them to form some kind of emotional relationship (to 'attach') with their offspring. Women may also be better prepared because throughout their own personal development they have been groomed, by society's expectations and reinforcements, for the role of care-giver and nurturer.

Men, in contrast, have a much greater struggle in making the transition to parenthood not because they are exploitative and immature (although some surely are) but because their energy and capacity to care are turned away from their most intimate relationships and into society and work. Men end up caring and nurturing the next generation through work and altruistic endeavour – and society expects this of them and rewards them accordingly. The capacity of men to care for their children and their motivation to become involved with them may well increase around the time of the birth of their children.[60] Kevin McKeown and his colleagues argue that 'The more that secure bonding and attachment occurs between father and child at this formative time, the greater the likelihood that the man will focus his capacity for caring within the family through active involvement with his children throughout the life-cycle'.[61]

It has been suggested that, although both women and men do more of what was traditionally deemed to be the role of the opposite sex, neither has totally given up their traditional roles within the family.[62] From the moment when fathers become fathers the division of roles is apparent. Up until the 1960s, few fathers were admitted into delivery rooms, as I know from my own experience. When my wife went into labour with our first child, my daughter Rachel, I stayed with her until late in the evening. I was then firmly shown the door of the Dublin nursing home and told to go home. I extricated a promise from the matron that she would call me when delivery seemed imminent – but no one called. When I was telephoned in the morning and was told I was a father, I inquired why they hadn't called me. 'We felt you should get a good night's sleep,' replied the matron.

Not until the 1970s did the situation alter on either side of the Atlantic. In 1972, about one in four fathers in the US was present at the birth of his child.[63] In Britain the trend was slower and, as Brockington reports, there was resistance in the maternity hospitals.[64] Professor Norman Morris was one of the first senior obstetricians to encourage the practice, declaring in 1960, 'If a husband wants to be with his wife in labour, I have no right to deny him this experience. I now actively encourage husbands to be present, provided they know what to expect.'[65] That last caveat reflects a male obstetrician's concern lest a father's strength fail him when he is confronted by the pain, blood and sheer physical effort associated with childbirth. Male squeamishness notwithstanding, by the late 1980s nearly two-thirds of British men were attending all the stages of the birth of their children, according to Charlie Lewis who carried out an interview study of 100 fathers of one-year-old children in Nottingham.[66] Many fathers admitted to being anxious. Most had been encouraged by their wives to attend. The majority found it a positive experience. One father, quoted by Lewis, admitted that he had been surprised by the hard work and trauma but added:

> I felt by the end of the experience that I had done a full day's work and was absolutely washed out, but nonetheless I wouldn't miss being there a second time.[67]

Is there any evidence that it matters one whit whether the father is present or not? Most fathers who are present describe feelings of elation and pride, and weep with happiness. Studies of fathers after childbirth report paternal absorption, fascination and preoccupation with the newborn. In one study the term 'engrossment' was used to describe the process whereby fathers were drawn to gaze repeatedly at their baby, obtained extreme pleasure from touching, picking up and holding it, and commented repeatedly on its unique features and resemblance to themselves.[68] In another study, 15 fathers who were given their newborn child immediately after Caesarean section were filmed.[69] They behaved 'just like mothers in the same situation',[70] touching the baby, seeking eye contact and murmuring to it. Such early postpartum bonding may be important for long-term father–child and indeed father–mother relationships. We just do not know. Such evidence as there is is flimsy but suggestive. In a study of 45 infants delivered by Caesarean section, half were presented to the father to hold for 10 minutes while the other half were put in incubators, the fathers only being allowed to visit and look, not touch. At three months, those fathers who had held their babies were much more involved with their infants than those who had not.[71]

In Lewis's Nottingham study, there was little correlation between the father being present at the birth and being more involved with childcare after the baby came home. It was the mother who did the feeding, changing, cleaning and getting up at night. Only when the mother was also working outside the home did the father do more. But Lewis also noted that the mothers (and the fathers too) identified the tasks of caring for and cleaning the baby as tasks requiring maternal expertise. And if the mothers were breastfeeding this was self-evidently a reasonable position to adopt.

Lewis compared his data, obtained in 1980, to similar data obtained in an earlier study some 20 years previously. The greatest changes are shown in Table 2. The most obvious relate to the husband's help in the period after childbirth and his willingness to get up at night. There are few changes over the 20 years in men's involvement in nappy-changing and bathing.

Table 2 Changes in father involvement in childcare 1960–80

	1960 N = 100	1980 N = 100
Husband helps in the period after birth	30	77*
Husband gets up for baby at night	49	87*
Husband rarely/never puts baby to sleep	29	26
Husband often involved in bathing baby	20	29
Husband often involved in nappy changing	20	28

* highly significant change
N = total number of respondents

Source: C. Lewis, *Becoming a Father*, Open University Press, Milton Keynes, 1986.

Remarkably pessimistic perceptions of the extent to which men are available in the home persist. It is certainly true that by the middle of the twentieth century the vast majority of fathers were routinely absent from the daytime activities of family life. Scott Coltrane, a researcher interested in men's work within the home, suggests that, since men were not supposed to be responsible for routine childcare, accounts of what men did at home in the 1950s and 1960s were extremely rare.[72] There are few studies of father–child interactions during that period and no reliable information on the extent of paternal participation in various childcare tasks. One much-quoted study suggested that fathers spent an average of an hour or less per week taking sole responsibility for their children, compared with mothers, who reported an average of 40 hours a week.[73] Other studies appeared to show that, whereas fathers often helped out, fewer of them took on full and regular responsibility for one or more specific tasks relating to the care of their children.[74] John Robinson's estimates of American men's involvement in household chores in 1965 suggested that husbands averaged just over one hour a week in meal preparation (compared to eight hours a week for their wives), contributed less than 10 per cent of the time spent by their wives cleaning up after meals or washing dishes in the average week, and only 5 per cent of the time doing house cleaning. They rarely did any laundry or ironing, averaging about five hours per year compared to over five hours per week for their wives. In effect, wives did over 90 per cent of the family and domestic chores.[75]

But these studies may already be dated. A US Census Bureau survey suggests that fathers there now provide the primary childcare for 25 per cent of preschool children and 11 per cent of school-age children whose mothers work part time, and 5 per cent of school-age children whose mothers work full time.[76] It is still true that American women are likely to spend fewer hours than men working outside the home and American men are likely to put in fewer hours than women on domestic work, but the total numbers of hours are converging.[77] Snarey, commenting on these figures, points out that fathers' childcare time is higher when their wives work part time rather than full time because couples are better able to use a shift-work system between them when mothers work part time, whereas they often need a more highly structured system of outside care (crèches, nannies, etc.) when both parents work full time.[78] Not merely do over 12 per cent of men report taking 'all or most' of the responsibility for childcare when their children are sick and home from school, and 28 per cent of men report taking 'all or most' of the responsibility for disciplining their children, but the estimates offered by women agree with them.[79] The growth of dual-earner families is almost certainly the engine driving this increase in the time spent by fathers caring for their children; the amount of time fathers carry the sole responsibility for the care of their children is almost double for those in dual-earner families compared with those in single-earner families.[80] There is evidence, too, that the time that fathers spend in specific childcare tasks is increasing. One study, admittedly of somewhat less traditional families,[81] reported that the participation by fathers in such childcare functions as helping to bath their infant children, reading to them and taking them on trips averaged 2.25 hours per day rather than the similar figure quoted per week in another study.[82]

In Ireland, a study carried out by the Family Studies Unit at University College Dublin looked at mothers' accounts of what fathers do in the home.[83] Almost 70 per cent of the 513 urban mothers said their partners participated in household tasks as much as they, the mothers, would like. However, when these responses were explored in greater depth it was clear that, although they carried out household repairs, fathers took little responsibility for such tasks as preparing breakfast, washing dishes, shopping or ironing.

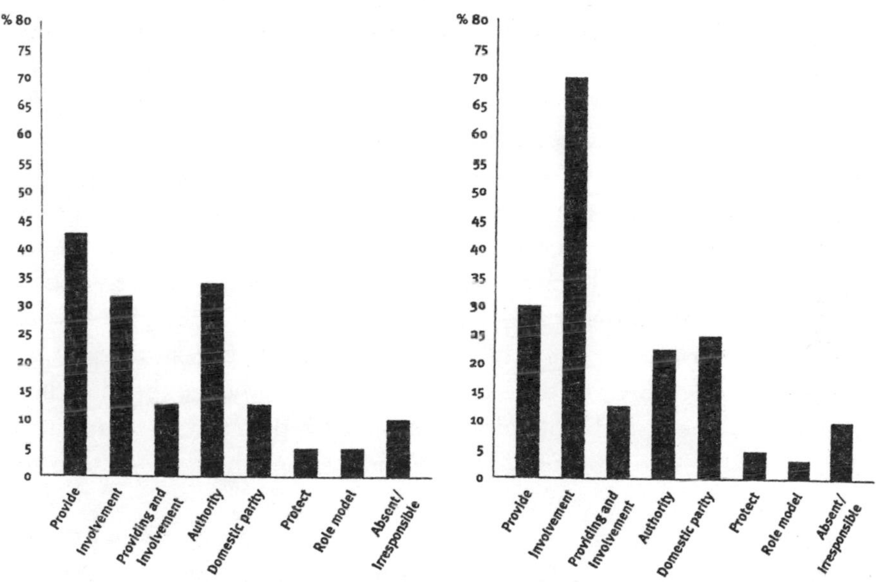

Figure 2: Fathers' response to the question, 'What do people expect of fathers these days?' (62 respondents, response categories as percentages)

Figure 3: Mothers' responses to the question, 'What do people expect of fathers these days?' (67 respondents, response categories as percentages)

Source: J. Warin, Y. Solomon, C. Lewis and W. Langford, *Fathers, Work and Family Life*, Family Policy Studies Centre/Joseph Rowntree Foundation, London, 1999.

'What do people expect of fathers these days?' was the question asked by researchers from the Family Policy Studies Centre of family members in Rochdale, England.[84] Most fathers identified their role as that of provider. Most mothers in contrast wanted fathers to be involved (Figures 2 and 3). However, that study, along with a number of others, has shown that 'involvement' does not just mean men doing things with children and developing relationships with them, it also means 'being there' or 'being available'. Having a father around completes a family but, in addition, a father should be there to participate in family interactions, discipline and in case of emergencies. There is considerable confusion between just being available, practical involvement and a psychological commitment. Many contemporary fathers realise that they are expected to spend time with their children but some do not know quite how such time is supposed to be spent, while others identify this kind of involvement with some type of 'feminine' model of fathering. The Rochdale study showed how long work hours can impoverish relationships – it is difficult to make a relationship with someone who is not there – but some of the negative effects of work on the quality of family relationships can be overcome in many instances with effort. Some respondents in the Rochdale study put the relative absence of fathers down to factors such as the man's personality, the relationship between father and mother and reluctance on the part of some mothers to involve the father. A few did challenge the idea that work patterns constrain the role of the father in the modern family and insisted that it is possible for gender differences in who does what to be eliminated.

But is there really any evidence of a change in men's behaviour *vis-à-vis* the care of their children? Yes, there is some. There are studies which show that fathers' engagement time increased in the years between 1924 and 1977 and between the mid-1960s and the early 1980s in the United States.[85] A more recent comparison corroborates the increase in paternal responsibility since the late 1970s.[86] But this does not necessarily mean that, overall, children are receiving as much or more attention from their parents. The greater involvement of fathers may reflect the trend towards less involvement of mothers due to the demands of the workplace. Indeed concern is now being expressed that just as more men have been persuaded of the benefits for them, their partners and their children of greater participation by fathers in the care and development of their children, the spectre of child sexual abuse has made men fearful of getting too close to their children, especially daughters, and anxious about the expression of affection. It is still not clear whether the growing concern in recent years regarding the physical and sexual abuse by men of infants and children has had an impact on the changing involvement of fathers in the direct care of their children.

Father the Protector

The terrible epidemic of child sexual abuse, in which an estimated 95 per cent of girls and 80 per cent of abusers of boys are male,[87] has resulted in a public atmosphere in which even to whisper of men as protectors of families risks a howl of derisive mockery. Men may still consider protection as one of the key tasks of being a father but that is not how it looks from the perspective of many working in the child and family services. Adrienne Burgess, author of *Fatherhood Reclaimed*, tells the story of a group of senior social work professionals who were shown a poster of a man holding a baby to his chest. The poster was designed to deter young men from rushing into fatherhood, but the advertising agency responsible for it felt there was a problem with it. The professionals were asked what they thought the problem might be. Their first response was to ask where was the man's other hand? The image of a young man holding a child quite simply conjured up the image of abuse. The looked-for answer was that the black-and-white poster had exaggerated the appeal of fatherhood and therefore, from the point of view of the campaign, was deemed ineffective.[88]

This intensification of anxiety concerning male abusiveness coincides with the growing desire in contemporary society to break down male views, particularly young male views, of childcare as a feminine activity. Media images that depict bare-chested young men cradling their infant children in their strong, muscular arms[89] are seen to be consistent with the emerging need that some fathers have to create the impression that they are good fathers and spend time with their children in public.

In another example provided by Burgess, a sample of workers from the Australian family services were asked what percentage of fathers abused their own children. The answer given was an astonishing 25 per cent! The actual figure is around 2 per cent. This discrepancy is worrying for it can contribute to a negative stereotyping of all fathers as real or potential abusers. But it is understandable given the remarkable rise in reported figures for child abuse. According to data from studies within the US, physical abuse of children increased by 58 per cent and sexual abuse by 300 per cent between 1980 and 1986.[90] A national survey in Ireland revealed that up to 6 per cent of the population claimed to have been sexually abused as children.[91] Fathers were the reported abusers in 35 per cent of the cases, mothers in 3 per cent. The remaining abusers included other family members and individuals outside the immediate family. This study, like many, did not distinguish between biological fathers and non-biological fathers. It has been suggested that, while it is unfortunately true that some biological fathers do molest their children, what magnifies the risk to children is not the presence of a biological father in the home but his absence.[92] It is the absence of married fathers and the increasing presence of stepfathers, cohabitees, common-law fathers, boyfriends and other transient males, so this argument goes, that raises the risks to children.[93] A study of a random sample of nearly 1,000 women living in San Francisco revealed that not only was the prevalence of sexual abuse by stepfathers much greater than abuse by biological fathers but the nature of the abuse committed by the stepfathers was more serious.[94] An early study in the United Kingdom provided only partial support for such an argument. Michael Gordon of the University of Connecticut and Susan J. Creighton of the National Society for the Prevention of Cruelty to Children studied all 198 cases of father–daughter abuse contained in the NSPCC's 1983–85 registers of child abuse.[95] Non-biological fathers were indeed disproportionately represented among paternal abusers but in this study they were not disproportionately found amongst those who indulged in the most severe forms of abuse.

Child sexual abuse increases significantly when biological fathers withdraw from the family. One of the most consistent findings, not only in child sexual abuse but in the even more common problems of child neglect and child physical and emotional abuse, is family disruption. In 1981, 43 per cent of children reported as abused in the US were living in female-headed, single-parent families compared to only 18 per cent of children in the overall population.[96] A number of factors may be at work here. Children in single-parent families may receive less supervision and such supervision as they do receive may be of inferior quality. In most single-parent families, fathers are not around to provide protection and, after all, protecting daughters from the sexual overtures of other men has been a culturally recognised role of fathers over the centuries. Single mothers often have to rely on providers of childcare who are not biological relatives of their child. One study of child sexual abuse in Iowa found that male babysitters were responsible for five times as much abuse as female sitters even though they performed only a very small proportion of childcare.[97]

A major problem in assessing the issue of child sexual abuse is that such research as is being undertaken is rapidly exploited by committed and ideological pressure groups. The crime of sexual abuse against children is described by the more extreme of such advocates as the inevitable consequence of having fathers in the home. Implicit in such a view is the belief that sexual molestation of children, particularly daughters, is 'an exaggeration of patriarchal family norms, but not a departure from them'.[98] The very presence of fathers is seen as the cause of the disaster. In contrast, there are members of the fathers' rights movement who appear to argue that an abusive father is better than no father at all. There are studies which support both sides – many men use the issue of child custody to continue to harass and intimidate their ex-wives; but some men who abuse their partners can be good parents to their children. The issues are extraordinarily complicated and Kathleen Sternberg is undoubtedly right when she argues that children's interests would be better served if advocates for various positions 'were more careful in the presentation of research findings and more open to the complexities of violence and its impact on family relationships'.[99]

But what can be said is that, while some of the most appalling cases of sexual abuse have been of children by their biological fathers, the overwhelming majority of fathers do *not* abuse their children, and there is powerful evidence to indicate that the presence of biological fathers in the home *reduces* rather than raises the risk of such abuse.

Father as Provider

Most fathers, as we have seen, define fatherhood in terms of providing for their families. It is one of the justifications men use for going out to work. Mothers are much more likely to cite the social side as a reason for why they choose to work outside the home: getting out of the house, enjoyment and companionship at work, a sense of independence and achievement. For many men, including those who are sick, disabled, unemployed and poorly paid, being unable to provide for their families severely affects their confidence in their ability to be good fathers. But, as we saw in Chapter 4, when it comes to occupying the jobs that are going, women are on the march. According to Suzanne Franks, the modern capitalist economy is actually creating more and more jobs for which women are preferred.[100] As she puts it, with characteristic pungency,

> The stereotypical image of a modern workplace features rows of women with headphones answering queries or selling services at a customer call centre, instead of men in overalls smelting steel or mining coal.

She quotes economists who predict that eventually men will be forced to accept lower levels of pay and conditions and that the 'reservation wage', the level of pay below which they are not prepared to work, will drop. The notion of 'women's work', diminishing fast, will disappear. Not surprisingly many young men are apprehensive about being parents because they feel they will be unable to secure the kind of job that will enable them to fulfil what they still see as a crucial marker of being a father, namely the breadwinner role. The issue is desperate for men with limited educational or work skills. It is not going to get any easier. And if men continue to invest so much of their identity in work (see Chapter 4) then the outlook for more and more of them is grim indeed.

Male problems with work are usually identified in terms of the availability of work, of pay and conditions, of work-related stresses and of the need for professional skills, experience and training. In the British government's Voices initiative, which was one of the most comprehensive consultation exercises with women throughout the UK during the first half of 1999, many women noted the extent to which working for a living was still assumed to be the benchmark of what it is to be male.[101] Admittedly, the report began with a characteristic and understandable female emphasis:

> Proving you care by working long hours represents a 'macho' culture that adds to the stresses women face – especially when they travel home late. And the man always wants to take the car.

But then it changed direction and suggested that 'Male employers' might be persuaded not to write off flexible working patterns as something only women want. I have little doubt that a similar 'Voices' exercise, involving 30,000 men instead of women, would yield very similar dissatisfactions with the realities of work for modern-day men. The problem is that men, largely responsible for the way work is structured and organised, are stuck with a notion of masculinity that is impregnated with the notion of sweat and effort and commitment. Even to contemplate a more balanced life, in the way that the women in the 1999 survey clearly did, is to call for the kind of radical public examination of what it is to be a twenty-first-century male that is almost inconceivable. But if men are to negotiate the transition from patriarchy to gender equality, then they must subject the current imbalance between their public and private lives to a radical re-evaluation and change.

They must also analyse what it is that they, as fathers, provide to their children. The value of the modern father has less to do with breadwinning and income generation and more to do with such qualities as involvement, consistency, awareness and ability to care.[102] *Involvement* means time – time spent with children, playing with them, helping them with homework and worries, conversing with them and sharing certain interests including reading, television and sport. The elements include engagement, a structured form of activity during which father and child do something together; accessibility, an unstructured form, which describes the child's sense that his or her father is approachable and reachable; and responsibility, which covers the more routine forms: providing allowances, reassuring worries and looking after children's physical well-being. *Consistency* is important: children need to be able to depend on their fathers to be predictable and reliable, if they are to grow up secure and confident. However, it is emotional consistency rather than always being physically there when needed that seems to be crucial. One 11-year longitudinal study of fathering concluded that, 'Fathers who maintain a close and stable emotional bond with adolescents over time protect adolescents from engaging in delinquent behaviour'.[103] *Awareness* concerns the extent to which fathers take note of their children as individuals in their own right. Some children sometimes feel that their fathers hardly know them. They fear they only exist as representations of individuals their fathers want them to become rather than who they actually are.

> Stephen came to see me because his mother felt he was depressed. He had done well at school but during his first year at university had become listless, apathetic and socially withdrawn. Both his parents were high achievers – his mother was a senior social worker and his father was a judge. When I saw Stephen, he complained of lacking any sense of purpose, worried that he might have chronic fatigue syndrome and insisted that nobody but himself was to blame for the way he felt. He was nonplussed when asked how he thought his parents felt about him, eventually answering that he doubted that they knew how he felt as he did not think they really knew much about him at all.
>
> In further sessions, Stephen admitted that he felt his parents, particularly his father, didn't care about him, citing as evidence the fact that his father only ever showed interest in his grades at school and his work at college. He could not recall his father ever showing any physical affection towards him nor asking him for his views. His father admitted that he had had little time for Stephen on account of his work. He knew little about Stephen's interests or hobbies or indeed about his friends. However, he pointed out that Stephen had not wanted for any material thing, had received an excellent education and that in his view a father should be judged not on how he demonstrated his feelings towards his children but on how he provided for their physical well-being. Stephen's mother took her husband's side and felt that Stephen was shifting responsibility for his inability to get his life going from himself on to his parents.
>
> During a number of family sessions, both parents revealed something of their own upbringing which had strongly encouraged personal independence, emotional control and a disinclination to express feelings. Stephen appeared to benefit from learning more about what his parents regarded as of most value in parenting although he never came to share their conclusions. It remains to be seen, when his turn comes to be a parent, how he will function.

Caring involves the formation of intimate bonds and is expressed in touching, encouraging, comforting and affirming. Many a father's ability or inability to nurture depends to a considerable extent on how he was nurtured by his own father. At the heart of such caring concern is discipline. Fathers still retain a core role of providing the discipline within a family. Problems arise, however, if discipline is provided in the absence of awareness, consistency and true affection. Some fathers believe that it is only as disciplinarians that they have a role; the consequences are almost invariably catastrophic. Effective fathers are those who are able to express their concern for, faith in and admiration of their children *and* can also make plain where the boundaries lie between acceptable and unacceptable behaviour. Close and stable emotional bonds between fathers and their children enable discipline to be enforced without recourse to physical threat and violence. Conversely, in families where the father is distant, uninvolved and unaware, discipline is difficult to enforce and verbal and physical confrontations common.

The overwhelming conclusion from research is that fathers do matter. But the reasons why they matter are not necessarily the reasons why many fathers think they matter! The emotional and psychological impoverishment that comes from paternal loss tells us much about the importance of fatherhood. And what it is telling us is that what matters for health, welfare and happiness 'is not whether your father was rich or poor but whether you had a father at all'.[104]

Conclusion

There is a role for men as fathers. They can help sons learn to be better men, daughters to feel better about themselves. They can protect their families and their communities from the depredations of unattached and poorly socialised fellow-males. They can provide and protect and do so more competently and more effectively than did their own fathers. And they can, through the process of becoming fathers, develop and cultivate empathy, altruism, sensitivity and emotional expressiveness. This needs to be said and argued, for the public image of men as fathers is not a favourable one. One commentator in the United States, himself a psychiatrist and writer on family issues, has described the television image of the contemporary father thus:

> when we watch Dad on TV sitcoms and the accompanying ads, he's a rather foolish man. He's not quite with it; a piece of him is astray. Commentators on contemporary fatherhood complain that he is being deliberately made to look foolish and antiquated . . . wives are shown to be more practical and connected, children to be more with it and savvy. Even if he's a good guy, Dad is a little dumb.[105]

It need not be like this. There is such a thing as a 'good enough father' even if it is no easier to be one than to be a good enough man. To be a good enough father requires being there on a reasonable basis, being protective of your children in the face of harm and danger, and supportive in the face of challenge and opportunity. The suggestions below as to how to be a good enough father are deceptive in their commonsense simplicity (Table 3). At the heart of a father's relationship with his children is the same notion of attachment that Bowlby all those years ago formulated in relation to mothers. A fellow-psychiatrist, Sebastian Kraemer, has described this attachment well:

> A secure attachment is like an invisible elastic which can stretch and contract depending on the need for protection. So when you are ill or in pain, tired or afraid, you move towards the person with whom you feel secure and when all is well you can move away to explore the world around. Clearly this applies to all of us, but most of all to small children.[106]

Table 3 How to be a better dad

Being a role model

A father is a role model. How he behaves teaches his children how to behave when adults. If he handles problems through talking, his children are more likely to do the same when they grow up. If he copes by losing his temper, being abusive or violent, his children will be more likely to grow up to do the same.

- Children learn mainly from what their fathers do, not what they say.
- Fathers who treat their daughters with love and respect will rear girls who when they grow up will expect to be treated the same way by boys and men.
- Fathers who teach their sons that a man is caring and fair, who is a friend to his children and treats children with respect, will bring up young men who will regard women positively.

Fathers at work and in the family

Work is tiring, stressful and can be worrying. However, it is neither fair nor wise to pass on such worries and stresses, no matter how real they are, to one's children.

- Fathers should put aside time to recharge their batteries.
- Fathers should look after their own health.
- Fathers should try and leave the hassles of work at work.

A father shows he cares

By getting involved with his children a father shows them that he cares.

- Fathers do things their children want them to do.
- Fathers hug their children and tell them they are great.
- Fathers help their children with their homework.
- Fathers play sports and games with their children.

- Fathers go to school functions, parent/teacher interviews, watch their children play sport, music, act on stage, etc.
- Fathers learn their friends' and teachers' names.

Fathers and partnerships

Being a parent is a partnership. Children cannot cope with parents who put each other down. Fathers should remember always to

- respect their child's mother;
- avoid arguing in front of the children;
- do something about relationship problems;
- get professional advice if things are not working out.

Fathers spending time with their children

The time fathers spend with their children is a good investment in their future. Fathers can show their love for their children by getting involved in their sports and hobbies or involving their children in their own interests. Children grow up quickly and fathers often leave becoming involved with their children until it is too late – when their children are not children any more.

- Fathers and children should share a regular meal.
- Fathers should talk to their children.
- Fathers should listen to their children's views without criticising them.
- Fathers should praise their children's efforts.
- Fathers should encourage their children and help them make decisions.[107]

But even if we accept the importance and value of the father – and many, I feel sure, will remain dubious – what are we to make of the facts that many women prefer to have a child without having a commitment to its father, many opt to leave marriage and negotiate the perils and hazards of single life and parenthood rather than stay and cope with marital abuse and violence, and many struggle to care for their children with little or no financial, emotional or social support from the man who has fathered them? If men can be so committed to their families and if their commitment can be so vital to the health and vitality of all concerned, then why *aren't* they so committed? Why, instead, do so many men display such indifference and incompetence in relation to their responsibilities and duties as fathers? Why, if marriage and family life is so good for men, do so many of them mess them up? What makes so many men such unattractive bets as life partners, lovers, mentors and mates? What is left of phallic power if more and more women find the challenge of living with and loving men more trouble than it is worth?

CHAPTER 8

MEN AND LOVE

As a man I love women, enjoy their company, admire their emotional frankness. I grew up an only son with two sisters, and although I went to a single-sex Jesuit school the major influences in my earliest years were female. Perhaps that is why in so many ways I feel more comfortable in female company and recognise that the number of close male friends I have is modest. Many men I know feel similarly, although others clearly prefer and seek out male camaraderie at work, in clubs, pursuing sporting and other interests.

But all men, myself included, do not just love women. We do not see them only as colleagues, friends, lovers; as sexually desirable, physically attractive, mentally stimulating. We fear them, hate them, marginalise them, denigrate them and categorise them. And we continually strive to control and dominate them. The call to us as men, at the beginning of the twenty-first century, to turn away from violence, to get in touch with our feelings, to express our fears and admit our inadequacies, is a doomed call if it is made, as it tends to be made, predominantly by women. Men, apart from a minority, seem fearful of making the changes that the death of patriarchy demands. Yet that is the scale of the challenge. Men can only save themselves. They cannot rely on women to save them.

The Male Fear of Women

Male fear of women and femininity is no modern phenomenon, no by-product of the rise in feminism and the onslaught on patriarchy. It can be traced back to (and beyond) the Greeks and Greek mythology in which the loveliness of the Muses was counterbalanced by the murderousness of the Sirens, Harpies, Furies and Gorgons. Nor are such visions of female murderousness restricted to Greek mythology. The Goddess Kali dances on the corpses of slain men. Samson, whom no man could destroy, is robbed of his strength by Delilah. Judith decapitates Holofernes after seducing him. Psychoanalyst and classical historian, Bennett Simon, suggests that these and related myths embody a deeply held child fantasy of the mother – as powerful, dangerous and equipped both with breasts and with penis – 'the phallic mother'.[1] Down through the ages, men have struggled to cope with their fear by objectifying and justifying it. Women become sinister, destructive, malignant, witches, vampires, succubi, insatiable – the very personification of the dreaded.

When in 1925 Freud came to examine the source of this male hostility to women, he attributed to it a fear of castration. His analysis, unfortunately, only served to be both demeaning and contemptuous. It was anatomy, he decided not unreasonably, that dictated the relationship between men and women. His paper on the subject 'Some psychical consequences of the anatomical distinction between the sexes' provides a revealing insight into his views of women. Freud argues that when a little boy first catches sight of a girl's genitals nothing very much happens. It is only later, 'when some threat of castration has obtained a hold on him' (a consequence of the need to separate from the mother, for example), that he is forced to believe in the reality of the danger. Such castration anxiety serves permanently to determine the boy's relations to women: 'horror of the mutilated creature or triumphant contempt for her'.[2] In his later 1931 paper on female sexuality he returns to the theme, noting that what is left over in the adult man of the young boy's anxiety relating to his discovery of the female genitals 'is a certain amount of disparagement in [men's] attitude towards women'.[3] A little girl, however, behaves differently. When she sees the little boy's penis she makes her judgement and her decision in a moment. 'She has seen it and knows that she is without it and wants to have it.' Freud continues:

> Here what has been named the masculinity complex of women branches off. It may put great difficulties in the way of their regular development towards femininity, if it cannot be got over soon enough. The hope of some day obtaining a penis in spite of everything and so of becoming a man may persist to an incredibly late age and may become a motive for strange and otherwise unaccountable actions . . . After a woman has become aware of the wound to her narcissism, she develops, like a scar, a sense of inferiority. When she has passed beyond her first attempt at explaining her lack of a penis as being a punishment personal to herself and has realized that that sexual character is a universal one, she begins to share the contempt felt by men for a sex which is the lesser in so important a respect and, at least in holding that opinion, insists on being like a man.[4]

True, Freud did concede, towards the end of his paper, that all human individuals, 'as a result of their bisexual disposition and of cross-inheritance', combine masculine and feminine characteristics but the damage had been done. Women were to be blamed for their sense of inferiority. It was women's fault, and not due to centuries of male domination and control. And the cause of all a woman's woes? Her realisation of 'the wound to her narcissism', of the fact that she does not possess the instrument of phallic power, the penis. Despite the suggestions of some recent feminists, sympathetic to his otherwise generally enlightened views on women, that he modified his views as he got older, Freud's emphasis on the importance of penis envy to any understanding of women remained unequivocal. In describing some of the consequences of this envy, Freud placed himself squarely within the ranks of those who had long argued that female inferiority is a biological fact. He speculated that because women's psychological development differed from that of men, so for women 'the level of what is ethically normal is different from what it is in men'. He went further:

> Character-traits which critics of every epoch have brought up against women – that they show less sense of justice than men, that they are less ready to submit to the great exigencies of life, that they are more often influenced in their judgements by feelings of affection or hostility – all these would be amply accounted for by the modification in the formation of their super-ego which we have inferred from above. We must not allow ourselves to be deflected from such conclusions by the denials of the feminists, who are anxious to force us to regard the two sexes as completely equal in position and worth.[5]

Freud did go on to add that all human individuals 'as a result of their bisexual disposition and of cross-inheritance' actually combine both masculine and feminine characteristics and that pure masculinity and feminity 'remain theoretical constructions of uncertain content' but by this stage of his paper the damage was done. The paper reeks for the most part of what Freud elsewhere describes as projection, that mental defence mechanism whereby impulses or ideas unacceptable to the self are projected into or located within somebody else. What is being projected here is male anxiety – anxiety about the actual basis of phallic superiority, male sexual and biological potency. By a deft piece of projection, it ends up in *women*, where it is portrayed as a female anxiety about the lack of a penis! The truly astonishing feature of

Freud's paper is its complete neglect of any consideration of the subservient social and personal position experienced by women down the centuries, a neglect which may of course be explained by reference to Freud's implicit assumption of the inevitability of women's inferiority. Freud's psychological explanation, enunciated in a series of papers and lectures throughout the 1920s and 1930s, neatly complemented the insistent biological explanations in medicine at that time (see Chapter 4).

One male–female relationship which Freud exempted from his otherwise pessimistic analysis of gender relationships was that between a mother and her son. He described this as 'the most perfect, easily the most ambivalence-free of all human relationships', an observation which biographer Peter Gay suggests seems more like a wish than a sound inference from clinical material.[6] Maternal feelings towards sons are often complicated by unrealistic expectations, profound disappointments, intense fears and extraordinary emotional demands. In a young son's efforts to satisfy his mother can be identified many of the seeds of an adult male's difficulties in relating to his female equals. Freud was astonishingly productive and inventive when it came to analysing a son's relationship with his father, a daughter's with both parents, siblings' relationships with each other and the greater demands of society on the individual's psychological development. But about a son's relationship with his mother, other than his Oedipal desire for her, he is relatively silent. In his 1931 paper on female sexuality he did refer to a boy's ambivalent feelings towards his mother, but only to argue that males deal with them by 'directing all their hostility on to their father' (which of course is what he himself appears to have done: see Chapter 8, p. 162ff.).

It was left to one of the first female psychoanalysts, Karen Horney, to challenge Freud's male-oriented and phallocentric analysis of the relationship between the sexes. The year after Freud's 1925 paper, Horney produced her own, entitled 'The flight from womanhood', which served as a protest against what her biographer Susan Quinn terms 'the joyless picture of female experience that psychoanalysis has painted'.[7] In it Horney countered Freud's preoccupation with penis envy in women by suggesting an equivalent envy of the womb in men:

> When one begins, as I did, to analyze men only after a fairly long experience of analyzing women, one receives a most surprising

> impression of the intensity of this envy of pregnancy, childbirth, and motherhood, as well as of breasts and of the act of suckling.[8]

Perhaps the depreciation of womanhood is just a case of male sour grapes? And, rubbing salt into the wound of male pretensions, Horney added:

> Is not the tremendous strength in man of the impulse to creative work in every field precisely due to their feeling of playing a relatively small part in the creation of living beings, which constantly impels them to an overcompensation in achievement?

For Horney, women's discontent with their lot reflected not penis envy but the actual disadvantages women experienced in their social lives. Exposed from birth onward to the suggestion of her inferiority, a woman has no obvious means to sublimate her feelings given that, in Horney's words, 'all the ordinary professions have been filled by men'. The control and subjugation of women have predictable consequences not merely for women in general but for women as mothers. Angry and resentful women raising young males can be expected to displace their disappointment with husbands, fathers and brothers on to their sons or to rear them to be instruments of revenge against the men in their lives. Ambitious, intelligent, talented mothers, dissatisfied with the inferior status and social constraints of housebound motherhood, cultivate ambition and desire for dominance in their sons (and in their daughters too). Greek myth and tragedy, from which Freud quarried his Oedipus complex, are rich in the theme of mothers who use their sons to get back at their husbands. The son can so easily become an object of displacement and rage against a husband and father who has failed a woman's expectations. Such a son becomes a mother's great hope, a surrogate phallus that may provide the pride and prestige that marrying her husband has singularly failed to produce. Such a son was Freud to his mother.

Yet every boy needs to negotiate the separation from his mother or risk being 'emasculated' as a mother's boy. A son who remains, beyond childhood, with his mother, 'tied to the apron-strings', castrates himself. In the separation process of son from mother are sown some of the seeds of male fear and anger with women, a fear and an anger not turned against the father, despite Freud's insistence, but consciously or otherwise harboured against women.

Both sexes begin life in close physical and psychological proximity to their mother. But the consequent issues of gender identity differ crucially for boys and girls. A girl forms her identity through identification and integration with her mother. A boy defines himself as masculine as he separates from his mother. Built into core male gender identity is, in the words of the feminist critic, Nancy Chodorow,

> an early, non-verbal, unconscious and almost somatic sense of primary oneness with the mother, an underlying sense of femaleness that continually, usually unnoticeably but sometimes consistently challenges and undermines the sense of maleness. Thus, because of the primary oneness and identification with his mother . . . a boy's and man's core gender identity . . . is an issue.[9]

From such a perspective, boys and young men are consciously or otherwise coping with an earlier intimate identification with their mother which threatens their identity as men and compromises their sense of self. Herein, it is argued, lie the seeds for men's avoidance of intimacy and self-revelation. Having had to negotiate a withdrawal from the intuitiveness and intimacy of the mother–son relationship, the male youth protects himself from the pain of future separations by constructing a protective barrier of emotional control. If he has no adult mentor, if, particularly, his father is absent or incapable of assuming an alternative nurturing, supportive and involved role, such a young man may encounter considerable difficulties in making and maintaining emotionally bonding and rewarding heterosexual relationships. Later relationships may revive yearnings for the mother and the result may be the kind of seeking emotional substitutes for mother-love which I discussed earlier (Chapter 7).[10]

But does this mean that a fear and even hatred of women is a ubiquitous phenomenon with deep roots common to every male in his earliest physical and psychological development? Does this mean men are condemned to misogyny? Some influential contemporary commentators, such as Adam Jukes and Dorothy Dinnerstein, certainly believe so.[11] They go further and argue that once the male child discovers that his desire to possess his mother genitally and orally is doomed, and his view of her as 'madonna' or 'princess' switches to 'witch' or 'whore', he relinquishes and devalues her and all womanhood. Male sadism becomes the driving impulse behind all man's relationships with women.

Sadly, there is some truth in this gloomy view but it is only part, albeit a disagreeable part, of the story. Men do split women into good and bad, mother and monster, saint and sinner, madonna and whore, but the split is never resolved in favour of either. What may be required is for men to acknowledge their ambivalence rather than to rely on sentimental and/or bitter visions of Mother. What is required is for men to examine what Horney and those analysts who have followed her have described, namely their possible envy and fear of women's biological creativity and identity.

Another source of male fear of, and hostility towards, women relates to the female ability to turn male sexual desire on and off. The French philosopher, Michel de Montaigne, back in the middle of the sixteenth century, drew attention to the 'disobedience of this member which thrusts itself forward so inopportunely when we do not want it to, and which so inopportunely lets us down when we most need it'.[12] There is a passage in Virginia Woolf's novel *Orlando* in which the hero/heroine muses on the effect the sight of her splendid bare calf has on men. A sailor high on the ship's mast started so violently that he missed his footing and only saved himself by the skin of his teeth. 'If the sight of my ankles means death to an honest fellow who, no doubt, has a wife and family to support, I must, in all humanity, keep them covered,' Orlando says.

> And she fell to thinking what an odd pass we have come to when all a woman's beauty has to be kept covered lest a sailor may fall from a mast-head. 'A pox on them', she said, realising for the first time what, in other circumstances, she would have been taught as a child, that is to say, the sacred responsibilities of womanhood.[13]

The 'sacred responsibilities of womanhood', which include the control of otherwise uncontrollable and incorrigible male sexual drive, provide the justification for some men to regard every woman as a potential whore who has it within her sexual power to ennoble or degrade him. The routine, unthinking use by men of words such as cunt, pussy, snatch, beaver, slash, synonyms for the female genitals, as swear words and obscenities denoting women as objects of contempt and intended to denigrate and degrade, reflects the rooted male hostility towards, and fear of, female sexual power. That which is desired is detested, for that which is desired exercises a terrible, nagging, insistent, irresistible temptation and poses an immense challenge to the male sense of control. The preoccupation of men with pornography provides an example of how men can and do turn their own self-disgust against women. The argument that pornography is 'part of the violation and exploitation of women as a class'[14] is a familiar one with much to support it but as one feminist critic, Deirdre English, has suggested, the exploitation can be seen as two-way:

> Actually since there are so few women (but hundreds and thousands of pictures of them) the overwhelming feeling is one of the commercial exploitation of male sexual desire. There it is, embarrassingly desperate, tormented, demeaning itself, begging for relief, taking any substitute and *paying* for it. Men who live for this are suckers and their uncomfortable demeanour shows they know it. If as a woman you can detach yourself . . . you see how totally tragic they appear.[15]

Men know only too well how tragic they appear, know too the extent to which they feel enslaved by their libidos. The newspapers, television newsreels and the stuff of prurient gossip constitute a daily catalogue of that legion of men, great and small, who risk personal relationships, public reputations and lifetime achievements for a sexual experience which almost inevitably proves transient. Men in thrall to sex exhibit self-disgust and disgust with what is seen to be the cause of their degradation: women. Men know they need women, depend on them. But for some men, many men (all men?), the female fulfilment of adult male dependency is shameful, with its connotations of a return to infancy and helplessness. Such disgust varies from man to man. But what seems uncomfortably true is that men differ from other men only in terms of the *extent* to which they hold hostile and resentful views of women, and not in terms of whether they do or do not.

Men and Control

Increasingly in my life as a man and my work as a psychiatrist I find myself wondering not so much what women want, the question that perplexed Freud, but why men need so much to be in control. Perhaps it is the nature of male sexuality, the anarchic penile response to trivial erotic stimuli, the autonomous, insistent, itching sexual urge that dominates so much of a young man's life, that holds the key. So much of male sexuality is bound up with a desire to be – indeed a need to be – in control, to master and possess the other while simultaneously seeming to yield, surrender, capitulate. One of the biological imperatives of being a man is that he feels compelled to go on proving his manhood to women. A man has to *do* something in order to fulfil himself. 'The ideal of efficiency', noted Horney, 'is a typical masculine ideal – oriented towards the materialistic, the mechanistic, toward action'.[16] Psychologist Liam Hudson has observed that at every turn men seem naturally to adopt an 'instrumental' mode of address to the world around them. As he puts it:

> Wherever a culture offers a choice between activities that are a matter of impersonal manipulations or control and one of personal relationship and caring, it is men who are drawn towards the first, women towards the second.[17]

This preoccupation with remaining in control coupled with the urgings of an insistent sexuality together lie at the core of male aggression, both turned outwards in sexual and other forms of violence, and turned inwards in suicidal destruction. Consider the clinical case history of Sean, the young man who preferred to try and kill himself rather than admit he might need help, which I described in Chapter 4. Or consider a man at the other end of the life cycle.

> **Andrew had recently retired when he came to see me. He had been a competent surgeon who had anticipated reaching his retirement age of 65 with enthusiasm. He had a variety of interests and hobbies including shooting, tennis and collecting antiques. However, shortly after retiring, he became impotent. It was a tremendous shock. He began to panic, could not concentrate, complained of poor memory and feared he was developing Alzheimer's disease. During his first consultation, he explained that he had never had a problem getting an erection before. 'Whenever I needed to perform it answered the call.' He was unaware of the fact that by his age the majority of men have experienced some degree of erectile dysfunction (impotence) and by 70 years of age only about one in three men describes himself as completely and reliably potent.[18] With explanation and reassurance, Andrew began to relax and sexual function returned. However, he continued to have a degree of impotence from time to time, aggravated by his irritation that his penis 'which always obeyed me before' now showed a wayward, less predictable pattern of behaviour.**

For Andrew, as for so many men, the ultimate control is sexual. And, like so many men, Andrew chose to discuss his impotence purely in terms of instrumental malfunction – the extent to which it did or did not impair his ability to pleasure and satisfy his partner never entered into the discussion. Discussions about impotence rarely refer to the mutuality of sexuality, to the fact that sexual activity, unless it is masturbatory, intimately involves another person. Not surprisingly, some vehement feminist critics of male sexuality accuse men of being either ignorant of, or indifferent to, female sexual impotence, the difficulty many women have in achieving orgasm. 'The sad fact', Phyllis Chesler bitterly observes, 'is that most human beings have been conceived with only *one* parent having an orgasm',[19] and, for the most part, men couldn't care less. So when a man develops impotence, even at the age of 70 years, the entire apparatus of sexual therapy, from vacuum pumps to Viagra, is wheeled into action; whereas if a woman is anorgasmic, even in the full reproductive years of her life, she is soon informed that this is a biological reality for many women that cannot be changed.

The burden of pleasuring women is often too much for many men, who then resort to prostitutes. Amongst the many motivations is the undeniable fact that the monetary nature of the transaction frees the man from any need to consider the woman's pleasure. Of course there are men who love women to the point of desiring to satisfy them sexually but even amongst these there lurks the conviction that turning on a woman is the ultimate proof of male sexual power and superiority. At the heart of much male sexual fantasy – of domination, bondage, flagellation, rape – is control in the service of phallic narcissism. And the ideal sexual object, the perfect woman to fulfil such a fantasy, is a fantasy woman – constantly available, forever lubricated, ever ready, in a state of perpetual desire but immediately dispensable on completion of the act.

Quite apart from the question of impotence, few men are in complete sexual control. But the ideal notion of what it is to be a man embodies a notion of such control. When we attempt to answer the question of why men rape or engage in the molestation and sexual assault of women and young children, we again encounter the issue of masculine control and conflicts around it. Four blame models are usually described – societal blame, offender blame, victim blame and situation blame. Relevant to our discussion, societal blame suggests that sexual assault is the consequence of cultural and social attitudes and values which legitimise sexual force and coercion. Such a view suggests that all men are potentially if not actually rapists.[20] There is disquieting support for this to be found in studies which show an overlap of attitudes and behaviours between sex offenders and other men.[21] Research findings from the University of Alabama Rape Research Group indicate a marked similarity between offenders and the general norms of male populations on scales measuring attitudes towards women.[22] Some seemingly normal men show approval of the commission of rape and hold beliefs that tend to minimise the violent and negative impact of rape on women.[23] Such men generally have little anxiety about the expression of aggression and are more controlling, more 'masculine' and 'dominant', characteristics which lend support to the view that sex stereotyping is related to rape attitudes and to rape.[24]

The findings relating to the sexual molestation by adult males of children are disconcertingly similar. The most consistent finding in recent years is that most sexually abused children are abused by an adult they know and trust. The second most consistent finding is that there is less reason than was once thought to see the child molester as a sexual deviant or as somebody with severe psychological problems. Instead, it is his non-sexual motivation, such as the desire and need for domination and control, which is emphasised. There is, however, very often a sexual component in that child molesters do not, for the most part, restrict themselves to the physical assault of children but often sexually abuse and rape them. In addition, in much child abuse behaviour the offender is erotically excited by the child he is abusing. Many offenders have clearly documented patterns of deviant sexual arousal. But before we men seek reassurance in the belief that sex offenders are a class apart and categorically distinct from the rest of us, we would do well to consider this conclusion from one of the most eminent researchers in the area of sexual deviance:

> Caught and convicted sex offenders are those who are the most compulsive, repetitive, blatant and extreme in their offending, and thus also those whose behaviour stems from the most deviant developmental experiences. We now know much better than before how widespread sexual abuse is and how small a fraction of offenders are ever apprehended let alone convicted. Although they have not been studied, it seems very probable that undetected offenders are persons with much less conspicuous psychological abnormality. The widespread existence of sexual abuse forces one away from an exclusive reliance on theories of psychopathology and towards the possibility that normative factors are at work. Widespread and conventional patterns of socialisation and cultural transmission also play a part in creating sexual abusers.[25]

Behind such bland terms as 'conventional patterns of socialisation' and 'cultural transmission' lurk power and control – twin themes that reverberate through the analysis of male sexual aggression, male culture, male preoccupations, indeed every aspect of male life. Men immersed in the public reality of a rampant capitalist and materialist economy appear driven by a neurotic overcompensation, a preoccupation with the biggest and the best, to keep at bay a profound, nagging sense of inadequacy. To be successful, a man is required to obsessively build, accumulate, hoard – whether it be money, achievement, status, approval or power. The consequences for modern man are predictable:

> This man cannot relax his efforts. He must always prove himself, always do something useful, always be hard at it, as though the least softening of effort would reveal a hidden weakness. His mind spins fantasies of new accomplishments, even when on the beach or the ski trail. He must have a telephone in his car, in his bathroom. He lays grid upon masculine grid, and grid upon that grid, not burnishing a delicate corner in a fine way, but endlessly manufacturing. He is heavy industry; pastoralia is foreign territory.[26]

Men, then, are not just fearful of, and angry with, women. They are fearful of, and angry with, each other. Men repudiate the feminine not only in women but in themselves. As the colonist despises the colonised for being weak, for having yielded to invasion and conquest in the first place, so men view women's apparent acquiescence with contempt. Such a view demands that any move towards identification with the oppressed, the colonised be promptly repudiated and stamped out. If a man feels he does not have *it* – masculine strength, masculine bravery, masculine achievement – he is a castrated male. He is a woman. When men are in the company of fellow-men, they characteristically cut each other down, mock. Competition, the mark of most male relationships – in business, sport, academic life, romance, social situations – is the antithesis of the domestic, the intimate, the exposed. Stereotypical male activities – drinking like a man, fighting like a man, striving to win like a man, dying like a man – involve the assertion of the self against constraint, against control. Collaborating, yielding, submitting, crying are for women. Many men sneer at and denigrate what they see as the suburban in the lives lived by child-bearing and child-rearing women. Many men seem afraid of making the transition from boy to man. The characteristics of marital family life – commitment, dependability, loyalty, self-sacrifice, tolerance, love itself – are seen as soft, limited, boring, threatening. Much of the introspective male literature of the late twentieth century – one thinks of Richard Ford and John Updike in the US, Nick Hornby and Tony Parsons in Britain – is an exploration of male inadequacy, of men's failure as husbands and fathers, of fear of the constraints and chains of the intimate and the domestic, of personal commitment and of children remorselessly reminding the man of the passage of time, of ageing and mortality – and of an overwhelming, inchoate terror of losing control. Nor is there much evidence to suggest that homosexual male attitudes to women are much more positive. One of the largest studies of homosexual men, commissioned by the US National Institute of Mental Health, found that homosexual men believed that men had in general better personalities than women and were more enjoyable to socialise with.[27] While not overtly hostile to women, most homosexual men were relatively indifferent.

It would be a mistake, too, to believe that male distaste for the feminine is restricted to macho sportsmen, competitive businessmen, thrusting professionals. It is to be found everywhere, even within the very heart of male sensitivity and sensibility, the world of poetry. In 1992, a number of male poets in Ireland set about the task of compiling a comprehensive anthology of Irish poetry, *The Field Day Anthology*, in part to correct the tendency in the larger English-speaking world whereby Irish poets writing in English are involuntarily recruited into the English poetic record and tradition. It led one of the country's finest female poets, Eavan Boland, to object strenuously at the under-representation of women. (She was one of only three female poets amongst the 34 males.) The failure to recognise the contribution to Irish poetry made by a bevy of distinguished women poets led her to observe:

> No post-colonial project, however distinguished, can sustain itself if it continues the exclusions for which it reproaches the original colony. I felt this was a post-colonial anthology which was not sufficiently alert to that contradiction. There were 28 sections, not one edited by a woman.[28]

The colonisation to which Boland referred was that of Ireland by Britain and that of women by men. She herself has deliberately identified the space and realities of the domestic life as a fit and proper subject for poetic concern, her work focusing on, among other things, the night feed of a baby, the loss of a child, the passing of a woman's reproductive life. It is a dimension of human experience which many men have, over the centuries, repressed, denied and, most ominously of all, derided. It is also a dimension that many men readily relinquish to women. This guarantees that public power remains in male hands, that in a two-sphere world composed of the public and the private domains men dominate the former and through such domination ensure that the latter is kept in a subordinate and devalued position.

Men, Women and Power

The belief in the necessity of a two-sphere world for the functioning of society has been strongly supported by a number of influential sociologists, including Talcott Parsons.[29] It has only recently been pointed out that much of the early family sociology ignored the fact that the ideology of a private, female-dominated sphere 'was kept in place by the simple fact of power'.[30] Modern female commentators wonder why such measures of male discontent as rising suicide rates are taken to reflect growing male anxiety at the increasing presence of women in the public sphere and the growing demand by women that men take a greater role in the private sphere. After all, men still pull the great majority of the levers in society. But so nervous are men about losing control, any control, that the merest suggestion that it might one day happen provokes the severest of reactions. One social commentator, W.J. Goode, reminds us just why men resist demands that they give up power and privilege:

> Boys and grown men have always taken for granted that what they were doing was more important than what the other sex was doing, that where they were was where the action was, that their women accepted the definition. Men occupied the center of the stage, and women's attention was focused on them.[31]

Boys and grown men have always taken for granted that what they were doing was more important than what girls and women were doing. This was particularly the case when what boys and men were doing was some altruistic and life-enhancing and intellectually demanding activity, such as medicine, while the 'other sex' was engaged at home bringing up the children. One of the most eminent physicians at the beginning of the twentieth century, Sir William Osler, was in no doubt about the priorities when he spoke to Canadian medical students in 1908 about how best to cope with the competing demands of professional and home life:

> What about the wife and babies if you have them? Leave them! Heavy as are your responsibilities to those nearest and dearest, they are outweighed by the responsibilities to yourself, to the profession, and to the public . . . Your wife will be glad to bear her share in the sacrifice you make.[32]

How easy it was for Osler then! But what would Osler say about today's medicine, with over half its students female? Would he exhort them to 'leave' their babies for 'a heavier responsibility'? In 1908 it was assumed that the centre of the public stage was occupied by men. But has this truly changed? Today's female doctor, like any woman wishing to make a public contribution, is still in effect asked to 'leave' her children – to leave them with nannies, to leave them with child-minders, to leave them in crèches, to leave them in nursery schools. And she is asked to do this because the value placed on public work, any public work, is still higher than that placed on caring for, attachment to and bonding with infants and small children. We still await a serious attempt to so modify the relationship between public and private work that the organisation of the former will reflect the needs of the latter, rather than insisting that one is subordinated to the other. *Men occupy the centre of the stage and women attend to them.* This is not the traditional way we used to envisage the relationship between the sexes. We imagined women as the gazed upon, the attended to, men as doing the gazing and attending. But think about it. Women, for the most part, occupied the worlds of fashion and glamour, of sexuality and pornography, where they could be gazed upon with little threat to male dominance. It was – and still is – in the powerful world of political control and economic might that men do the parading and provide the show, and women, for the most part, are the spectators. And in that powerful world, it is male values and male attitudes which dominate.

One of the consequences has been the steady diminution in value of such tasks and activities as child-bearing and child-rearing, family relationships, the use of quality time, the cultivation of intimacy between men and women and between parents and children. Even today, after women have made such efforts and some gains in blurring the divide between the two spheres of routine family life and admired life in the workplace, the fact remains that it is the public sphere that still is accorded the primary value. Many women who leave the home to work feel they are colluding in the view that the boardroom and the office *are* more important than the kitchen and the nursery. Some do not mind particularly. But many do. It is interesting to note, for example, that the Voices initiative undertaken by the Women's Unit in the Cabinet Office revealed that not only do many women want a working world that acknowledges the demands and realities of family life, they want one that recognises 'the work women do as carers as equal to any career'.[33] At the top of the 12 issues women said mattered to them was 'balancing paid work and home life'.

But balancing paid work and home life has become a problem for everyone, not only women. In a number of studies reported on by the Henley Centre in London, over half of adults in the UK say they don't seem to have enough time to get anything done, while over one in three claim their working hours continue to increase. Many recognise that while they are richer in monetary terms, they are losing in terms of available time – the so-called 'decoupling' of economic growth and satisfaction from personal growth and satisfaction.[34] Many women, in particular, feel they have sacrificed the chance of having children, or even forming relationships, for the sake of their career. Many men lose out on home life, due to the demands of work and work-related travel. Families are sacrificed in the name of putting work before domestic and personal life. Substantial numbers of men and women believe they have missed out on their children's early years and development, and many others blame the pressures and demands of the workplace for divorce and other difficulties in their relationships (Table 4).

Table 4 The high cost of work

'What is the single biggest personal sacrifice in your home life you have made in your career so far?' (%)

	Men	Women
Missed children growing up	23.7	22.2
Work put before family	23.8	21.3
Moving home for employer	10.8	4.0
Missed leisure/hobby time	7.0	15.7
Away from home, short term	8.9	3.1
Divorce/relationship strain	7.1	7.3
Away from home, long term	4.7	1.3
Time spent on work-related education	2.7	2.5
Not having/postponing children	1.2	1.2
Unable to form relationships	1.2	3.7

Source: WFD/Management Today, *The Great Work/Life Debate*, 1998, from *The Paradox of Prosperity*, The Henley Centre/Salvation Army, London, 1999, p. 25

So, whatever the premium put on public life as opposed to private, the great majority of people still wish for a traditional family structure and home life. When asked, 'Which do you think is the most desirable way to live?', 69 per cent considered it to be marriage with children,[35] despite the fact that more and more people are failing to achieve this desired state. Indeed, the predictions are sobering. Fewer people will form families, there will be a 33 per cent increase in single-parent households and a 55 per cent increase in one-person households by 2011 (as against 1991) and by 2010 some 22 per cent of 45-year-old women will remain childless compared with 16 per cent in 1997. Now, increasingly if belatedly, men, too, want the workplace to recognise the demands and realities of family life – but do men, and particularly our (predominantly male) political masters, wish equal recognition to be given to the work women do as carers? Most of the talk emanating from Tony Blair's Supporting Families initiative still smacks of the desire of his government to attract more and more women into a workforce which desperately needs them rather than recognising the need to keep a ravenous capitalist job market from sucking the dynamic out of personal and family life. It is the problem of feeding the labour demand of an ever-expanding free-market economy, rather than any real desire to improve the quality and indeed quantity of family and personal life, that does appear to be the motivating force behind a policy ostensibly about protecting family values. The demand for equal recognition of what women do as carers in the home, which in effect means appropriate financial remuneration, is never directly addressed in the Voices document, nor anywhere else for that matter. Such neglect of a crucial issue is hardly surprising. It is political and financial dynamite to any government intent on maximising the yield of labour to be mined from the many hundreds and thousands of women who remain full time or virtually full time at home, when they could be out manning the factories and businesses of Great Britain Inc. The Blair government may talk of family-friendly policies and strengthening the basic unit of society but what the public world of work wants to hear is that more women will be directed towards its insatiable maw. Such a reality bodes ill for the men who would like to see the cultivation of a more civilised and balanced view of the two spheres of public and private life.

In her book, *The Second Shift*, Arlie Hochschild, Professor of

Sociology at the University of California, warns about this very development.[36] In the United States the assertive job culture that is at the very heart of capitalism has remorselessly expanded at the expense of family culture. More recently, Hochschild has considered the profound consequences in the United States of the increase in work time over the last 20 years.[37] Amongst these consequences is the re-emergence of the so-called 'latchkey kids'. One study of nearly 5,000 children and their parents found that children who were home alone for 11 or more hours a week were three times more likely than other children to abuse cannabis, alcohol or tobacco. The findings were unaffected by whether the children were upper-class or working-class.[38] Many parents in the less well paid jobs in the US, Britain and elsewhere cannot afford to purchase childcare, and even if they could it is not widely available. But even when working parents use others to care for their children, are we to assume that the balance between the inexorable demands of work and the more subtle demands of home and family life is thereby met? Hochschild describes the rise in self-help books designed to allay parental guilt and insecurity and to help young children gain fresh insights into, and appreciation of, how hard their parents are trying to balance work and parenting. In one such book, entitled *Teaching Your Child to Be Home Alone*, two psychotherapists write a section clearly designed to be read not just by the parents but by their children:

> The end of the workday can be a difficult time for adults. It is natural for them to sometimes be tired and irritable . . . Before your parents arrive at the Center, begin to get ready, and be prepared to say good-bye to your friends so that pick-up time is easier for everyone.[39]

The truth about both parents working in the world of work as it is presently structured is that the world of home and family is invaded by the very time and organisational modes that make work efficient. I cannot better Hochschild's account which, though reflecting American experience, readily matches my own on this side of the Atlantic.

> To be efficient with whatever time they do have at home, many working parents try to go faster if for no other reason than to clear off some space in which to go slowly. They do two or three things at once . . . In their efficiency, they may inadvertently trample on the emotion-laden symbols associated with particular times of day or particular days of the week. They pack one activity closer to the next and disregard the 'framing' around each of them, those moments of looking forward or looking back

> on an experience, which heighten its emotional impact. They ignore the contribution that a leisurely pace can make to fulfillment, so that a rapid dinner, followed by a speedy bath, and a bedtime story for a child – if part of 'quality time' – is counted as 'worth the same' as a slower version of the same events. As time becomes something to 'save' at home as much as or even more than at work, domestic life becomes quite literally a second shift.[40]

The need is not for more imaginative and seductive initiatives masquerading as family-friendly policies which are actually devised to get more and more people to work longer and longer away from their families and community. The need is for a more fundamental reassessment of the way work and domestic life relate. Such a reassessment could have profound implications for the way men organise and live their lives.

As for the question of cost, that in turn is a question of values. We decide, or rather men for the most part decide, that it is worth spending billions on the production of weapons and the design and deployment of instruments of mass destruction. We decide to spend billions on a penal and welfare system which is a *reaction* to social and personal ills, a great many of which result from the persistent devaluation and neglect of individual and family priorities. The argument for the protection and the enhancement of the personal and the intimate is in constant danger of being dismissed on grounds of economic cost when it needs to be endorsed on grounds of human value.

At the heart of the crisis in masculinity is a problem with the reconciliation of the private and the public, the intimate and the impersonal, the emotional and the rational. Peter Marris, a sociologist with a particular interest in the tension between personal and public life, puts the issue squarely:

> The rationalism of scientific management denies the validity of personal affection and loyalties in most of the work that men do, while the idealisation of domesticity denies the validity of rational self-interest in a woman's management of her mothering. Men want the chance to be loving and women to be self-interested, so that both can find themselves in some meaningful structure of relationships. But each seems to threaten the other, as men fear that feminists want to drag the only relationships uncontaminated by buying and selling into the market-place of professional child care, wages for housework, and take-home fast foods; and women, that men, once again, are undermining sexual equality by their age-old romance with mothering.[41]

Out of the Crisis

Some months ago I was contacted by the wife of a middle-aged company director. Her husband was becoming unpredictable, irritable, was drinking heavily and on a number of occasions had been physically violent. I was sufficiently alarmed by her story to ask her to come and see me (she had adamantly refused to take any legal action, such as informing the police or taking out a barring order, insisting that her husband was ill and needed to see a doctor).

She dated the onset of the change in her husband to about twelve months previously. She attributed it to strain associated with a take-over bid for her husband's company, a bid which, after many difficulties and setbacks, had proved successful, leaving him a very wealthy man. She had met her husband when they were both university students – she studying languages, he accountancy. He was ambitious, bright and energetic. On qualification, he set up his own business which rapidly expanded, until the take-over by a major bank. They had four children, relatively close together, and when the youngest started school the wife returned to her work as a teacher. She described the marriage as happy but admitted that she did not feel she really knew her husband – or rather that he kept his emotions under a tight rein and avoided introspection. She doubted he would come and see me.

He did, however, respond to my invitation, possibly because I couched it in terms of needing information to help me help his wife. When he arrived in my office he exuded the air of a man in a hurry. He made it plain that time was at a premium. He answered questions tersely and to the point. He saw himself as the provider and protector of his family and insisted that he was a good father and that his wife had nothing to worry about. I learned that he was the youngest of five, that his father, a farmer, was over 60 years old when he was born and that he was never close to his mother. In the middle of the interview, he suddenly admitted that when he was growing up he had always felt that there was something odd about his family. No-one ever talked of feelings and he had always felt, as he put it, 'a goose amongst swans'. Of all the children he had the most drive and determination and was the only one to obtain a university education. But he spoke no more about it, insisted that he felt fine, assured me that there were no problems in his marriage, business or family life and left.

Some weeks later he telephoned my office, seeking an appointment. When he arrived, he seemed very different. He was flustered and ill at ease. He took an age to get going and then blurted out that he had discovered that his father was not his father nor his mother his mother. His real mother was his 'eldest sister', a woman some sixteen years older than he. He had, as yet, not learned the identity of his real father.

Following our first interview, he had gone to get his full birth certificate and discovered the identity of his mother. No father was stated on the certificate. When I asked why he had chosen to seek this information now, he replied that for some months he had wondered about his identity. At the time of the take-over, there had been much praise of his talents by his employees and by his new managing director and colleagues. He had again pondered the origins of these talents and felt uneasy when he considered what he termed his 'genetic inheritance' – the rural simplicity and homespun habits of his father and the lack of drive, initiative and educational flair exhibited by his mother and siblings. He began to feel depressed, started to drink heavily and to argue with his wife and children. At the end of this interview, he told me he had decided to search for his father.

I did not hear from him for several months. Then he rang and made an appointment. On this occasion he appeared relaxed and at ease. He talked calmly and with emotion. He had traced his father's family. From them he had discovered that his father was dead and the tragic details of what had happened. His father had killed himself at the age of 23 after making his mother, then a sixteen-year-old schoolgirl, pregnant. His father had been about to qualify as a doctor and was at his family home for the summer, where my patient's mother worked as a summer domestic. The pregnancy and suicide had been a major scandal. Members of his father's family were highly successful and politically powerful; his mother's poor and on the margins. His maternal grandparents sent their pregnant daughter away to England to have her child and when she returned made out that the child was theirs. He had lived this lie his entire adult life.

The importance for my patient of his learning the truth of his origins was illustrated by his demeanour and his behaviour. He said he felt for the first time 'authentic'. He believed that much of the ambition and energy that drove him to compete in business originated in his deep sense of insecurity and self-doubt, and that at last he could relax as he no longer had anything to prove. He still wanted to know more about his father – reassured that he had been talented, popular and ambitious, worried that he had taken advantage of his mother and might even have raped her. There were many questions he wanted to ask his mother, but never having been close to a person he had long believed to be an older sister, he was finding this difficult.

I have not seen this man since. But I received a letter from his wife indicating that he was very much improved, had not hit her since, and that their relationship was better than it had ever been.

The story illustrates so much about fathers – real, imagined and dead. For this man, the identity of his father was highly significant; he needed it to help make sense of himself. When he discovered his father, he was both reassured and disturbed – but despite the dramatic and ambiguous story he felt he could better cope with the reality of a father who might have committed a terrible crime than with the fantasy of a reliable father who was not a father at all. And yet, this man's biological father contributed nothing to him save half his genes, whereas the man he had taken to be his father, who in fact was his grandfather, had provided him with a home, an education and a start in life. So much is written about the importance of the mother, and understandably so. But our fears and fantasies, expectations and idealisations of fathers are rich, complex and formative too. We can be as shaped by the father we never had as by the father who is ever present. We can project onto a fantasy father our resentments and aspirations as we reach for and push away the father in reality. This man had two fathers – one of whom had stood by him and helped nurture and educate him. But until he himself had searched for and found his biological father, he had felt incomplete and alien.

Why had all of this come to a head at the time of his greatest business success? Perhaps the feelings of separatedness and isolation he had felt as a child had flooded back. He had become depressed and had lashed out at his wife. He had come as near as he had ever come to falling apart.

I began this book reflecting on the threat to the survival of men. I end it by reflecting on the survival of men and women struggling to protect their private, personal, intimate, domestic lives in the context of an increasingly voracious economic system. It is a struggle between the world of personal love, intimacy, empathy, magnanimity and self-sacrifice, and the terrible pressures of conspicuous consumption to achieve, possess, display. Thomas Lynch, an Irish-American poet who is also an undertaker – 'the last one to let you down', as his father, also an undertaker, was fond of saying – has observed of America in the late twentieth century that never have so many lives been lived with such little appreciation of what living is about. Never, for example, have so many young couples worked so hard to build and furnish their dream homes when, in fact, there is nobody to live in them. The babies are in daycare, the adolescents in summer camp and the elders in condominiums in Florida. And the adults are at work. Everything works better in this technologically stunning world, even the people, but nobody seems to know what for.[42]

The very social changes being aggravated and exacerbated by this distortion in priorities seem set to ensure that the current fractured relationship between men and women persists and even intensifies. The economic gap between rich and poor, healthy and sick, widens. The least well off financially are sucked more and more into a cycle of unemployment, poverty, separation, divorce, family breakdown, crime. The family is under intense strain from within and without. The links with violence have been well established. To those adults brought up in acrimonious and divided families at the hands of a violent father or a depressed mother, the urge to commit violence against figures in, and institutions of, authority is ever present. The personalities of many of our most vulnerable children are badly warped before they reach primary school. Projects for parents who have problems with their children are either poorly funded or non-existent. The cost of such psychological and social neglect is horrendous – violent adolescents expelled from school for disruptive behaviour, aggressive young males with time on their hands fathering and then leaving children, a growing tendency to resort to penal rather than political solutions.

We spend vast sums of money on killing machines and wonder why our youngsters are so aggressive and our young men so murderous. We insist that our children, from the earliest of years, familiarise themselves with the intricacies of human biology, yet we ensure that they learn little or nothing of human psychology until their own personalities are distorted beyond correction. And, rather than acknowledge the neglect and indifference we have shown towards structures such as marriage and family life, we resort to doubting and undermining their importance in the sum of human health and happiness.

Freud's legacy is a controversial one and his ultimate place in the history of ideas remains to be established. But his speculative hypothesis concerning female penis envy and male misogyny have served neither women nor men well. In so far as women have envied men it has been male power and autonomy that they have envied – and resented. In so far as men hate women it is in part at least because women represent a powerful and seemingly more biologically rooted and authentic vision of what life is about and in part because men know that they cannot survive without them. Men need women and children to be complete, to express their sexuality and humanity, to obtain that sense that everyone needs: the sense that one matters.

Mature male sexuality in turn is related to the success with which a son negotiates the separation from his mother and identification with his father. Such a development assumes there is a father there to be identified with. Finkelhor's reference to the 'widespread and conventional patterns of socialisation and cultural transmission' does not just apply to the pathology of the abuse of children by adult males. It refers to the warps and abnormalities in the values and behaviours which men in general and individual fathers in particular transmit and transfer to their sons. Cultures which exult in the belief in the intrinsic maleness of such values as control, indifference to feelings and a ruthless pursuit of power produce a psychopathic masculinity from which not merely women but many men turn away.

So where do we men go from here? First, we must acknowledge where we are. And where we are marks the beginning of the end of male control. That is the reality. As men we can deny it, struggle against it, project our frustrated and angry feelings against what we see as the source of our growing weakness, be it the individual women in our lives or the feminist movement in general. But if men insist on doing any or all of these things, then men are doomed. Acknowledge the end of patriarchal power and participate in the discussion of how the post-patriarchal age is to be negotiated and there is hope. And we can learn from women who, over the past century, have subjected the strained and unbalanced relationship between the public political world, from which they were largely excluded, and the private domestic world, in which they were largely immersed, to a vigorous and continuing analysis. Men must do the same. There are, thankfully, signs that this is indeed starting to happen, that men and women together are beginning to identify their true desires and needs and the real obstacles to their fulfilment. And men can do it. There is nothing intrinsically, innately, biologically incorrigible about male aggression and violence that means that the current ways in which men live their lives cannot be modified and changed. Such biological differences as exist between men and women are not of an order that casts in stone men as phallic supremacists, as sexual predators, as violent killers. Most men are not violent. But, as Joanna Bourke reminds us, most men can be made to be violent – by training and conditioning them to idealise war, to admire heroic martial figures, to hate the enemy, to love their country and identify with and support their comrades.[43] The very fact that being a killer depends less on one's genes and hormones and more on one's training and conditioning does mean that, given the right circumstances, women can be every bit as violent and murderous as men.

We need to introduce our children to an understanding of the ways their minds as well as their bodies work far earlier than we do. Ours is a culture which believes that from the earliest years it is important that children know something of human biology. But what of human psychology? We worry about what to tell our children about love and hate, tolerance and intolerance, friendship and bullying, romance and relationships. We earnestly demand that experts talk to them about drugs and alcohol, cannabis and Ecstasy, HIV and AIDS. Yet the courses we devise are uninspiringly described as civic instruction, health education or social biology and are stuck on to or within the curriculum in a haphazard and fragmented fashion. Not surprisingly, when it is suggested – usually in response to some crisis, real or imaginary – that a course or series of lectures be given on a controversial topic, such as homosexuality or AIDS or drug dependence, there is anxiety and dissent. What is needed is a proper, systematic and co-ordinated introduction to human psychology – the psychology of personality, the psychology of behaviour, the psychology of feelings, the psychology of individuals and groups, the psychology of memory and will and impulse control, the psychology of sexuality. It could begin in primary school and be taught as an examination subject in secondary education. We teach our children the history of war, but little of its psychology. We teach our children the relationship between states, but little of love and marriage, divorce and remarriage, heterosexuality and homosexuality. We teach our children the intricacies of the human body, but little of the functioning (and malfunctioning) of the human mind. We need to use the curriculum to teach our children the totality of having children – not just the biology of reproduction, but the psychology of human relationships. We need to start teaching our children how to be better men and women, better lovers and partners, better mothers and fathers.

We need to recognise that the private, personal, intimate domain of children and family and extended family and friendship and community is as valid and important and satisfying and fulfilling a world as the arena of power and achievement, status and money. Too often the talk is of the *demands* of family, the *costs* of children, the *frustrations* of parenthood, the *burdens* of family. For many parents, children have become an obstacle, a babysitting problem, a barrier to self-advancement and career promotion. Yet, as I have argued, the rewards of family life are substantial, in terms of health, satisfaction and happiness. 'You can attach the whole of moral philosophy to a commonplace private life', declared Montaigne, 'just as well as to one of richer stuff'. Or, as Alain de Botton observed in his splendid essay on the wise Frenchman, 'A virtuous, ordinary life, striving for wisdom but never far from folly, is achievement enough.'[44]

We need to rekindle in men a belief in the importance to them and to their children of fatherhood. For most men, to be a father will have a more positive impact on their health and happiness than career achievement. And, contrary to much popular opinion, fathers do matter. Fatherhood remains a central civilising force in every society. The responsibilities, opportunities, duties, emotional demands and rewards involved in being a father can and, in many cases, do help young males develop into mature, constructive and caring social beings.

I realise that in describing fatherhood and family life in this way I am at risk of dismissing the worth and value of all those men, and women too, who by reason of nature or choice do not become parents. Many gay men, for example, will never be fathers – although some do enter into heterosexual relationships to fulfil that role, while others campaign for the right of gay couples to adopt children or arrange to have a surrogate mother bear children for them. I have no firm views one way or another concerning the fitness or otherwise of gay or lesbian couples to be parents. But it does seem likely to me that some will prove very much more committed, concerned and caring parents than many heterosexual couples who conceive their offspring in a drunken or violent encounter and go on to be entirely unsuitable as parents. What is important is that men, straight and gay, take seriously their parental role.

Politicians must take much more seriously the impact of policies on marriage and the family. So much of politics concerns itself with the consequences of parental and family failure – educational failure, crime, violence, physical and mental ill health, isolation, lack of support for the elderly. Homeless children are frequently the product of fractured families or unhappy stepfamilies. And the demands of an entrepreneurial, capitalistic, individualistic economy exact their own price. The British working week is already the longest in Europe; how much worse can the time pressures of work on personal and family life become? More, much more, needs to be done to create a working environment that takes seriously the reality of family life, the need for parents, particularly mothers, to be able to take time out and re-enter the work arena with appropriate retraining, for greater job flexibility and for a taxation system which would support marriage and enable women to make a genuine choice between caring personally for their children during the preschool and school years and paying for professional childcare. But when it comes to the issue of professional childcare, those same politicians and the influential voices that support them will need to consider the increasing scarcity of people to fill other caring jobs in modern society – nurses, social workers, teachers, health visitors. Such a scarcity seems certain to make the necessary army of skilled and committed professional childcare professionals exceedingly difficult to recruit. The tasks of doing a job and caring for one's children are likely to lie heaviest on the shoulders of parents themselves. Politicians would do well to stop talking piously about the need for family-friendly work policies, flexible working hours and proper parental leave arrangements and start implementing them. Some two months before the birth of her son, Leo, Cherie Blair declared to an audience of lawyers: 'Our children need their male role models as well as their female ones'. Well said, and even better was her demand that men should start 'to challenge the assumption that the nurturing of children has nothing to do with them.'[45] The problem is that most governments, including the one led by her husband and Leo's father, Tony Blair, so arrange their working hours and choose their political priorities as to make it abundantly plain that the nurturing of children has nothing to do with them.

Unless men wake up to what is happening all around them they will find themselves in even greater trouble. The omens are not good. Richard Scase is but one of a number of social analysts who believes that current trends spell disaster for men. In his recently published book, *Britain Towards 2010*, Scase predicts that there will be more single persons, fewer children, persistently high rates of divorce and a 'churning' of partners (repeated changing rather than any consistent commitment).[46] Most of these single people will be male – one in three men will be living alone by 2010. Some one and a half million men will be permanently excluded from the workforce, either because of early retirement or because they just will not have the education and skills necessary for employment. And given the growing demand for skilled people able to work creatively and collaboratively rather than in a hierarchical, competitive and status-obsessed fashion, men may find themselves redundant in the job recruitment market.

Freud once asked what it was women wanted. As a man, I hesitate to answer but I nourish the suspicion that respect from men would figure high on any list of responses. And what do men want? Well, what I want as a man, and what I want for men, is that we become more capable of expressing the vulnerability and the tenderness and the affection we feel, that we place a greater value on love, family and personal relationships and less on power, possessions and achievement, and that we continue to place faith in wider social and communal values in so far as they enable and empower us all to live more generous and fulfilling lives. There is no need to create a 'new man' in the image of woman. There is a need for the 'old man' to re-emerge. Such a man employs his physical, intellectual and moral strength not to control others but to liberate himself, not to dominate but to protect, not to worship achievement but to enlist it in the struggle to find meaning and fulfilment. 'A man can't go out the way he came in,' says Willy Loman in *Death of a Salesman*, 'a man has got to add up to something'.[47] And he still can.

NOTES

CHAPTER 1

1 C.G. Jung, 'America facing its most tragic moment', *New York Times*, 19 September 1912. Reprinted in *C.G. Jung Speaking: Interviews and Encounters*, ed. W. McGuire and R.F.C. Hull, Thames & Hudson, London, 1978, p. 19.

2 United Nations Development Programme, *Human Development Report*, United Nations, New York, 1999, p. 225, Table 24.

3 A.E. Jukes, *Why Men Hate Women*, Free Association Books, London, 1994, pp. 300–1; S. Jefferies, *Anticlimax*, The Women's Press, London, 1990, pp.289–97; E. Kelly, 'The continuum of male violence', in *Women, Violence and Social Control*, J. Hanmer and M. Maynard, Macmillan, London, 1987, pp. 46–60.

4 G. Greer, *In the Psychiatrist's Chair*, BBC Radio 4, BBC, London, 1989.

5 J. Lacan, *Ecrits. A Selection*, Tavistock, London, 1977.

6 M. Maguire, *Men, Women, Passion and Power*, Routledge, London, 1995, p. 63.

CHAPTER 2

1 B.T. Lahn and K. Jegalian, 'The key to masculinity', *Scientific American*, 10, 2, (1999): 20–25.

2 J.M. Reinisch, M. Ziemba-Davis and S.A. Sanders, 'Hormonal contributions to sexually dimorphic behavioral development in humans', *Psychoneuroendocrinology*, 16, 1–3 (1991): 216.

3 S. Goldberg, *The Inevitability of Patriarchy*, Morrow, New York, 1973, p. 78.

4 G. Greer, *The Whole Woman*, Doubleday, London, 1999, p. 327.

5 T.N. Wiesel, 'Genetics and behavior' (editorial), *Science*, 264 (1994): 1647.

6 G. Giordano and M. Giusti, 'Hormones and psychosexual differentiation', *Minerva Endocrinologica*, 20, 3 (1995): 179.

7 D.B. Kelley, 'Sexually dimorphic behaviors', *Annual Review of Neurosciences*, 11 (1988): 225–51.

8 B.A. Gladue and J.M. Bailey, 'Aggressiveness, competitiveness and human sexual orientation', *Psychoneuroendocrinology*, 20, 5 (1995): 475–85.

9 L. Ellis, 'Developmental androgen fluctuations and the five dimensions of mammalian sex (with emphasis upon the behavioral dimension and the human species)', *Ethology and Sociobiology*, 3 (1982): 171–97; M. Hines, 'Prenatal gonadal hormones and sex differences in human behavior', *Psychological Bulletin*, 92 (1982): 56–80; J.M. Reinisch, 'Influence of early exposure to steroid hormones on behavioral development', in *Development in Adolescence: Psychological, Social and Biological Aspects*, ed. W.

Everaerd, C.B. Hindley, A. Bot and J.J. van der Werff Ten Bosch, Martinus Nijhoff, Boston, 1983, pp. 63–113.

10 E.P. Monaghan and S.E. Glickman, 'Hormones and aggressive behavior', *Behavioral Endocrinology*, ed. J.B. Becker, S.M. Breedlove and D. Crews, MIT Press, Cambridge, Mass., 1992, pp. 261–86.

11 A.A. Ehrhardt, H.F. Meyer-Bahlburg, L.R. Rosen, J.F. Feldman, N.P. Veridiano, E.J. Elkin and B.S. McEwen, 'The development of gender-related behavior in females following prenatal exposure to diethylbestrol (DES)', *Hormones and Behavior*, 23, 4, (1989): 526–41.

12 J. Money and A.A. Ehrhardt, *Man and Woman, Boy and Girl. The Differentiation and Dimorphism of Gender Identity from Conception to Maturity*. Johns Hopkins University Press, Baltimore, Maryland, 1972. A.A. Ehrhardt and H.F. Meyer-Bahlburg, 'Effects of prenatal sex hormones on gender-related behavior', *Science*, 211 (1981): 1312–18. R.G. Dittman, M.H. Kappes, M.E. Kappes, D. Borger, H. Stegner, R.H. Willis and H. Wallis, 'Congenital adrenal hyperplasia 1: gender-related behavior and attitudes in female patients and their sisters', *Psychoneuroendocrinology*, 15 (1990): 401–20.

13 S.A. Berenbaum and M. Hines, 'Early androgens are related to childhood sex-typed toy preferences', *Psychological Science*, 3 (1992): 203–6.

14 R. Bleier, *Science and Gender: A Critique of Biology and its Theories on Women*, The Athene Press, Oxford, 1984, pp. 99–101.

15 J.E. Griffin, 'Androgen resistance. The clinical and molecular spectrum', *New England Journal of Medicine*, 326 (1992): 611–18.

16 J. Imperato-McGinley, R.E. Peterson, T. Gautier and E. Sturla, 'Androgens and the evolution of male-gender identity among male pseudohermaphrodites with 5a-reductase deficiency', *New England Journal of Medicine*, 300 (1979):1233–7.

17 Ibid., p. 1235.

18 N. Heim and C. Hursch, 'Castration for sex offenders. Treatment or punishment?' *Archives of sexual behavior*, 8 (1979): 281–304.

19 P. Brain, 'Hormonal aspects of aggression and violence', in *Understanding and Preventing Violence*, Vol. I, ed. A. Reiss Jr, K. Miczek and J. Roth, National Academy Press, New York, 1994.

20 A. Roesler and E. Witztum, 'Treatment of men with paraphilia with a long-acting analogue of gonadotropin-releasing hormone', *New England Journal of Medicine*, 338, 1998: 416–22. A. Cooper and Z.E. Cernovsky, 'Comparison of cyproterone acetate (CPA) and leuprolide acetate (LHRH agonist) in a chronic pedophile: a clinical case study', *Biological Psychiatry*, 36 (1995): 269–72. F. Thibaut, B. Cordier and J.M. Kuhn, 'Gonadotrophin hormone releasing hormone agonist in cases of severe paraphilia: a lifetime treatment', *Psychoneuroendocrinology*, 21 (1996): 411–19.

21 Giordano and Giusti, 'Hormones'.

22 D. Simon, P. Preziosi, E. Barrett-Connor, M. Roger, M. Saint-Paul, J. Nahoul and K. Papoz, 'The influence of aging on plasma sex hormones in men', *American Journal of Epidemiology*, 135 (1992): 783–91.

23 K.N. Pike and P. Doerr, 'Age-related changes and inter-relationships between plasma testosterone, oestradiol and testosterone-binding globulin in normal adult males', *Acta Endocrinologica*, 74 (1973): 792–800.

24 J. Wilson and R. Herrnstein, *Crime and Human Nature*, Simon & Schuster, New York, 1985.

25 D. Simon, P. Preziosi, E. Barrett-Connor, M. Roger, M. Saint-Paul, J. Nahoul and K. Papoz, 'The influence of aging on plasma sex hormones in men: the Telecom study', *American Journal of Epidemiology*, 135 (1992): 783–91.

26 R. O'Carroll, C. Shapiro and J. Bancroft, 'Androgens, behavior and nocturnal erection in hypogonadal men: the effects of varying the replacement dose', *Clinical Endocrinology*, 23 (1985): 527–38.

27 R.A. Anderson, J. Bancroft and F.C.W. Wu, 'The effects of exogenous testosterone on sexuality and mood of normal men', *Journal of Clinical Endocrinology and Metabolism*, 75 (1992): 1503–7.

28 J. Archer, 'The influence of testosterone on human aggression', *British Journal of Psychology*, 82 (1991): 1–28.

29 J.M. Dabbs, Jr, S. Carr, R. Frady and J. Riad, 'Testosterone, crime and misbehavior among 692 male prison inmates', *Personality and Individual Differences*, 18 (1995): 627–33. T. Scaramella and W. Brown, 'Serum testosterone and aggressiveness in hockey players', *Psychosomatic Medicine*, 40 (1978): 262–3. A. Booth and J.M. Dabbs, Jr, 'Testosterone and men's marriages', *Social Forces*, 72 (1993): 463–77. A. Booth and D. Osgood, 'The influence of testosterone on deviance in adulthood', *Criminology*, 31 (1993): 93–117. J.M. Dabbs, Jr and R. Morris, 'Testosterone, social class and antisocial behavior in a sample of 4,462 men', *Psychological Sciences*, 3 (1990): 209–11. A. Mazur, 'Biosocial models of deviant behavior among army veterans', *Biological Psychology*, 41 (1995): 271–93.

30 W. Jeffcoate, N. Lincoln, C. Selby and M. Herbert, 'Correlation between anxiety and serum prolactin in humans', *Journal of Psychosomatic Research*, 29 (1986): 217–22.

31 H. Pope Jr and D. Katz, 'Psychiatric and medical effects of anabolic-androgenic steroid use', *Archives of General Psychiatry*, 51 (1994): 375–82.

32 E. Susman, C. Inoff-Germain, E. Nottelmann, D. Loriaux, G. Cutler, Jr. and G. Chrousos, 'Hormones, emotional dispositions and aggressive attributes of young adolescents', *Child Development*, 58 (1987): 1114–34.

33 C. Halpern, J. Udry, B. Campbell and C. Suchindran, 'Testosterone and pubertal development as predictors of sexual activity', *Psychosomatic Medicine*, 55

(1993): 436–47.
34 J. Constantino, D. Grosz, P. Saenger, D. Chandler, R. Nandi and F. Earls, 'Testosterone and aggression in children', *Journal of the American Academy of Child and Adolescent Psychiatry*, 32 (1993): 1217–22.
35 Anderson et al., 'Effects'.
36 A. Mazur and A. Booth, 'Testosterone and dominance in men', *Behavioral and Brain Sciences*, 21 (1998): 353–97.
37 A. Booth, C. Shelley, A. Mazur, G. Tharp and R. Kittok, 'Testosterone and winning and losing in human competition', *Hormones and Behavior*, 23 (1989): 556–71.
38 B. Campbell, M. O'Rourke and M. Rabow, 'Pulsatile response of salivary testosterone and cortisol to aggressive competition in young males'. Paper presented at the annual meeting of the American Association of Physical Anthropologists, Kansas City, Missouri, 1988. M. Elias, 'Serum cortisol, testosterone and testosterone-binding globulin responses to competitive fighting in human males', *Aggressive Behavior*, 7 (1981): 215–24.
39 A. Mazur, A. Booth and J.M. Dabbs, Jr, 'Testosterone and chess competition', *Social Psychology Quarterly*, 55 (1992): 70–7.
40 J. Fielden, C. Lutter and J.M. Dabbs, Jr, 'Basking in glory: testosterone changes in World Cup soccer fans', Psychology Department, Georgia State University, 1994.
41 R.E. Nisbett and D. Cohen, 'Men, honor and murder', *Scientific American*, 10,2 (1999): 18.
42 R.E. Nisbett and D. Cohen, *Culture of Honor: The Psychology of Violence in the South*, Westview Press, Boulder, Colorado, 1996.
43 J.M. Dabbs and R. Morris, 'Testosterone, social class and antisocial behavior in a sample of 4,462 men', *Psychological Science*, 1 (1990): 209–11.
44 D. Cohen, 'Shaping, channelling and distributing testosterone in social systems', *Behavioral and Brain Sciences*, 21, 3 (1998): 367.
45 R. Sapolsky, 'The trouble with testosterone', in *The Trouble with Testosterone and Other Essays*, Simon & Schuster, New York, 1997, p. 155.
46 Ibid., pp. 151–2.
47 Mazur and Booth, 'Testosterone', p.353.
48 J.M. Dabbs, Jr, 'Testosterone and the concept of dominance', *Behavioral and Brain Sciences*, 21, 3 (1998): 370–1. A.A. Berthold, 'Transplantation of testes' (1849), Trans. D.P. Quiring, *Bulletin of the History of Medicine*, 16 (1994): 399–401.
49 V. Grant, 'Dominance runs deep', *Behavioral and Brain Sciences*, 21 (1998): 376–7.
50 Archer, 'Influence of testosterone'.
51 J. Ehrenkranz, E. Bliss and M. Sheard, 'Plasma testosterone. Correlation with aggressive behavior and social dominance in men', *Psychosomatic Medicine*, 36 (1974): 469–73.
52 L.A. Jensen-Campbell, W.G. Graziano and S. West, 'Dominance, prosocial orientation and female preference: do nice guys really finish last?' *Journal of Personality and Social Psychology*, 68 (1995): 427–40. E.K. Sadalla, D.T. Kenrick and B. Vershure,

'Dominance and heterosexual attraction', *Journal of Personality and Social Psychology*, 52 (1987): 730–8. J.M. Townsend, 'Gender differences in mate preferences among law students', *Journal of Psychology*, 127 (1993): 507–28.

53 F. Purifoy and L. Koopmans, 'Androstenedione, testosterone and free testosterone concentrations in women of various occupations', *Social Biology*, 26 (1979): 179–88.

54 E. Cashdan, 'Hormones, sex and status in women', *Hormones and behavior*, 29 (1995): 354–66.

55 J.M. Dabbs Jr and M. Hargrove, 'Age, testosterone and behavior among female prison inmates', *Psychosomatic Medicine* (1999)

56 J.M. Dabbs Jr, R.B. Ruback, R.L. Frady, C.H. Hopper and D.S. Sgoutas, 'Saliva testosterone and criminal violence among women', *Personality and Individual Differences*, 9 (1988): 269–75.

57 Cashdan, 'Hormones'.

58 V. Grant, 'Maternal dominance and the conception of sons', *British Journal of Medical Psychology*, 67 (1994): 343–51. V. Grant, 'Sex of infant differences in mother–infant interaction: a reinterpretation of past findings', *Developmental Review*, 14 (1994): 1–26.

59 Grant, 'Dominance runs deep', p.377.

60 Booth and Dabbs Jr, 'Testosterone'.

61 Mazur and Booth, 'Testosterone', pp.361–2.

62 J. Batty, 'Acute changes in plasma testosterone levels and their relation to measures of sexual behavior in the male house mouse (*Mus musculus*)', *Animal Behavior*, 26 (1978): 349–57.

63 S. LeVay, 'A difference in hypothalamic structure between heterosexual and homosexual men', *Science*, 253 (1995): 1034–7. D.H. Hamer, S. Hu, V.L. Magnuson, N. Hu and A.M. Pattatucci, 'A linkage between DNA markers on the X chromosome and male sexual orientation', *Science*, 261 (1993): 321–7.

64 R. Blanchard, J.G. McConkey, V. Roper and B. Steiner, 'Measuring physical aggressiveness in heterosexual, homosexual and transsexual men', *Archives of Sexual Behavior*, 12 (1985): 511–24. B.A. Gladue, 'Aggressive behavioral characteristics, hormones and sexual orientation in men and women', *Aggressive Behavior*, 17 (1991): 313–26.

65 B.A. Gladue and J.M. Bailey, 'Aggressiveness, competitiveness and human sexual orientation', *Psychoneuroendocrinology*, 20 (1995): 475–87.

66 L. Gooren, 'The endocrinology of transsexualism: a review and commentary', *Psychoneuroendocrinology*, 15,1 (1990): 3–14.

67 Giordano and Giusti, 'Hormones'.

68 E.E. Maccoby and C.N. Jacklin, *The Psychology of Sex Differences*, Oxford University Press, London, 1975.

69 D.K. Kimura, 'Sex differences in the brain', *Scientific American*, 10 (1999): 28.

70 College Board, *College-bound Seniors* 1984–1985, College Board, Princeton, New Jersey, 1985. E.G.J. Moore and A.W. Smith, 'Sex and ethnic group differences in mathematics achievement: results from the National

Longitudinal Study', *Journal for Research in Mathematics Education*, 18 (1987): 25–36.

71 C.P. Benbow, 'Sex differences in mathematical reasoning ability in intellectually talented preadolescents: their nature, effects and possible causes', *Behavioral and Brain Sciences*, 2 (1988): 169–83.

72 C.P. Benbow and J.C. Stanley, 'Sex differences in mathematical ability: fact or artifact?' *Science*, 210 (1980): 1262–4.

73 Bleier, *Science and Gender*, p. 104.

74 J. McGlone, 'Sex differences in human brain asymmetry', *Behavior and Brain Sciences*, 3 (1980): 215–63.

75 M. Hines and R.A. Gorski, 'Hormonal influences on the development of neural asymmetries', in *The Dual Brain*, ed. F. Benson and E. Zaidel, The Guilford Press, London, 1985, pp.75–96.

76 C. de LaCoste-Utamsing and R.L. Holloway, 'Sexual dimorphism in human corpus callosum', *Science*, 216 (1982): 1431–2.

77 J. Baack and C. de LaCoste-Utamsing, 'Sexual dimorphism in fetal corpus callosum', *Society of Neurosciences Abstracts*, 8 (1982): 213.

78 S.G. Gould, 'Cardboard Darwinism', in *An Urchin in the Storm*, W.W. Norton & Co., New York, 1987.

79 E.O. Wilson, *On Human Nature*, Harvard University Press, Cambridge, Mass., 1978, p.125.

80 L. Tiger, *Men in Groups*, 2nd ed, Marion Boyars, London, 1984, p.182. A. Storr, *Human Aggression*, Penguin Books, Harmondsworth, Middlesex, 1968, p.88.

81 K. Lorenz, *On Aggression*, Methuen, London, 1966, p.209.

CHAPTER 3

1 T. Maden, 'Women as violent offenders and violent patients', in *Violence in Society*, ed. P. Taylor, Royal College of Physicians, London, 1993, Ch. 5, pp. 69–80.

2 R.E. Nisbett and D. Cohen, 'Men, honour and murder', *Scientific American*, 10, 2 (1999): 16–19.

3 P. Fusell, 'On war and the pity of war', *Guardian*, 1990: 25–6.

4 E. Stover and G. Peress, *The Graves: Srebrenica and Vukovar*, Scalo, Zurich, 1998, p. 182.

5 E.O. Wilson, *On Human Nature*, Harvard University Press, Cambridge, Mass. 1978, p. 114.

6 National Research Council Panel on the Understanding and Control of Violent Behavior, *Understanding and Preventing Violence*, National Academy Press, Washington, DC, 1993, p.2.

7 D. Walsh, 'Crime in Limerick', Anglo-Irish Encounter Conference, Limerick, 1998.

8 G. Mezey and S. Bewley, 'Domestic violence and pregnancy'. Editorial, *British Medical Journal*, 314 (1997): 1295.

9 World Bank, *World Development Report: Investing in Health*, Oxford University Press, Oxford, 1993, p. 50.

10 P.A. Hillard, 'Physical abuse in pregnancy', *Obstetrics and Gynecology*, 66 (1985): 185–90.

11 A.S. Helton, J. McFarlane and E.T. Anderson, 'Battered and pregnant: a prevalence study', *American Journal of Public Health*, 77 (1987): 1337–9. L.B. Norton, J.F.

Peipert, S. Zierler, B. Lima and L. Hume, 'Battering in pregnancy: an assessment of two screening methods', *Obstetrics and Gynecology*, 85 (1995): 321–5.
12 E. Stark, A. Flitcraft and W. Frazier, 'Medicine and patriarchal violence: the social construction of a "private" event', *International Journal of Health Services*, 9 (1979): 461–93.
13 D.C. Berrios and D. Grady, 'Domestic violence: risk factors and outcomes', *Western Journal of Medicine*, 155 (1991): 133–5.
14 J.A. Gazmarian, M. Adams, L.E. Saltzman, C.H. Johnson, F.C. Bruce, J.S. Marks, et al for PRAMS Working Group, 'The relationship between pregnancy intendedness and physical violence in mothers of newborns', *Obstetrics and Gynecology*, 85 (1995): 1031–8.
15 World Bank (1993), Ibid., p. 50.
16 M. Cheasty, A.W. Clare and C. Collins, 'Relation between sexual abuse in childhood and adult depression: case-control study', *British Medical Journal*, 316 (1998): 198–201.
17 D. Halperin, P. Bouvier, P.D. Jaffe, R-L. Mounod, C.H. Pawlak, J. Laederach, H.R. Wicky and F. Astie, 'Prevalence of child sexual abuse among adolescents in Geneva: results of a cross-sectional survey', *British Medical Journal*, 312 (1996): 1326–9.
18 J. Lalor, 'Study suggests culture of sexual aggression towards girls'. Report in the *Irish Times*, Friday, 13 November 1998: 7.
19 N. Walter, 'Three per cent of men say they're rapists', *Observer*, 18 January 1998: 1.
20 Home Office, *Domestic Violence: Findings from a New British Crime Survey Self-completion Questionnaire* (Home Office Research Study 191). Home Office, London, 1999.
21 L. Magdol, T.E. Moffitt, A. Caspi, D.L. Newman, J. Fagan and P.A. Silva, 'Gender differences in partner violence in a birth cohort of 21-year-olds: bridging the gap between clinical and epidemiological approaches', *Journal of Consulting and Clinical Psychology*, 65 (1997): 68–78.
22 C.T. Snowden, 'The nurture of nature: social, developmental and environmental controls of aggression', *Behavioral and Brain Sciences*, 21,3 (1998): 385.
23 C.W. Harlow, *Female Victims of Violent Crime*, Bureau of Justice Statistics, Washington, DC, 1991, p.4.
24 United States Centers for Disease Control and Prevention, *Morbidity and Mortality Weekly Report*, 43,8 (1994): 135.
25 O.M. Linaker, 'Dangerous female psychiatric patients: prevalences and characteristics', *Acta Psychiatrica Scandinavica*, 101 (2000): 67–72.
26 J. Waters, reported in the *Irish Times*, 12 January 1999, p. 14.
27 H. Johnson and V.F. Sacco, 'Researching violence against women: Statistics Canada's national survey', *Canadian Journal of Criminology*, 37 (1995): 281–304.
28 Australian Bureau of Statistics, *Women's Safety – Australia 1996*, Australia Bureau of Statistics, Canberra, 1996.
29 A.E. Jukes, *Men Who Batter Women*, Routledge & Kegan Paul,

London, 1999.
30 D. Edgar, *Men, Mateship and Marriage*, HarperCollins, Sydney, 1997, p. 65.
31 Jukes, *Men Who Batter Women*, p. 83.
32 N. Tinbergen, 'Of war and peace in animals and men', *Science*, 160 (1968): 1411–18.
33 K. Lorenz, 'Uber das Toten von Artgenossen', *Jahrbuch d. Max-Planck-Ges*, 1955, pp. 105–40.
34 K. Lorenz, *On Aggression*, Harcourt Brace, New York, 1963.
35 L. Tiger, *Men in Groups*, 2nd edn, Marion Boyars, New York, 1984, p. 182.
36 F. de Zulueta, *From Pain to Violence*, Whurr Publishers, London, 1993, p.32.
37 D. Morris, *The Naked Ape*, McGraw-Hill, New York, 1967. I. Eibl-Eibesfeldt, *On Love and Hate: The Natural History of Behavior Patterns*, trans. G. Strachan, Holt, Rinehart & Winston, New York, 1972. R. Ardrey, *The Territorial Imperative: A Personal Inquiry into the Animal Origins of Property and Nations*, Atheneum, New York, 1966. A. Storr, *Human Aggression*, Penguin Books, Harmondsworth, 1968. Wilson, *On Human Nature*.
38 P. Gay, *Freud: A Life of Our Times*, J.M. Dent & Sons, London, 1988, pp. 395–6.
39 S. Freud, *Beyond the Pleasure Principle*, Standard Edition of the Complete Works of Sigmund Freud, ed. J. Strachey, Hogarth Press and the Institute of Psychoanalysis, London, 1920, Vol. XVIII, p. 38.
40 S. Freud, *Civilization and Its Discontents*, ibid., Vol. XXI, pp. 118–19.
41 Freud, *Beyond the Pleasure Principle*, p. 24.
42 S. Freud, *New Introductory Lectures on Psychoanalysis* ibid., Vol. XXII, 1933.
43 N. Ferguson, *The Pity of War*, Allen Lane, London, 1998, pp. 357–8.
44 Ibid., p. 447.
45 S. Freud, *Why War?* Standard Edition, ed. J. Strachey, Hogarth Press and Institute of Psychoanalysis, London, 1939, Vol. XXII, pp. 214–15.
46 E. Fromm, *The Anatomy of Human Destructiveness*, Jonathan Cape, London, 1973.
47 H. Arendt, *On Violence*, Allen Lane, London, 1969, p. 64.
48 Fromm, *Anatomy*, p. 187.
49 I. Suttie, *The Origins of Love and Hate* (1935), Free Association Books, London, 1999, p. 15.
50 M. Rutter, 'A fresh look at "maternal deprivation"', in *The Development and Integration of Behaviour*, ed. P. Bateson, Cambridge, Cambridge University Press, 1991, pp. 331–74.
51 M. Daly and M. Wilson, 'Machismo', *Scientific American*, 10,2 (1999): 9–14.
52 R.J. Lifton, *The Nazi Doctors: A Study of the Psychology of Evil*, Macmillan, London, 1986, Ch. 19, pp. 418–29.
53 Ibid., p. 428.
54 R. Morgan, *The Demon Lover: On the Sexuality of Terrorism*, Methuen, London, 1985, p. 84.
55 S. Nechaev, *The Catechism of a Revolutionist*, 1869 quoted ibid.
56 C. Guevara, 'Socialism and Man in Cuba', quoted in foreword to *Reminiscences of the Cuban Revolutionary War*, Monthly

Review Press, New York, 1968.
57 B. Allen, *Rape Warfare: The Hidden Genocide in Bosnia-Herzegovina and Croatia*, University of Minnesota, Minneapolis, 1996.
58 Documents on British Foreign Policy 1919–1939 3rd series, VII, HMSO, London, 1954: 257–60. (Original text sent to the Foreign Office, 25 August 1939.)
59 Nisbett and Cohen, 'Men, honor and murder', pp. 18–19.
60 D. Hamburg, 'Human aggression', in *The Development and Integration of Behaviour*, ed. P. Bateson, Cambridge University Press, Cambridge, 1991, Ch. 17, pp. 419–57.
61 J. Demos, 'Child abuse in context: an historian's perspective', in *Past, Present and Personal: The Family and the Life Course in American History*, Oxford University Press, New York, 1986, pp. 68–91.
62 Ibid., p. 72.
63 Ibid., pp. 83–4.
64 Wilson, J. and Howell, J., 'Comprehensive strategy for serious, violent and chronic juvenile offenders' in *Serious, Violent and Chronic Juvenile Offenders*, ed. J. Howell, B. Krisberg, D. Hawkins and J. Wilson, Sage, London, 1995.
65 *Carnegie Quarterly*, 39, 1 (1994).
66 S. Asquith, personal communication, 1999.
67 Boswell, G., *Young and Dangerous – the backgrounds and careers of Section 53 offenders*, Avebury, Aldeshot, 1996.
68 G. Sereny, *Cries Unheard: Why Children Kill*, Henry Holt, New York, 1998. B. Morrison, *As If*, Granta Books, London, 1997.
69 J. Garbarino, *Lost Boys: Why Our Sons Turn Violent and How We Can Save Them*, Free Press, New York, 1999.
70 M. Meaney, quoted in 'Why the young kill', *Newsweek*, 3 May 1999: 81.
71 J. Bertrand, *Born to Win* (as told to Patrick Robinson), Bantam Books, Sydney, NSW, 1985, p. 136.
72 Lorenz, *On Aggression*, p. 243.
73 I. Reid, *Social Class Differences in Britain*, 3rd edn, Fontana Press, London, 1989, p. 385.
74 J. Updike, *Golf Dreams*, Penguin, London, 1998, p. 125.
75 National Research Council, *Understanding . . . Violence*, p. 358.
76 D.P. Farrington, L. Gallagher, R.J. St Leger Morley and D.J. West, 'Are there any successful men from criminogenic backgrounds?' *Psychiatry*, 51 (1988): 116–30.
77 J.S. Milner, K.R. Robertson and D.L. Rogers, 'Childhood history of abuse and child abuse potential', *Journal of Family Violence*, 5 (1990): 15–34.
78 Monahan, J. 'The Causes of Violence' in *Drugs and Violence in America*, ed. U.S. Sentencing Commission, Government Printing Office, Washington, D.C., pp. 77–85.
79 N. Edley and M. Wetherell, *Men in Perspective: Practice, Power and Identity*. Prentice-Hall Harvester Wheatsheaf, London, 1995.

CHAPTER 4

1 J. Strouse, *Alice James: A Biography*, Jonathan Cape, London, 1980, p. 101.
2 A.D. Wood, '"The fashionable diseases". Women's complaints

and their treatment in nineteenth-century America', *Journal of Interdisciplinary History*, 4,1 (1973): 25–52.
3 E.H. Clark, *Sex in Education: or a Fair Chance for Girls*, Boston, 1878.
4 W.P. Dewees, *A Treatise on the Diseases of Females*, 17.14 Philadelphia, 1843.
5 W.H. Byford, *A Treatise on the Chronic Inflammation and Displacements of the Unimpregnated Uterus*, Philadelphia, 1864, pp. 22–44.
6 J. Sadgrove, 'What makes women sick?' *Lancet*, 346 (1995): 890.
7 P. Horn, 'Maternal mortality', in *Women in the 1920s*, Alan Sutton Publishing, Stroud, 1995.
8 M. Hall, *Commentaries on Some of the Views Imparted of the Diseases of Females*, London, 1827.
9 I. Irwell, 'The competition of the sexes and its results', *American Medical Bulletin*, 10 (1896): 319.
10 *Lancet*, 30 March 1867.
11 G. Engelmann, *The American Girl of Today: Modern Education and Functional Health*, Washington, 1900, pp. 9–10.
12 K. Dalton, 'Menstruation and examinations', *Lancet*, 2 (1968): 1386–8.
13 C. Smith-Rosenberg and C. Rosenberg, 'The female animal: medical and biological views of woman and her role in 19th century America', *Journal of American History*, 60 (1973): 332–56.
14 H. Maudsley, in the *Fortnightly Review*, 15 (1874): 467.
15 B. Harrison, 'Women's health and the women's movement in Britain: 1840–1940', in *Biology, Medicine and Society*, ed. C. Webster, Cambridge University Press, London, 1981, pp. 206–7.
16 Board of Regents, University of Wisconsin, *Annual Report for the Year Ending September 30 1877*, Madison, Wisconsin, 1877.
17 C.F. Taylor, 'Emotional prodigality', *The Dental Cosmos*, July 1879, pp. 4–11.
18 H. James, Sr, in *Putnam's Monthly*, 1 March 1853, pp. 279–88.
19 Strouse, *Alice James*.
20 G.M. Beard, *American Nervousness*, G.P. Putnam & Sons, New York, 1881.
21 S. Wessely, 'Old wine in new bottles: neurasthenia and ME', *Psychological Medicine*, 20 (1990): 35–53.
22 A. James, *The Diary of Alice James*, ed. L. Edel, Northeastern University Press, Boston, Mass., 1964, pp. 206–7.
23 Ibid., p. 207.
24 J. Critchley, quoted in D. Orr, 'Take a good look at yourself', *Independent* (*The Friday Review*), 4 June 1999: 5.
25 C. Moynihan, 'Testicular cancer: the psychosocial problems of patients and their relatives', *Cancer Survey*, 6 (1987): 477–510.
26 C. Moynihan, 'Theories of masculinity', *British Medical Journal*, 317 (1998): 1072–5.
27 M. Kaplan and G. Marks, 'Appraisal of health risks: the roles of masculinity, femininity and sex', *Social Health and Illness*, 17 (1995): 206–21.
28 Moynihan, 'Theories'.
29 C. Mitchel, 'Relationship of femininity, masculinity and gender

to attribution of responsibility', *Sex Roles*, 16 (1987): 151–63.

30 F. Korzenny, 'AIDS communication, beliefs, and behaviours', paper presented at the symposium on Science Communication: Environment and Health Research, University of Southern California, Los Angeles, 1988.

31 Contraception Education Service, *Use of Family Planning Services*, Family Planning Association, London, 1998.

32 A. Prince and A.L. Bernard, 'Sexual behaviors and safer sex practices of college students on a commuter campus', *Journal of the American College Health*, 47 (1998): 11–21. G. Yamey, 'Sexual and reproductive health: what about boys and men?' *British Medical Journal*, 319 (1999): 1315–16.

33 K. Dunnell, 'Are we healthier?' in *The Health of Adult Britain*, ed. J. Charlton and M. Murphy, Vol 2, Government Statistical Service, HMSO, London 1997, Ch. 25, p. 174.

34 A.R.P. Walker, 'Women – how far still to go?' *Journal of the Royal Society of Medicine*, 92, 2 (1999): 57–9.

35 *United Nations Human Development Report*, Oxford University Press, New York, 1966, pp. 135–7.

36 A. Booth, D.R. Johnson and D.A. Granger, 'Testosterone and men's health', *Journal of Behavioral Medicine*, 22,1 (1998): 1–19.

37 J.M. Dabbs, 'Testosterone and occupational achievement', *Social Forces*, 70 (1992): 813–24.

38 I. Joung, J. Mackenback, K. Stronks, J. van de Mheen and F. van Poppel, 'The contribution of intermediary factors to marital status differences in self reported health', *Journal of Marriage and the Family*, 59 (1997): 476–90.

39 J.M. Dabbs and R. Morris, 'Testosterone, social class and antisocial behavior in a sample of 4,462 men', *Psychological Sciences*, 3 (1990): 209–11.

40 V. Chandra, M. Szklo, R. Goldberg and J. Tonascia, 'The impact of marital status on survival after an acute myocardial infarct', *American Journal of Epidemiology*, 117 (1983): 320–5.

41 H. Carter and P. Glick, *Marriage and Divorce: A Social and Economic Study*, Harvard University Press, Cambridge, Mass., 1970.

42 M. Koskenvuo, J. Kaprio and S. Sarna, 'Causes of specific mortality by marital status and social class', *Journal of Chronic Disease*, 33 (1980): 95–106.

43 C.M. Parkes, B. Benjamin and R.G. Fitzgerald, 'Broken heart: a statistical study of increased mortality among widowers', *British Medical Journal*, 1 (1969): 740–3.

44 C.F. Mendes de Leon, A.W.P.M. Appels, F.W.J. Otten and E.G.W. Shouten, 'Risk of mortality and coronary heart disease by marital status in middle-aged men in the Netherlands', *International Journal of Epidemiology*, 21 (1992): 46–466.

45 A.V. Horwitz and H.R. White, 'Becoming married, depression and alcohol problems among the young', *Journal of Health and Social Behavior*, 32 (1991): 221–37.

46 M.T. Temple, K.M. Fillmore, E. Hartka, B. Johnstone, E.V. Leino and M. Motoyoshi, 'The collaborative alcohol-related longitudinal project. A meta-analysis of changes in marital and employment status as predictors of alcohol consumption on a typical occasion', *British Journal of Addiction*, 86 (1991): 1269–81.
47 A. Rosengren, H. Wedel and L. Wilhelmsen, 'Marital status and mortality in middle-aged Swedish men', *American Journal of Epidemiology*, 129, 1 (1989): 54.
48 D.A. Leon, *Longitudinal Study: Social Distribution of Cancer 1971–1975*, OPCS LS Series, no. 3, HMSO, London, 1988. A.J. Fox and P.O. Goldblatt, *Longitudinal Study: Socio-demographic Mortality Differentials 1971–1975*, OPCS LS Series no. 1, HMSO, London, 1982.
49 J.S. Goodwin, W.C. Hunt, C.R. Key and J.M. Samet, 'The effect of marital status on stage, treatment and survival of cancer patients', *Journal of the American Medical Association*, 258,21 (1987): 3125.
50 W. Gove, M. Hughes and C.B. Style, 'Does marriage have positive effects on the psychological well-being of the individual?' *Journal of Health and Social Behavior*, 24 (1983): 122–31.
51 D. Jewell, 'Adult life', in *Men's Health*, ed. T. O'Dowd and D. Jewell, Oxford University Press, Oxford, 1998, Ch.3, pp. 46–8.
52 The NHS Health Advisory Service, *Suicide Prevention: the Challenge Confronted*, HMSO, London, 1999.
53 R. Desjarlais, L. Eisenberg, B. Good and A. Kleinman, *World Mental Health: Problems and Priorities in Low-Income Countries*, Oxford University Press, Oxford, 1995.
54 E. Isometsa, M. Henriksson, M. Marttunen, M. Heikkinen, H. Aro, K. Kuoppasalmi and J. Lonnqvist, 'Mental disorders in young and middle-aged men who commit suicide', *British Medical Journal*, 310 (1995): 1366–7.
55 A.D. Lesage, R. Boyer, F. Grunberg, C. Vanier, R. Morissette, C. Menard-Buteau and M. Loyer, 'Suicide and mental disorders: a case-control study of young men', *American Journal of Psychiatry*, 151 (1994): 1063–8.
56 C.L. Rich, D. Young and R.C. Fowler, 'San Diego suicide study: young v. old subjects', *Archives of General Psychiatry*, 43 (1986): 577–82.
57 E. Fombonne, 'Suicidal behaviours in vulnerable adolescents: time trends and their correlates', *British Journal of Psychiatry*, 173 (1998): 154–9.
58 H. Hendin, *Suicide in America*, W.W. Norton, New York, 1999.
59 The Samaritans, *Young Men Speak Out*, The Samaritans, London, 1999.
60 Ibid., p. 3.
61 Jewell, 'Adult Life', p. 50.
62 D.J. Levinson, C.N. Darrow, E.B. Klein, M.H. Levinson and B. McKee, *The Seasons of a Man's Life*, Ballantine Books, New York, 1978, p. 335.
63 A.P. Bell and M.S. Weinberg, *Homosexualities: A Study of Diversity among Men and Women*, Mitchell Beazley, London, 1978, p. 175.
64 D. Ornish, *Love and Survival*,

Vermilion, London, 1999.
65 L.F. Berkman and S.L. Syme, 'Social networks, host resistance and mortality: a nine year follow-up study of Alameda County residents', *American Journal of Epidemiology*, 109 (1979): 186–204.
66 G.A. Kaplan, J.T. Salonen, R.D. Cohen, et al, 'Social connections and mortality from all causes and from cardiovascular disease: prospective evidence from eastern Finland', *American Journal of Epidemiology*, 128 (1984): 370–80.
67 B.W. Penninx, T. van Tilburg, D.M. Kriegsman, et al, 'Effects of social support and personal coping resources on mortality in older age: the Longitudinal Aging Study Amsterdam', *American Journal of Epidemiology*, 146 (1997): 510–19.
68 T.E. Oxman, D.H. Freeman, Jnr and E.D. Manheimer, 'Lack of social participation or religious strength and comfort as risk factors for death after cardiac surgery in the elderly', *Psychosomatic Medicine*, 57 (1995): 5–15.
69 Ornish, p. 24.
70 D. Gilmore, *Manhood in the Making: Cultural Concepts of Masculinity*, Yale University Press, London, 1990, pp. 10–12.
71 N. Mailer, *Armies of the Night*, New American Library, New York, 1968, p. 25.
72 Gilmore, *Manhood*, p. 19.
73 Central Statistics Office, *Statistical Bulletin*, Dublin, December 1998.
74 Higher Education Statistics Agency, Cheltenham, 1999.
75 M. Baxter, *Women in Advertising*, Institute of Practitioners in Advertising, London, 1990.
76 J. O'Connor, 'Women making a difference? Reflections on the glass ceiling', paper read to the Irish Medical Organisation annual conference, Killarney, 9 April 1999.
77 Central Statistics Office, *Statistical Bulletin*, Dublin, December 1998.
78 L. Brooks, 'Some are more equal than others', *Guardian* G2, 11 November 1999: 2.
79 L. Hodge, 'It's time for women to turn the tables', *Independent*, Education Supplement, 11 November 1999: 7.
80 J.C. Mason, 'Women at work: knocking on the glass ceiling', *Management Review*, 82 (1993): 5.
81 P.J. Ohlott, M.N. Ruderman and C.D. McCauley, 'Gender differences in managers' development job experiences', *Academy of Management Journal*, 37 (1994): 46–67.
82 C.M. Dominguez, 'Women at work: knocking on the glass ceiling', *Management Review*, 31 (1992): 385–92.
83 S.B. Garland, 'How to keep women managers on the corporate ladder', *Business Week*, 3329 (1991): 64.
84 M. Brennan, 'Marriage, gender influence and career advancement for chemists', *Chemical and Engineering News*, 70 (1992): 46–51.
85 N.D. Marlow, E. Marlow and V.A. Arnold, 'Career development and women managers: does "one size fit all?"' *Human Resource Planning*, 18 (1995): 38–50.
86 O'Connor, 'Women making a

difference?' pp. 11–15.

87 *United Nations Human Development Report*, Oxford University Press, New York, 1999, p. 80.

88 A. Roddick, 'Fairness not equality', *Newsweek*, 18 May 1998: 23.

89 *United Nations Human Development Report*, Oxford University Press, New York, 1996, p. 52.

90 A.R. Hochschild, *The Time Bind: When Work Becomes Home and Home Becomes Work*, Henry Holt, New York, 1997.

91 'Superwoman squashed on the glass ceiling', *Sunday Times*, 16 January 2000. Interview: Eleanor Mills meets Aisling Sykes.

92 F.M. Andrews and S.B. Withey, *Social Indicators of Well-being: Americans' Perception of Life Quality*, Plenum Press, New York, 1976, p. 124. A. Campbell, P.E. Converse and W.I. Rodgers, *The Quality of American Life*, Russell Sage, New York, 1976, pp. 380–1.

93 R.E. Lane, *The Loss of Happiness in Market Democracies*, Yale University Press, New Haven, Conn., 2000, p. 336.

CHAPTER 5

1 S. Farrar, in the *Sunday Times*, 10 January 1999.

2 C. Smith-Rosenberg and C. Rosenberg, 'The female animal: medical and biological views of woman and her role in nineteenth-century America', *Journal of American History*, 60 (1973): 332–56.

3 W.D. Haggard, 'Abortion: accidental, essential, criminal', address before the Nashville Academy of Medicine, Nashville, Tennessee, 4 August 1898, quoted in Smith-Rosenberg and Rosenberg, 'The female animal'.

4 B. Harrison, 'Women's health and the woman's movement', in *Biology, Medicine and Society*, ed. C. Webster, Cambridge University Press, Cambridge, 1981, Ch. 1, pp. 60–72.

5 Ibid., p. 64.

6 S. D'Cruze, 'Women and the family', in *Women's History: Britain 1850–1945. An Introduction*, ed. J. Purvis, UCL Press, London, 1995, Ch. 3, p. 56

7 G. Greer, 'Contraception – 1972', in *The Madwoman's Underclothes*, Picador, London, 1986, pp. 105–8.

8 A. Prince and A.L. Bernard, 'Sexual behaviors and safer sex practices of college students on a commuter campus', *Journal of American College Health*, 47 (1998): 11–21.

9 Centers for Disease Control and Prevention, 'Increases in unsafe sex and rectal gonorrhoea among men who have sex with men, San Francisco 1994–1997', *Journal of the American Medical Association*, 281 1999: 696–707.

10 C. AbouZahr and E. Ahman, 'Unsafe abortion and ectopic pregnancy', in *Health Dimensions of Sex and Reproduction*, ed. C.J.L. Murray and A.D. Lopez, Harvard University Press, Cambridge, Mass., 1998, Ch. 8, p. 277.

11 C.F. Westoff and L.H. Ochoa, *Demographic and Health Surveys. Unmet Need and the Demand for Family Planning*. Comparative studies, 5. Institute for Resource Development/Macro International Inc., Columbia, Maryland, 1991.

12 S.K. Henshaw and K. Kost,

'Abortion patients in 1994–95: characteristics and contraceptive use', *Family Planning Perspectives*, 28 (1996): 140–58.

13 G. Yamey, 'Sexual and reproductive health: what about boys and men?' *British Medical Journal*, 319 (1999): 1315–16.

14 E.C. Small and R.N. Turskov, 'A view of artificial insemination', *Advances in Psychosomatic Medicine*, 12 (1985): 105–23. H. Waltzer, 'Psychological and legal aspects of artificial insemination (AID): an overview', *American Journal of Psychotherapy*, 36 (1982): 91–102.

15 A.F. Guttmacher, 'Artificial insemination', *Annals of the New York Academy of Science*, 97 (1962): 623.

16 R. Snowden and E. Snowden, *The Gift of a Child*, Allen & Unwin, London, 1984.

17 British Medical Association, 'Annual Report of the Council (1973) Report of the Panel on Human Artificial Insemination', Appendix V, *British Medical Journal (Suppl.)*, 2 (1973): 3–5.

18 *Report of the Committee of Inquiry into Human Fertilisation and Embryology* (The Warnock Report) HMSO, London, 1984, recommendation no. 13, p. 82.

19 P. Petersen and A.T. Teichmann, 'Our attitude to fertilization and conception', *Journal of Psychosomatic Obstetrics and Gynaecology*, 3 (1984): 59–65.

20 The Warnock Report, para 4. 12, p. 21.

21 D. Callahan, 'Bioethics and fatherhood', *Utah Law Review*, 735 (1992).

22 R.J. Edelmann, 'Psychological aspects of insemination by donor', *Journal of Psychosomatic Obstetrics and Gynaecology*, 10 (1989): 3–13.

23 D. van Berkel, L. van der Veen, I. Kimmel and E. te Velde, 'Differences in the attitudes of couples whose children were conceived through artificial insemination by donor in 1980 and in 1996', *Fertility and Sterility*, 71, 2 (1999): 226–31.

24 A. Brewaeys, S. Golombok, N. Naaktgeboren, J.K. de Bruyn and E.V. van Hall, 'Donor insemination: Dutch parents' opinions about confidentiality and donor anonymity and the emotional adjustment of their children', *Human Reproduction*, 12, 7 (1997): 1591–7.

25 S. Golombok, A. Brewaeys, R. Cook, M.T. Giavazzi, D. Guerra, A. Mantovani, E. van Hall, P.G. Crosignani and S. Dexeus, 'The European study of assisted reproduction families: family functioning and child development', *Human Reproduction*, 11, 10 (1996): 2324–331.

26 C. Mihill, 'UK fertility doctors rule out test tube babies for older women because of fears for children's welfare', *Guardian*, 20 July, 1993.

27 B. Pedersen, A.F. Nielsen and J.G. Lauritsen, 'Attitudes and motivations of sperm donors in relation to donor insemination', *Ugeskr Laeger*, 157 (1995): 4462–5.

28 N. Farley, 'The sperm donor', *The Times*, Section 3 (1999): 37.

29 M. Hull, 'Ethics of egg and sperm donation', letter, *The Times* Thursday, 19 August 1999: 23.

30 A. Baran and R. Pannor, *Lethal Secrets: The Psychology of Donor Insemination, Problems and Solutions*, Amistad Press, New York, 1993.

31 M. Morton and M.A. Irving, 'Common questions that arise at adoption', in *Secrets in the Genes: Adoption, Inheritance and Genetic Disease*, ed. O. Turnberry, British Agencies for Adoption and Fostering, London, 1995, pp. 166–75.

32 R. Landau, 'Secrets, anonymity and deception in donor insemination: a genetic, psychosocial and ethical critique', *Social Work in Health Care*, 28, 1 (1998): 75–89.

33 P. Turnpenny, 'Introduction', in *Secrets in the Genes* ed. Turnpenny, pp. 1–8.

34 C. Bennett, 'Every sperm has a past', *Guardian*, 29 July 1999, p. 5.

35 Baran and Pannor, *Lethal Secrets*.

36 S. Michie and T. Marteau, 'Knowing too much or knowing too little. Psychological questions raised for the adoption process by genetic testing', in *Secrets in the Genes*, ed. Turnberry, pp. 166–75.

37 T. Hedgley, 'Should sperm donors be traceable?' *Guardian*, Saturday Review, 11 September 1999: 2.

38 B.D. Whitehead, *The Divorce Culture*, Alfred A. Knopf, New York, 1996, p. 146.

39 J. Mattes, *Single Mothers by Choice: A Guidebook for Single Women Who Are Considering or Have Chosen Motherhood*, Times Books, New York, 1994, p. 156.

40 K.R. Daniels and K. Taylor, 'Secrecy and openness in donor insemination', *Politics Life Sciences*, 12 (1993): 155.

41 K.R. Daniels, G.M. Lewis and W. Gillett, 'Telling donor insemination offspring about their conception: the nature of couples' decision-making', *Social Science and Medicine*, 40, 9 (1995): 1213–20.

42 Bennett, 'Every sperm has a past'.

43 C.V. Frost, H. Moss and R. Moss, *Helping the Stork: The Choices and Challenges of Donor Insemination*, Macmillan, New York, 1997.

44 M. Warnock, *A Question of Life: The Warnock Report on Human Fertilisation and Embryology*, Blackwell, Oxford, 1984, p. 11.

45 C. Strong, *Ethics in Reproductive and Perinatal Medicine*, Yale University Press, New Haven, Conn., 1997, pp. 86–97.

46 *Regulation of Assisted Human Reproduction Bill*, introduced by M. Henry, Government Publications Office, Dublin, 1999.

47 M. Henry, personal communication, 1999.

48 J. Savulescu, 'Should we clone human beings? Cloning as a source of tissue for transplantation', *Journal of Medical Ethics*, 25 (1999): 87–95.

49 J. Burley and J. Harris, 'Human cloning and child welfare', *Journal of Medical Ethics*, 25 (1999): 108–13.

50 J.P. Kassirer and N.A. Rosenthal, 'Should human cloning research be off limits?' *New England Journal of Medicine*, 338, 13 (1998): 905–6.

51 R. Winston, editorial: 'The promise of cloning for human medicine', *British Medical Journal*, 314 (1997): 913–14.

52 J.D. Watson, 'The future of

asexual reproduction', *Intellectual Digest*, October 1971: 69–74.

53 Ibid., p. 73.

54 R. Williamson, 'Human reproductive cloning is unethical because it undermines autonomy: commentary on Savulescu', *Journal of Medical Ethics*, 25 (1999): 96–7.

55 C. Dyer, 'Whose sperm is it anyway?' *British Medical Journal*, 313 (1996): 837.

56 E. Corrigan, E. Mumford and M.G.R. Hull, 'Posthumous storage and use of sperm and embryos: survey of opinion of treatment centres', *British Medical Journal*, 313 (1996): 24.

57 NIH Consensus Development Panel on Impotence, 'Impotence', *Journal of the American Medical Association*, 270 (1993): 83–90. P. Nettelbladt and N. Uddenberg, 'Sexual dysfunction and sexual satisfaction in 58 married Swedish men', *Journal of Psychosomatic Research*, 23 (1979): 141–7.

58 'Just how safe is sex?' *Newsweek*, 22 June 1968: 42.

59 J. Warden, 'Viagra unlikely to be prescribed by GPs in Britain', *British Medical Journal*, 317 (1998): 234.

60 J. Bressan, 'Hard and true facts on Viagra', *Medicine Weekly*, 20 October 1999: 36.

61 'Sexual chemistry', *Focus Magazine*, 22 August 1998: 31.

62 G. Greer, *The Whole Woman*, Doubleday, London, 1999, p. 181.

63 E.S. Person, 'Male sexuality and power' (1986), in *The Sexual Century*, ed. E.S. Person, Yale University Press, New Haven, Conn., 1999, Ch. 18, p. 316.

64 R. English, 'I lost everything after bungled sex operation', *Express*, 24 November 1998: 7.

65 C. Dyer, '£3m claim over penis operation', *Guardian*, 24 November 1998: 5.

66 P. Kedem, M. Mikulincer and Y.E. Nathanson, 'Psychological aspects of male infertility', *British Journal of Medical Psychology*, 63 (1990): 73–80.

67 L.P. Salzer, *Infertility: How Couples Can Cope*, G.K. Hall, Boston, Mass., 1986.

68 S. Irvine, E. Cawood, D. Richardson, E. MacDonald and J. Aitken, 'Evidence of deteriorating semen quality in the United Kingdom birth cohort study in 577 men in Scotland over 11 years', *British Medical Journal*, 312 (1996): 467–70. L. Bujan, A. Mansart, F. Ponteonnier and R. Mieusset, 'Time series analysis of sperm concentration in fertile men in Toulouse, France between 1977 and 1992', *British Medical Journal*, 312 (1996): 471–2.

69 E. Carlsen, A. Giwerman, N. Keiding and N.E. Skakkeback, 'Evidence of decreasing quality of semen during the past 50 years', *British Medical Journal*, 305 (1992): 609–13.

70 World Health Organisation Task Force on Methods for the Regulation of Male Infertility, 'Contraceptive efficacy of testosterone-induced azoospermia in normal men', *Lancet*, 336 (1990): 955–9.

71 Ministry of Environment and Energy, Denmark, *Male Reproductive Health and Environmental Chemicals with Estrogenic Effects*, Danish Environmental Protection Agency,

Copenhagen, 1995.
72 D.M. de Krester, 'Declining sperm counts', *British Medical Journal*, 312 (1996): 457–8.
73 J.A. Thomas, 'Falling sperm counts', *Lancet*, 346 (1995): 635.
74 H.J. Menger, 'Sexual revolution and sperm count', letter to *British Medical Journal*, 308 (1994): 1440–1.
75 R. Baker, 'The brave new world of sexual relations', *Independent* Weekend Review, 8 May 1999: 7.

CHAPTER 6

1 C. Pateman, *The Sexual Contract*, Cambridge University Press, Cambridge, 1988, pp. 77–92
2 P. Aries, *Centuries of Childhood*, Jonathan Cape, London, 1960.
3 L. Stone, *The Family, Sex and Marriage in England 1500–1800*, Weidenfeld & Nicolson, London, 1977, pp. 652–3.
4 J. Demos, *Past, Present and Personal: The Family and the Life Course in American History*, Oxford University Press, New York, 1986.
5 Ibid., p. 46.
6 P. Laslett, *Family Life and Illicit Love in Earlier Generations*, Cambridge University Press, 1977.
7 A. Burgess, *Fatherhood Reclaimed: The Making of the Modern Father*, Vermilion, London, 1997, p. 55.
8 J. Tosh, *A Man's Place: Masculinity and the Middle Class Home in Victorian England*, Yale University Press, New Haven and London, 1999.
9 Ibid., p. 6.
10 Demos, J., (1986), Ibid., p. 58.
11 Demos, J., Ibid., p. 57.
12 J. Bourke, 'Family values seminar', *Cusp Review*, Autumn 1997: 10–11.
13 Demos, *Past, Present and Personal*, p. 58.
14 Burgess, *Fatherhood Reclaimed*, p. 73.
15 D. Blankenhorn, *Fatherless America*, HarperPerennial, New York, 1996, p. 15.
16 D. Yankelovich, 'How changes in the economy are reshaping American values', in *Values and Public Policy*, ed. H.J. Aaron, T.E. Mann and T. Taylor, Brookings Institute, Washington, DC, 1994, p. 34.
17 'Home sweet home: the family', *Economist*, 9 September 1995: 21.
18 *Social Trends*, 29, Government Statistical Service, London, 1999: 42.
19 *Daily Telegraph*, 24 June 1998.
20 *The Times*, 24 June 1998.
21 *Bright Futures: Promoting Children and Young People's Mental Health*, Mental Health Foundation, London, 1999.
22 M. Richards and M. Dyson, *Separation, Divorce and the Development of Children: A Review*, Child Care and Development Group, University of Cambridge, 1982.
23 N.R. Butler and J. Golding, *From Birth to Five: A Study of the Health and Behaviour of Britain's Five Year Olds*, Pergamon, Oxford, 1986.
24 J.W.B. Douglas, 'Early disturbing events and later enuresis', in *Bladder Control and Enuresis*, ed. I. Kolvin, R.C. McKeith and S.R. Meadows, Spastics International Medical, London, 1973.
25 Butler and Golding, *From Birth to Five*.
26 D.A. Dawson, *Family Structure and Children's Health United*

States 1988, Series 10:178, Vital and Health Statistics Public Health Service, Maryland, 1991.

27 L.E. Wells and J.H. Rankin, 'Families and delinquency: a meta-analysis of the impact of broken homes', *Social Problems*, 38,1 (1991): 71–93.

28 M.E.J. Wadsworth, 'Early stress and associations with adult health behaviour and parenting', in *Stress and Disability in Childhood*, ed. N.R. Butler and B.D. Corner, John Wright & Sons, Bristol, 1984, pp. 100–4.

29 B.J. Elliott and M.P.M. Richards, 'Children and divorce: educational performance and behaviour before and after parental separation', *International Journal of Law and the Family*, 5 (1991): 258.

30 M. Cockett and J. Tripp, *The Exeter Family Study: Family Breakdown and its Impact on Children*, University of Exeter Press, Exeter, 1994, p. 61.

31 Ibid., p. 53.

32 S. McLanahan and G. Sandefur, *Growing Up with a Single Parent: What Hurts, What Helps*, Harvard University Press, Cambridge, Mass., 1994, p. 49.

33 J. Campion and P. Leeson, 'Marriage, morals and the law', paper prepared for Empowering People in Families conference, University of Plymouth. Family Law Action Group, West Sussex, 1994.

34 *Second Commission on the Status of Women Report to Government 1993*, Government of Ireland, Stationery Office, Dublin, 1993, p. 170.

35 D.P. Moynihan, *The Negro Family: The Case for National Action*, Office of Planning and Research, United States Department of Labor, Washington, DC, 1965.

36 McLanahan and Sandefur, *Growing Up with a Single Parent*, p. 1.

37 Ibid., p. 141.

38 Ibid., p. 29.

39 P. Uhlenberg, 'Changing configurations of the life course', in *Transitions: The Family and the Life Course in Historical Perspective*, ed. T.K. Hareven, Academic Press, New York, 1978, pp. 78–9.

40 S. Coontz, *The Way We Never Were: American Families and the Nostalgia Trap*, Basic Books, New York, 1992, pp. 183–4.

41 McLanahan and Sandefur, *Growing Up with a Single Parent*, p. 66.

42 B.D. Whitehead, *The Divorce Culture*, Alfred A. Knopf, New York, 1997, p. 98.

43 E.M. Hetherington, W.G. Clingempeel, E.R. Anderson, J.E. Deal, M.S. Hagan, E.A. Hollier and M.S. Lindner, 'Coping with marital transitions', in *Impact of Divorce, Single-parenting and Step-parenting on Children*, Lawrence Erlbaum, Hillsdale, NJ, 1992.

44 P. Hill, 'Recent advances in selected aspects of adolescent development', *Journal of Child Psychology and Psychiatry*, 34, 1 (1993): 84–5.

45 *Social Trends*, Government Statistical Service, London, 1998, pp. 50–1.

46 Cockett and Tripp, *The Exeter Family Study*, p. 41.

47 B. Bergman, *The Economic Independence of Women*, Basic

Books, New York, 1986.
48 J.S. Wallerstein and S. Blakeslee, *Second Chances: Men, Women and Children, a Decade after Divorce*, Bantam Press, London, 1989.
49 C. Masheter, 'Post-divorce relationships between ex-spouses: the roles of attachment and interpersonal conflict', *Journal of Marriage and the Family*, 53 (1992): 103.
50 R.E. Emery and P. Dillon, 'Conceptualizing the divorce process: renegotiating boundaries of intimacy and power in the divorced family system', *Family Relations*, 43 (1994): 374.
51 J.A. Seltzer, 'Relationships between fathers and children who live apart: the father's role after separation', *Journal of Marriage and the Family*, 53 (1991): 79.
52 *Marital Breakdown and the Health of the Nation*, ed. F. McAllister, One Plus One, London, 1995.
53 Seltzer, p. 246.
54 Family Policy Studies Centre, *Family Policy Bulletin*, March 1991.
55 *Marital Breakdown and the Health of the Nation*, p. 28.
56 P. Bronstein, M.F. Stoll, J. Clauson, C.L. Abrams and M. Briones, 'Fathering after separation or divorce: factors predicting children's adjustment', *Family Relations*, 43, 4 (1994): 469.
57 Blankenhorn, *Fatherless America*, p. 148.
58 D. Donnelly and D. Finkelhor, 'Does equality in custody arrangements improve the parent–child relationship?' *Journal of Marriage and the Family*, 54, 4 (1992): 837.
59 Wallerstein and Blakeslee, *Second Chances*.
60 Blankenhorn, *Fatherless America*, p. 155. F.F. Furstenberg, Jnr and A.J. Cherlin, *Divided Families: What Happens to Children When Parents Part*, Harvard University Press, Cambridge, Mass., 1991.
61 D.H. Demo and A.C. Adcock, 'The impact of divorce on children', in *Contemporary Families: Looking Forward, Looking Back*, National Council on Family Relations, Minneapolis, Minnesota, 1991.
62 S. Gable, K. Ornic and J. Belsky, 'Co-parenting within the family system: influences on children's development', *Family Relations*, 43, 4 (1994): 380.
63 A.J. Stewart, A.P. Copeland, N.L. Chester, J.E. Malley and N.B. Barenbaum, *Separating Together: How Divorce Transforms Families*, Guilford Press, London, 1997.
64 L.A. Kurdek, 'The relationship between reported well being and divorce history, availability of proximate adult and gender', *Journal of Marriage and the Family*, 53 (1991): 71.
65 McLanahan and Sandefur, *Growing Up with a Single Parent*, pp. 30–1.
66 M. Gallagher, 'The importance of being married', in *The Fatherhood Movement*, ed. W.F. Horn, D. Blankenhorn and M.B. Pearlstein, Lexington Books, New York, Ch. 6, p. 62.
67 Wallerstein and Blakeslee, *Second Chances*, p. 238.
68 R. Pickford, *Fathers, Marriage and the Law*, Family Policy Studies Centre/Joseph Rowntree Foundation, London, 1999.
69 Department of Social Security, *Child Support Agency: Quarterly*

Summary of Statistics, Analytical Services Division, Government Statistical Service, May 1966.

70 A. Marsh, R. Ford and L. Finlayson, *Lone Parents, Work and Benefits*, Department of Social Security Research Report 61, HMSO, London, 1997.

71 J. Bradshaw, C. Stimson, J. Williams and C. Skinner, 'Non resident fathers in Britain', paper presented to ESRC Programme on Population and Household Change seminar, 13 March 1997.

72 Pickford, *Fathers, Marriage and the Law*, p. 35.

73 L. Burghes, L. Clarke and N. Cronin, *Fathers and Fatherhood in Britain*, Family Policy Studies Centre, London, 1997, pp. 72–3.

74 D. Popenoe, *Life without Father*, The Free Press, New York, 1996.

75 K. McKeown, H. Ferguson and D. Rooney, *Changing Fathers? Fatherhood and Family Life in Modern Ireland*, The Collins Press, Dublin, 1998, p. 26.

76 J. Warin, Y. Solomon, C. Lewis and W. Langford, *Fathers, Work and Family Life*, Family Policy Studies Centre/Joseph Rowntree Foundation, London, 1999, p. 34.

CHAPTER 7

1 J. Knitzer, *Unclaimed Children*, Children's Defense Fund, Washington, DC, 1982.

2 P.J. Caplan and I.H. McCorquodale, 'Mother-blaming in major clinical journals', *American Journal of Orthopsychiatry*, 53 (1985): 345–53.

3 S.M. Bianchi, in *The New York Times*, 11 December 1998: A11–13.

4 S. Freud, *An Outline of Psychoanalysis*, Hogarth Press, London, 1938, cited in J. Bowlby, 'The nature of the child's tie to his mother', *International Journal of Psychoanalysis*, 39 (1958): 350–73.

5 R.W. Clark, *Freud, the Man and the Cause*, Jonathan Cape and Weidenfeld & Nicolson, London, 1980, p. 19.

6 P. Gay, *Freud. A Life For Our Time*, J.M. Dent and Sons, London, 1988, pp. 11–12.

7 J. Bowlby, *Maternal Care and Mental Health*, Monograph Series (2), World Health Organization, Geneva, 1951.

8 Ibid., p. 7.

9 Ibid., p. 46.

10 R. Karen, *Becoming Attached*, Warner Books, New York, 1994, p. 110.

11 C. Ernest, 'Are early childhood experiences overrated? A reassessment of maternal deprivation', *European Archives of Psychiatry and Neurological Sciences*, 237 (1988): 80–90.

12 A.S. Rossi, 'Gender and parenthood', *American Sociological Review*, 49 (1984): 1–19.

13 R. Baker and E. Oram, *Baby Wars: Parenthood and Family Strife*, Fourth Estate, London, 1998.

14 K. Holmquist, 'Single mothers rule OK', *Irish Times*, 2 February 1998.

15 S. Kraemer, *Active Fathering for the Future*. The Seven Million project. Working paper 7, DEMOS, London, 1995.

16 L. Burghes, L. Clarke and N. Cronin, *Fathers and Fatherhood in Britain*. Occasional Paper 23, Family Policy Studies Centre,

London, 1997, p. 11.

17 J. Haskey, 'Estimated numbers of one-parent families and their prevalence in Great Britain in 1991', *Population Trends*, 71, HMSO, London, 1994.

18 R. Pickford, *Fathers, Marriage and the Law*, Family Policy Studies Centre/Joseph Rowntree Foundation, London, 1999, p. 44.

19 M.E. Lamb, 'Fathers and child development: an introductory overview and guide', in *The Role of the Father in Child Development*, ed. M.E. Lamb, John Wiley & Sons, New York, 1997, Ch. 1, p. 5.

20 A. Misterlich, *Society without the Father: A Contribution to Social Psychology*, HarperCollins, New York, 1993.

21 D. Dawson, 'Family structure and children's well-being: data from the 1988 National Health Survey', *Journal of Marriage and the Family*, 53 (1991). US Department of Health and Human Services, National Center for Health Statistics *Survey of Child Health*, US Government Printing Office, Washington, DC, 1988.

22 US Department of Health and Human Services, National Center for Health Statistics *National Health Interview Survey*, US Government Printing Office, Hyattsville, Maryland, 1988.

23 J. Garfinkel and S. McLanahan, *Single Mothers and Their Children*, Urban Institute Press, Washington, DC, 1986.

24 C.L. Tishler, P.C. McKenry and K.C. Morgan, 'Adolescent suicide attempts: some significant factors', *Suicide and Life Threatening Behavior*, 11 (1981): 86–92.

25 A. Botsis, M. Plutchik, M. Kotler and H. van Praag, 'Parental loss and family violence as correlates of suicide and violence risk', *Suicide and Life Threatening Behavior*, 25 (1995): 253–60.

26 H. Abramovitch, 'Images of the "Father" in psychology and religion', in *The Role of the Father in Child Development*, ed. Lamb, Ch. 2, p. 21.

27 N. Dennis, *Rising Crime and the Dismembered Family*, Institute of Economic Affairs, London, 1993.

28 Abramovitch, 'Images', pp. 19–32.

29 M.E. Lamb, 'Introduction. The emergent American father', in *The Father's Role: Cross-cultural Perspectives*, ed. M.E. Lamb, Lawrence Erlbaum, Hillsdale, NJ, 1987, pp. 3–25.

30 N. Radin, 'Primary-caregiving fathers in intact families', in *Redefining Families: Indications for Children's Development*, ed. A.E. Gottfried and A.W. Gottfried, Plenum, New York, 1994, pp. 55–97.

31 J.K. Nugent, 'Cultural and psychological influences on the father's role in infant development', *Journal of Marriage and the Family*, 53 (1991): 475–85.

32 A.E. Gottfried, A.W. Gottfried and K. Bathurst, 'Maternal employment, family environment and children's development. Infancy throughout the school years', in *Maternal Employment and Children's Development: Longitudinal Research*, ed. A.E. Gottfried and A.W. Gottfried, Plenum, New York, 1988, pp. 11–58.

33 E. Williams, N. Radin and T.

Allegro, 'Sex-role attitudes of adolescents raised primarily by their fathers', *Merrill-Palmer Quarterly*, 38 (1992): 457–76.

34 J. Mosley and E. Thomson, 'Fathering behavior and child outcomes. The role of race and poverty', in *Fatherhood: Contemporary Theory Research and Social Policy*, ed. W. Marsigkio, Sage, Thousand Oaks, Cal., 1995, pp. 148–65.

35 S. Glueck and E. Glueck, *Delinquents and Nondelinquents in Perspective*, Harvard University Press, Cambridge, Mass., 1968.

36 G.E. Vaillant, 'Natural history of male psychological health: VI. Correlates of successful marriages and fatherhood', *American Journal of Psychiatry*, 135 (1978): 653–9.

37 J. Snarey, *How Fathers Care for the Next Generation: A Four-Decade Study*, Harvard University Press, Cambridge, Mass., 1993.

38 E. Erikson, *Identity and the Life Cycle*, Norton, New York, 1959.

39 Snarey, *How Fathers Care*, pp. 18–19.

40 J. Kotre, *Outliving the Self: Generativity and the Interpretation of Lives*, Johns Hopkins University Press, Baltimore, Maryland, 1984.

41 D.H. Heath, 'What meaning and effects does fatherhood have for the maturing of professional men?' *Merrill-Palmer Quarterly*, 24, 4 (1978): 265–78.

42 D.H. Heath and H.E. Heath, *Fulfilling Lives: Paths to Maturity and Success*, Jossey-Bass, San Francisco, 1991, p. 227.

43 Ibid., p. 288.

44 Vaillant, 'Natural history'.

45 D. Popenoe, *Life without Father*, The Free Press, New York, 1996, p. 75.

46 D. Blankenhorn, *Fatherless America*, HarperCollins, New York, 1995, p. 38.

47 G. Vidal, 'Sex is politics', in *Pink Triangle and Yellow Star*, Heinemann, London, 1982, p. 150.

48 D.L. Gutmann, 'The species narrative', in *The Fatherhood Movement*, ed. W.F. Horn, D. Blankenhorn and M.B. Pearlstein, Lexington Books, Lanham, Maryland, 1999, pp. 141–2.

49 A.H. Halsey, in *Families without Fatherhood*, ed. N. Dennis, and G. Erdos, Institute of Economic Affairs, London, 1992.

50 H.B. Biller, *Fathers and Families. Paternal Factors in Child Development*, Auburn House, Westport, Conn., 1993, pp. 1–2.

51 L. Jardine, 'Mummy's boy', *Guardian*, Monday, 22 February 1999.

52 A.M. Nicoli, Jnr, 'The adolescent', in *The Harvard Guide to Psychiatry*, ed. A.M. Nicholi, Jnr, The Belknap Press of Harvard University Press, Cambridge, Mass., 1999, Ch. 28, p. 623.

53 D.L. Guttmann, 'The species narrative', in *The Fatherhood Movement*, ed. Horn, et al., Ch. 13, p. 138.

54 M.H. Huyck, 'Development and pathology in post-parental men', in *Older Men's Lives*, ed. E. Thompson, Jnr, Sage Publications, Thousand Oaks, Cal., 1994.

55 E.M. Hetherington, 'Effects of father absence on personality development in adolescent daughters', *Developmental Psychology*, 7 (1972): 313–26.

56 L. Tessman, 'A note of father's contribution to his daughter's way

of loving and working', in *Father and child: development and clinical perspectives*, ed. S. Cath, A.R. Gurwitt and J. Ross, 1982, pp. 219–38.

57 Ibid., p. 204.

58 Snarey, *How Fathers Care*, p. 323.

59 K. McKeown, H. Ferguson and D. Rooney, 'Fathers: Irish experience in an international context', in *Strengthening Families for Life*, final report of the Commission on the Family, The Stationery Office, Dublin, 1998, Ch. 18, p. 426.

60 A. Hawkins, S.L. Christiansen, K. Pond Sargent and E.J. Hill, 'Rethinking fathers' involvement in child care: a developmental perspective', in *Fatherhood: Contemporary Theory, Research and Social Policy*, ed. W. Marsiglio, Sage, London, 1995.

61 McKeown et al., 'Fathers: Irish experience', p. 427.

62 Burghes, et al., *Fathers and Fatherhood*, p. 88.

63 K.A. May and S.P. Perrin, 'Prelude, pregnancy and birth', in *Dimensions of Fatherhood*, ed. S. Hanson and F. Bozett, Sage, Beverly Hills, Cal., 1985, pp. 64–91.

64 J. Brockington, *Motherhood and Mental Health*, Oxford University Press, Oxford, 1996, p. 526.

65 N. Morris, 'Human relations in obstetric practice', *Lancet*, 1 (1960): 913–15.

66 C. Lewis, *Becoming a Father*, Open University Press, Milton Keynes, 1986.

67 Ibid., p. 70.

68 M. Greenberg and N. Morris, 'Engrossment: the newborn's impact upon the father', *American Journal of Orthopsychiatry*, 44 (1984): 520–31.

69 M. Roedholm and K. Larsson, 'Father-infant interaction at the first contact after delivery', *Early Human Development*, 3 (1979): 21–7.

70 Brockington, *Motherhood*, p. 528.

71 M. Roedholm, 'Effect of father–infant postpartum contact in their interaction 3 months after birth', *Early Human Development*, 5 (1981): 79–85.

72 S. Coltrane, *Family Man: Fatherhood, Housework and Gender Equity*, Oxford University Press, New York, 1996, p. 42.

73 M. Kotelchuck, 'The infant's relationship to the father: experimental evidence', in *The Role of the Father in Child Development*, 1st edn, ed. Lamb, John Wiley, New York, 1976, pp. 329–44.

74 M.E. Lamb, J. Pleck, E. Charnov and J. Levine, 'A biosocial perspective on paternal behavior and involvement', in *Parenting across the Life-span: Biosocial Dimensions*, ed. J. Lancaster, J. Altmann, A. Rossi and L.R. Sherrod, Aldine de Gruyter, New York, 1987, pp. 111–42.

75 J. Robinson, 'Who's doing the housework?' *American Demographics*, 10 (1988): 24–8.

76 Bureau of the Census, 'Child care arrangements: who's minding the kids?' *Child care arrangements: Winter 1986–1987* (1990) Current Population Reports, series P.7–no.20.

77 Coltrane, *Family Man*, p. 52.

78 Snarey, *How Fathers Care*, p. 36.

79 Ibid., pp. 36–7.

80 A.C. Crouter, M. Perry-Jenkins, T. Huston and S. McHale, 'Processes

underlying father involvement in dual-earner and single-earner families', *Developmental Psychology*, 23 (1987): 431–40.

81 F.K. Grossman, W.S. Pollack and E. Golding, 'Fathers and children: predicting the quality and quantity of fathering', *Developmental Psychology*, 24 (1988): 82–91.

82 G. Russell and N. Radin, 'Increased paternal participation: the father's perspective', in *Fatherhood and Family Policy*, ed. M.E. Lamb and A. Sagi, Lawrence Erlbaum, Hillsdale, NJ, 1983, pp. 139–65.

83 G. Kiely, 'Fathers in families', in *Irish Family Studies: Selected Papers*, ed. C. McCarthy, University College Dublin, Dublin, 1996, pp. 147–58.

84 J. Warin, Y. Solomon, C. Lewis and W. Langford, *Fathers, Work and Family Life*, Joseph Rowntree Foundation and Family Policy Studies Centre, London, 1999, p. 37.

85 M.E. Lamb, J.H. Pleck, E.L. Charnov and J.A. Levine, 'Paternal behavior in humans', *American Zoologist*, 25 (1985): 883–94.

86 J.H. Pleck, 'Paternal involvement: levels, sources and consequences', in *The Role of the Father in Child Development*, ed. Lamb, 1997 edn, p. 74.

87 D. Finkelhor, 'Current information on the scope and nature of child sexual abuse', *Future of Children*, 4, 2 (1994): 31–53.

88 A. Burgess, account provided by A. Thompson, in 'Father figures', *Community Care*, 5–11 August 1999: 20–1.

89 T. Knijn, 'Towards post-paternalism? Social and theoretical changes in fatherhood', in *Changing Fatherhood: An Interdisciplinary Perspective*, ed. G.A.B. Frinking, M. van Dongen and M.J.G. Jacobs, Thesis, Amsterdam, 1995, pp. 1–20. Quoted in W. Marsiglio and M. Cohan, 'Young fathers and child development', in *The Role of the Father in Child Development*, ed. Lamb, 1997 edn, Ch. 13. p. 242.

90 National Research Council, *Understanding Child Abuse and Neglect*, National Academy Press, Washington, DC, 1993, p. 81.

91 Market Research Bureau of Ireland, 1987, quoted in *Changing Fathers: Fatherhood and Family Life in Modern Ireland*, ed. K. McKeown, H. Ferguson and D. Rooney, Collins Press, Dublin, 1998, p. 186.

92 Blankenhorn, *Fatherless America*, p. 40. E. Sagarin, 'Incest: problems of definition and frequency', *Journal of Sex Research*, 13 (1977): 126–35.

93 R. Bachman and L.E. Salzman, *Violence against Women: Estimates from the Redesigned Survey*, Bureau of Justice Statistics Special Report NCJ–154348, US Department of Justice, Washington, DC, 1995.

94 D.E.H. Russell, 'The prevalence and seriousness of incestuous abuse. Stepfathers versus biological fathers', *Child Abuse and Neglect*, 8 (1984): 15–22.

95 M. Gordon and S.J. Creighton, 'Natal and non-natal fathers as sexual abusers in the United Kingdom: a comparative analysis', *Journal of Marriage and the Family*, 50 (1988): 99–105.

96 National Center on Child Abuse

and Neglect, *National Study of the Incidence and Severity of Child Abuse and Neglect*, National Center on Child Abuse and Neglect, Washington, DC, 1981.

97 L. Margolin, 'Child sexual abuse by nonrelated caregivers', *Child Abuse and Neglect*, 15 (1991): 213–21.

98 J.L. Herman, (with Lisa Hirschman), *Father–Daughter Incest* Harvard University Press, Cambridge, Mass., 1981.

99 K.J. Sternberg, 'Fathers: the missing parents in research on family violence', in *The Role of the Father in Child Development*, ed. Lamb, 1997 edn, p. 295.

100 S. Franks, *Having None of It: Women, Men and the Future of Work*, Granta Books, London, 1999.

101 *Better for Women, Better for All: Listening to Women*, Women's Unit, Cabinet Office, London, 1999, p. 11.

102 K.R. Canfield, 'Promises worth keeping', in *The Fatherhood Movement*, ed. Horn et al., Ch. 5, pp. 45–50.

103 K.M. Harris, F. Furstenberg, Jr., and J. Marmer, 'Paternal involvement with adolescents in intact families: the influence of fathers over the life course', paper presented at the annual meeting of the American Sociological Association, New York, 16–20 August 1996, p. 28.

104 L. Meade, 'The new politics of the new poverty', *The Public Interest*, 103 (1991): 10.

105 J. Hillman, *The Soul's Code: In Search of Character and Calling*, Random House, New York, 1996, p. 80.

106 S. Kraemer, 'Parenting yesterday, today and tomorrow', in *Families and Parenting*, Report of a conference, London, 26 September 1995, Family Policies Study Centre, London, 1995.

107 This is a modified and expanded form of a table used in the Government of South Australia's recent 'Six Ways to be a Better Dad' campaign, published by The Office for Families and Children, Southern Australia.

CHAPTER 8

1 B. Simon, *Mind and Madness in Ancient Greece*, Cornell University Press, Ithaca, NY, 1978, p. 246.

2 S. Freud, 'Some psychical consequences of the anatomical distinction between the sexes', in *Standard Edition of the Complete Works of Sigmund Freud*, ed. J. Strachey, Hogarth Press and the Institute of Psychoanalysis, London, 1925, Vol. XIX, pp. 252–3.

3 S. Freud, 'Female sexuality', in *Standard Edition*, ed. Strachey, Vol. XXI, p. 229.

4 Freud, 'Some psychical consequences', p. 253.

5 Ibid., pp. 257–8.

6 P. Gay, *Freud: A Life for Our Time*, J.M. Dent & Sons, London, 1988, p. 506.

7 S. Quinn, *A Mind of Her Own: The Life of Karen Horney*, Macmillan, London, 1987, p. 222.

8 K. Horney, 'The flight from womanhood', *International Journal of Psychoanalysis*, 7 (1926): 324.

9 N. Chodorow, *Feminism and Psychoanalytic Theory*, Yale University Press, New Haven, Conn., 1989, p. 109.

10 W. S. Pollack, 'Fatherhood as a transformation of the self: steps toward a new psychology of men', in *Masculinity and Sexuality: Selected Topics in the Psychology of Men*, ed. R.C. Friedman and J.I. Downey, American Psychiatric Press, Washington, DC, 1999, Ch. 4, p. 93.

11 A.E. Jukes, *Why Men Hate Women*, Free Association Books, London, 1994. D. Dinnerstein, *The Mermaid and the Minotaur*, Harper & Row, New York, 1976.

12 M. de Montaigne, quoted in Alain de Botton, *The Consolations of Philosophy*, Hamish Hamilton, London, 2000, p. 127.

13 V. Woolf, *Orlando*, Penguin, London, 1925, pp. 110–11.

14 C. MacKinnon, *Feminism Unmodified: Discourses on Life and Law*, Harvard University Press, Cambridge, Mass., 1987, p. 225.

15 D. English, 'The politics of porn: can feminists walk the line?' in *The Best of Mother Jones*, ed. R. Reynolds, Foundation for National Progress, San Francisco, 1985, pp. 49–58.

16 K. Horney, 'The dread of women: observations on a specific difference in the dread felt by men and by women for the opposite sex', *International Journal of Psychoanalysis*, 13 (1932): 348.

17 L. Hudson, *Bodies of Knowledge*, Weidenfeld & Nicolson, London, 1982, p. 19.

18 H.A. Feldman, I. Goldstein, D.G. Hatzichristou, et al., 'Impotence and its medical and psychosocial correlates: results of the Massachusetts Male Aging Study', *Journal of Urology*, 151 (1994): 54–61.

19 P. Chesler, *About Men*, The Women's Press, London, 1978, p. 221.

20 S. Brownmiller, *Against Our Will: Men, Women and Rape*, Simon & Schuster, New York, 1975. L. Clark and D. Lewis, *Rape: The Price of Coercive Sexuality*, The Women's Press, Toronto, 1977.

21 E.C. Nelson, 'Pornography and sexual aggression', in *The Influence of Pornography on Behaviour*, ed. M. Yaffe and E.C. Nelson, Academic Press, London, 1982, Ch. 9, p. 226.

22 Brodsky, S.L., and Hobart, S.C., 'Blame Models and Assailant Research', in *Criminal Justice and Behavior*, 5 (1978): pp. 379–88.

23 T. Tieger, 'Self-rated likelihood of raping and the social perception of rape', *Journal of Research in Personality*, 15 (1981): 147–58.

24 M.R. Burt, 'Cultural myths and supports for rape', *Journal of Personality and Social Psychology*, 38 (1980): 217–30.

25 D. Finkelhor, *Child Sexual Abuse: New Theory and Research*, Free Press, New York, 1984, p. 35.

26 E. Monick, *Castration and Male Rage: The Phallic Wound*, Inner City Books, Toronto, 1987, p. 110.

27 A.P. Bell and M.S. Weinberg, *Homosexualities: A Study of Diversity among Men and Women*, Mitchell Beazley, London, 1978, pp. 173–5.

28 E. Boland, 'The beauty of ordinary things'. Interview with Eileen Battersby *Irish Times*, 22 September 1998: 14.

29 T. Parsons, 'Age and sex in the social structure of the United States', *American Sociological*

Review, 7 (1942): 604–16. T. Parsons and R. Bales, *Family: Socialization and Interaction Process*, The Free Press, Glencoe, Ill., 1955.

30 M. Komarovsky, 'The new feminist scholarship: some precursors and polemics', *Journal of Marriage and the Family*, 50 (1988): 585–93. Quotation from H. Z. Lopata, 'The interweave of public and private: women's challenge to American society', *Journal of Marriage and the Family*, 55 (1993): 176–90.

31 W.J. Goode, 'Why men resist', in *Rethinking the Family: Some Feminist Questions*, ed. B. Thorne and M. Yalom, Longman, New York, 1982, pp. 130–50.

32 W. Osler, 'The student life', in *Aequanimitas: with Other Addresses to Medical Students, Nurses and Practitioners of Medicine*, 2nd edn, H.K. Lewis, London, 1908, p. 435.

33 *Voices*, Women's Unit, Cabinet Office, London, October 1999, p. 11.

34 *The Paradox of Prosperity*, The Henley Centre/Salvation Army, London, 1999, pp. 11–12.

35 Ibid., pp. 25–6.

36 A.R. Hochschild, *The Second Shift*, Avon, New York, 1989.

37 A.R. Hochschild, *The Time Bind: When Work Becomes Home and Home Becomes Work*, Henry Holt & Co., New York, 1997.

38 J. Richardson, K. Dwyer, K. McGuigan, W. Hansen, C. Dent, C.A. Johnson, S. Sussman, B. Brannon and B. Flay, 'Substance use among eighth-grade students who take care of themselves after school', *Paediatrics*, 84 (1989): 556–66.

39 E.A. Grollman and G.L. Sweder, *Teaching Your Child to Be Home Alone*, Macmillan, New York, 1983, p. 14.

40 Hochschild, *The Second Shift*, p. 212.

41 P. Marris, 'Attachment and society', in *The Place of Attachment in Human Behaviour*, ed. C. Murray Parkes and J. Stevenson-Hinde, Tavistock, London, 1982.

42 T. Lynch, *The Undertaker: Life Studies from a Dismal Trade*, Jonathan Cape, London, 1997.

43 Bourke, Jo., *An Intimate History of Killing: Face to Face Killing in Twentieth Century Warfare*, Granta, London, 2000.

44 de Botton, A., *The Consolations of Philosophy*, Hamish Hamilton, London, 2000.

45 Blair, C., quoted in 'Cherie fighting for a better family life', Natasha Walter, *Irish Independent*, 22 May 2000, p. 8.

46 Scase, R., *Britain Towards 2000*, Copstone Publishers, Oxford.

47 Arthur Miller, *Death of a Salesman*.

ACKNOWLEDGEMENTS

The original idea for this book emerged from musings, arguments, discussions and debates with many colleagues, friends and acquaintances down through the years. However, it was Professor Lesley Rees, a friend and colleague at St. Bartholomew's Hospital Medical College, whose views have been particularly influential. A superb endocrinologist as well as medical educator – at one stage she was to be co-author but as the book took shape it became increasingly clear that it had to be written by a man – she brought me in touch with the relevant and current literature on the hormonal basis of gender difference. Others who, wittingly and unwittingly, have stimulated my thinking include Joyce O'Connor, Leon Eisenberg, Felicity de Zulueta, Richard Scase, Adam Jukes, Adrienne Burgess, Steve Biddulph, Joanna Bourke and Joseph Veale. Kieran McKeown, Harry Ferguson and Dermot Rooney have been particularly influential – their courageous book, *Changing Fathers?* represents a particularly thoughtful contribution to the debate over fatherhood. My thanks are also due to Ian Fox, Aengus Fanning, Jack Dominian, John Quinn, Lia O'Hegarty of the Irish Law Reform Commission, Professor Stewart Asquith at the Centre for the Child and Society at the University of Glasgow, Rachel Clare and her colleagues at the Henley Centre, Professor John Monahan, Professor Paul Mullen, and the librarians at the British Medical Association, the Royal Society of Medicine, the Royal College of Physicians, the Trinity Medical School Library at St. James's Hospital, Dublin, the Joseph Rowntree Foundation, the Family Policy Studies Centre, and Esther Murnane of the *Irish Times*. My professional colleagues, the psychiatrists, nurses, psychologists, social workers and occupational therapists at St. Patrick's Hospital and at St. Edmundsbury Hospital in Dublin and in particular my own team, Yvonne Tone, Anne Buckley, Michael del Monte, and Teresa Peacock have been enormously helpful as have the numerous psychiatrists in training who over the years have kept me thinking, doubting and learning.

I gratefully acknowledge permission from W.W. Norton to quote from *Suicide in America* by Herbert Hendin, Random House for quotations from the *Standard Edition of the Complete Psychological Works of Sigmund Freud*, and from *Love and Survival* by Dean Ornish, the Society of Authors for *Orlando* by Virginia Woolf, Gerard McCauley Agency for quotations from John Demos's *Past, Present and Personal: the Family and Life Course in American History*, Simon & Schuster for quotations from Robert Sapolsky's *The Trouble with Testosterone*, David Finkelhor's *Child Sexual Abuse: New Theory and Research*, and Germaine Greer's *The Whole Woman*, Yale University Press for excerpts from Robert E. Lane's *The Loss of Happiness in Market Democracies*, John Tosh's *A Man's Place: Masculinity and the Middle Class Home in Victorian England* and Nancy Chodorow's *Feminism and Psychoanalytic Theory*. I thank Eric Stover and Gilles Peress for permission to quote from *The Graves: Srebrenica and Vukovar*, Inner City Books for permission to quote from Eugene Monick's *Castration and Male Rage*, the Family Policy Studies Unit for an excerpt from *Fathers, work and family life*, the Henley Centre for quotations from *The Paradox of Prosperity*, Thames & Hudson for the quotation from *C.G. Jung Speaking: Interview and Encounters*, and the Open University Press for a quotation and table from *Becoming a Father* by C. Lewis, Georges Borchardt Inc. for an excerpt from Arlie Russell Hochschild's *The Time Bind*, Northeastern University Press for a quotation from *The Diary of Alice James* edited by Leon Edel, Teacher's College Press for permission to quote from *Science and Gender* by Ruth Bleier and Penguin Press for permission to quote from John Updike's *Golf Dreams*.

I am indebted to Derek Johns and Anjali Pratap at A.P. Watt who persuaded me from the outset to write this book, editor Penny Hoare and assistant editor Stuart Williams who provided a unique blend of constructive criticism and nudging encouragement, my own secretary, Bernie Butler, who despite having to manage my clinical work with immense professionalism has coped uncomplainingly with the added burden of my chaotic planning and the librarian at St. Patrick's Hospital, Niamh Crowley who with patience and competence chased up references and identified sources and to all those patients whose experiences, triumphs and disasters I have been privileged to share.

Finally, to my wife, Jane, and my children, Rachel, Simon, Eleanor, Peter, Sophie, Justin and Sebastian, I owe an enormous debt. They have over the years helped me get my priorities right and in so far as I have been a good enough spouse and parent the achievement is theirs.

INDEX